Teaching
Controversial Issues

Teaching
Controversial Issues

The Case for Critical Thinking
and Moral Commitment
in the Classroom

Nel Noddings
Laurie Brooks

TEACHERS COLLEGE PRESS

TEACHERS COLLEGE | COLUMBIA UNIVERSITY

NEW YORK AND LONDON

Published by Teachers College Press, 1234 Amsterdam Avenue, New York, NY 10027

Copyright © 2017 by Teachers College, Columbia University

Cover design by David K. Kessler. Cover image by Alexander Palm / Getty Images.

Library of Congress Cataloging-in-Publication Data is available at loc. gov

ISBN 978-0-8077-5780-2 (paper)
ISBN 978-0-8077-5781-9 (hardcover)
ISBN 978-0-8077-7488-5 (ebook)

Printed on acid-free paper
Manufactured in the United States of America

24 23 22 21 20 19 18 17   8 7 6 5 4 3 2 1

Contents

Acknowledgments

I would like to thank my mother for the opportunity to at long last collaborate in our writing. My husband and children and their spouses gave valuable input—Karen on gender, Mark on race, and Jenny as a writing partner. Rob Capozzoli, marketing director at the Provident Bank in New Jersey, supplied data for Chapter 7 on the media; the students and teachers, especially Catkin Flowers, at Philip's Academy Charter School in Newark, New Jersey, provided inspiration and examples.

—Laurie Brooks

Introduction

Critical thinking appears as a primary aim of education over most of the world today. It is often described as a detached, skeptical, and analytical process, and many people believe that its main use is to win arguments. However, critical thinking is best thought of as a dedicated search for meaning and understanding. At its most basic, it probes for what words mean, how words connect to convey meaning in sentences, how sentences bring meaning to paragraphs and paragraphs to longer messages. When we apply critical thinking to what we hear or read, we are trying to interpret accurately, to understand.

A prime purpose of critical thinking in the public domain is to consider and evaluate the arguments made on controversial issues. This requires a continual search for meaning and understanding. The object is not necessarily to win a debate. Rather, it is to understand what is being said on all sides and, perhaps, to find a nucleus of agreement that will provide a starting point from which we can work together. The idea is to use critical thinking in contributing to healthy human relations and the maintenance of a strong participatory democracy. Citizens in such a democracy must be able to communicate effectively with one another, and this capacity should be developed in our schools.

Our approach might be called an *open system* approach. We do not start with a set of definitions, rules, or specific learning objectives, nor do we even specify topics. If we are serious about developing their capacity for critical thinking, we must give students opportunities to introduce questions, to challenge standard positions, to—at least occasionally—change the direction of a planned lesson.

Our approach is interdisciplinary. The broad set of human problems and controversies should be addressed across the disciplines. Too often today educators are urged to reduce—even avoid—controversy by keeping social/political problems sharply confined to one discipline if they are addressed at all. It has been suggested, for example, that matters of religion be sharply confined to classes on religion and that discussion of evolution be conducted only in science class. Where, then, will the exciting differences that arise between the two views be discussed? How will students work their way to a reasonable understanding when they are told x in one class and not-x in another with no discussion of the controversy?

An interdisciplinary approach places emphasis throughout the curriculum on the great ideas and central skills of a sound education. Consider what might be done in response to the Common Core recommendation that English classes should give more time to the reading of documents and less to literature. The purpose, ostensibly, is to encourage the exercise of critical thinking on political/social issues. We might support this new emphasis and yet deeply regret the loss of literature. Applying critical thinking—appreciative understanding—to this loss, teachers might work together to add great literature to all of the disciplines. Given our experience in math education, we (this mother-daughter author team) would be delighted to add Abbott's *Flatland*, Martin Gardner's *Annotated Alice*, a brief history of the Pythagoreans, or any of a number of books suggested by Douglas Hofstadter to our math curriculum. Similarly, science, history, art, music, and foreign language teachers could make suggestions that would enrich the whole curriculum. We fall into many educational traps by supposing that every topic, concept, or skill must be taught, learned, and tested in a specific place.

A second recommendation (see Noddings, 2013, 2015a) is to add a 4-year series of forums or seminars on social/moral issues to the high school curriculum. These classes would be carefully composed of students from all of the school's programs. The idea is to bring together students with different interests, talents, and likely futures to consider and think critically together on controversial issues. Many social critics today are deeply concerned about the increasing gap in communication across social classes in our country. The 4-year seminars would address this problem by promoting cross-class communication early on.

Guiding the discussion of controversial issues is challenging work. We warn early and often against indoctrination and emphasize pedagogical neutrality. But even the use of pedagogical neutrality is open to argument. Certainly there are views that should *not* be given a fair hearing—for example, racist recommendations, "scientific" claims that have been proven false, endorsement of cruel punishments, and permission to use nasty language in argumentation. Nor does the commitment to pedagogical neutrality forbid teachers to reveal their own position on the controversies under discussion. It does require them to remind students that there are competing positions and that they, too, are invited to contribute and defend their own.

Responsible teachers must also be concerned about the possible development of cynicism. Our object is to prepare students for active life in a participatory democracy. When we encourage a full and open discussion of controversial issues, we may unintentionally induce demoralization—what is sometimes referred to as "educated despair" with respect to the history of our country's or group's various transgressions. We want students to recognize the wrongdoings of their own country or group, but we also want them to see the best in their various traditions and find hope in the work of restoring, maintaining, and extending that best.

Although the importance of morality will be evident throughout our discussion, we will emphasize this importance in the first chapter on the sources of morality and again in the final chapter, where we will argue that critical thinking must be guided by moral commitment. Unfortunately, many skilled critical thinkers in our society use their skills to advance their own welfare at the expense of the less fortunate. Critical thinking—the search for meaning and understanding—can be used for good or evil purposes. We hope that attempts to teach critical thinking will be accompanied by a serious discussion of moral commitment. Again, moral education should not be thought of as a separate subject—one to be taught formally in, say, 7th grade. All of education should be guided by and imbued with moral dedication. Our aim is to produce better people, and what we mean by "better" people is itself a topic that should be open to continuing dialogue and generous argumentation.

In what follows, we will discuss controversies around such questions as these:

- How should children be taught to relate to authority? What function does choice play in this?
- Why do we teach almost nothing on parenting—one of the most important tasks undertaken by most adults? What should we teach about it?
- Could an avowed atheist be elected president of the United States? Why not? As we now include more about the world's great religions in our high school curriculum, should we also teach more about atheism, agnosticism, and deism? Should we say more about the influence of religion in our political history?
- Why is America experiencing an increasing communication gap—a situation in which we seem less and less able to talk with others across social classes? What can be done about this?
- What do we mean by "equality"? In what sense is it true that "all men are created equal"? Does equality imply the same education for everyone?
- Have Americans neglected our shameful history of racism and gender bias for too long? Can we apply critical thinking to that history in a way that will not produce "educated despair" but help us to identify and promote the best in our traditions? Should we remove statues and other tributes commemorating the lives of confirmed racists? Are there ways of recognizing their genuine contributions without endorsing their racism?
- Is it feasible to reshape public life along the lines suggested by women's traditional lives and thought? Or should we concentrate

on achieving women's equality in the male-defined world? What should we teach about gender/sex in our schools?

- Are we better informed by the enormous increase in messages received through electronic media? Or is our society becoming more polarized? What can schools do to address this?
- In what ways has technology improved our lives? Can technology be used to protect and improve the natural environment?
- Is socialism now more respectable? Can we select and promote the best elements of both capitalism and socialism? What are some of the objectionable features of each?
- Is there a way to eliminate poverty? Why does there seem to be a growing separation between our social classes? Are the poor partly responsible for their own poverty?
- Are some people resistant to freedom and/or liberation? Are they somehow afraid of freedom? Why? What can be done about this?
- Could we—should we—try to change the focus of patriotism away from pride in our nation as a political entity and toward a love for our country as a natural place? Might this change in emphasis encourage more devotion to Earth as home for all of us? Can we promote a vigorous form of global patriotism?

This book is an invitation to teachers to *think* and to explore ways in which to promote critical thinking in their students. A word of caution: If discussion becomes heated, if there are signs of cynicism or despair, close the conversation with the promise of revisiting the topic on another day and the reassurance that such difficult moments occur in adult deliberation among dedicated citizens. It is part of life in a participatory democracy.

A central claim in this book is that critical thinking must be guided by moral commitment. Chapter 1 will address the sources of morality. Many philosophers have claimed that *reason* is the main source of morality—"to know the good is to do the good." Others, with whom we largely agree, point out that it is *feeling* or passion that motivates us to act; reason is used to *direct* that action. Although we do not recommend character education as the main way to approach moral education, we heartily endorse the cultivation of character in all of the material we teach. All three of these sources of moral conduct will be important in what follows. Critical thinkers must be able to reason effectively but, if that thinking is to promote the common good, it must be directed by moral commitment.

CHAPTER 1

The Sources of Morality

Philosophers have long discussed three significant human capacities influencing moral life: reason, passion (feelings), and character. For centuries, debates have continued over which of the three is most fundamental in moral decisionmaking and conduct. Some have argued strongly that reason—the "moral law"—is innate in humans. Indeed, Immanuel Kant (1966/1781) contended that the universality of the "moral law within" is persuasive evidence for the existence of God, and a moral act is one that is done in obedience to the law defined by reason. In contrast, David Hume (1983/1751) argued that reason, as important as it is, cannot *motivate* moral action; we are motivated by what we feel, by passions. Finally, there are those who point to character as the main source of morality. "Character is defined by the quality of the intentions on which a person is moved to act, and virtues are described as those attributes of character that lead individuals to respond in ways that are labeled "good" or "bad."" All three of the inner sources of morality are subject to development or shaping by external forces.

Philosophical work on the sources of morality is voluminous, and we will not attempt a comprehensive review of any of these three fundamental positions. However, teachers need to know something about the history and philosophy of moral thought, and they need to consider carefully ways in which they might influence the moral growth of their students. In this book, we are particularly interested in the use of critical thinking on moral and political thought. What sort of citizens do we seek to develop, and how should we try to do this?

THE CLASSICAL INFLUENCE

The classical approach posited a strong connection between reason and character; it tended to equate knowledge with virtue. One of its basic ideas is that, using reason appropriately, a person will know what is good and right and thereby be moved to act morally; he or she cannot rationally do otherwise. We find this classical idea deeply entrenched in Christian religion and its educational practices. Indeed, this emphasis on the intimate connection between "true" knowledge and virtue was part of the Puritan thinking that pervaded 17th- and 18th-century education. Roger Geiger (2015, p. 8) notes that "the Aristotelian notion embedded in Puritan theology that the end of knowledge is praxis, or knowing how to act" remained central in Western collegiate education well into the 19th century. It is important to note that *knowledge* as it is used here is not mere information. True knowledge is virtue, and perfect knowledge describes the mind of God. When colleges were established through the joint efforts of church and government, the curriculum was considered to be a segment of the mind of God.

The classical view clearly puts great emphasis on the use of reason in moral decisionmaking and on the development of character. The connection between reason and character was described by Socrates as one of continual self-study and criticism. "Know thyself!" was the advice Socrates gave to those seeking knowledge; the unexamined life is not worth living. Socrates did not mean by this that we learn nothing from our parents and teachers, but we must think carefully about what they teach us. Socrates was an early and powerful advocate of critical thinking, especially such thinking turned on ourselves and our ways of life.

As colleges developed in the United States, the classical view was affirmed by religious support. Their main mission initially was to train ministers, but even when that mission expanded, the classical view held. The good man, it was held, strives to acquire, understand, and apply the knowledge offered, thereby acquiring virtue, and the best men come closer to it than the vast majority of humankind. The perfect mind was posited as a universal ideal for education, one of harmony and goodness (Geiger, 2015; Turner, 1985).

For many years, this sort of thinking also supported a reverence for kings and helped to maintain monarchies. The king was thought of as a substitute for God. As history increasingly revealed, however, kings were not always godlike in their wisdom and goodness, and people began to seek wiser leadership. As the classical ideals were interpreted in the early republics, kings—hereditary rulers—were to be replaced by people who possessed the knowledge and disinterest to promote the best interests of their subjects. The requirement of disinterest, a virtuous lack of concern for personal gain, made it likely that comfortably rich men would acquire leadership roles. Merchants and those who worked for wages were for the most part disqualified. As a prominent example, students should be aware that George Washington served without pay as commander of the colonial army and returned without monetary reward to private life. Indeed, he argued that he should receive no salary when he served as president of the new republic, but that offer was rejected.

As a young nation, the United States was deeply influenced by classical views. It hovered on the edge of democracy; that is, as a republic, it embraced the view that a nation should be governed by its citizens, but it leaned heavily toward the classical definition of who should qualify as a voting citizen. A strong republic, it was held, should be governed by its most knowledgeable citizens, those well educated and successful enough to own property and qualify as financially independent. These men (women were not even considered in this class) were thought most likely to put the welfare of the republic and its citizens above their own private concerns. It was recognized, however, that even the well-to-do might yield to corruption, and the founders spent much time and argumentation at the Constitutional Convention debating over the kinds of governmental structures that might weaken the temptation to engage in corrupt practices (Teachout, 2014).

Isaiah Berlin summarizes the classical-republican assumptions and their associated problems well:

> First, that all men have one true purpose, one only, that of rational self-direction; second, that the ends of all rational beings must of necessity fit into a single universal, harmonious pattern, which some men may be able to discern more clearly than others; third, that all conflict, and consequently all tragedy, is due solely to the clash of reason with the irrational or the insufficiently rational— the immature and the undeveloped elements in life—whether individual or communal, and that such clashes are, in principle, avoidable, and for wholly rational beings impossible; finally, that when all men have been made rational, they will obey the rational laws of their own natures, which are one and the same for all, and so be at once wholly law-abiding and wholly free. (1969, p. 154)

Clearly, we can see both valuable and dangerous elements in this picture. It is lovely to believe that at least some human beings have potential access to a godlike knowledge and virtue. It is reasonable, too, to assume that some people will come much closer to the ideal than most. What should worry us is the contention that people should have only one true purpose and that, without it, they are necessarily lesser beings. It should also worry us, perhaps even more, that this sort of thinking leads to the belief that the "truly rational" few should control the lives of the many who are unenlightened. As we talk about this, we should remind teachers to keep these worries in mind. Berlin points out that this sort of belief leads to paternalism and, at its worst, to dictatorship, totalitarianism, and even slavery.

If all "true" men share the purpose of seeking rational self-direction, what should be done with those who seem unwilling or unable to seek or achieve that desirable state? They should, it was held, be directed by their betters; they should accept instruction and keep trying. But in some cases, these unfortunates should learn to accept their inferior status and be thankful if they achieve a measure, at least, of usefulness. It is shocking to us today to recognize and admit that so many of our republican forbears— including many of our early presidents—were slaveholders and defended that practice as part of the republican tradition. Slaves were advised to accept their status as God's will. One preacher/slaveholder advised his Black congregation: "The great God above has made you for the benefit of the Whiteman, who is your lawmaker and law giver" (quoted in Baptist, 2014, p. 204). Such talk reinforced the belief of owners that their practice as slaveholders was sanctioned by God and gave some solace to slaves who were encouraged to believe that their subservience would be some day rewarded.

For teachers, it is important to be aware of the longstanding debate over the relation between knowledge and virtue. Certainly, the founders accepted as fact that supposedly well-educated men could go wrong morally, but there remained the lingering notion that the problem was largely one of proper shaping, proper education. That idea arose again and again and still appears in moral/political arguments. Today we do not worry about being burglarized or robbed on the street by college graduates, but our whole financial system has on occasion been put in jeopardy by the morally questionable activities of highly educated people. Should we reject the idea of knowledge as virtue? Or should we work to produce a population of highly virtuous people? What should we do?

Public school teachers may understand Berlin's worry about any form of government that advocates control over the undereducated or not entirely rational by those who apparently come closer to the rational ideal, but those who work with children and teenagers naturally have some sympathy with a view that recognizes the need to shape minds and encourage rationality. We must remember, however, that our purpose in shaping young minds is to produce people who can think for themselves and, eventually, reject further attempts to control their decisions or prescribe the form of their rationality and purposes. That is why so much attention must be given to critical thinking and its connections to moral life. I (Noddings, 2015a) have recommended that our main educational purpose should be to produce "better adults," but I have left open the description of what is meant by "better" over the entire dimension of human life. It requires a never-ending critical discussion.

There is another problem with the classical-republican view that has been so influential in our moral/political thought, and that is its supposition that our moral actions are motivated by reason—that "knowledge is virtue." Not all philosophical thinkers agree, and we will discuss the matter more fully in a later section. Suffice it here to say that we agree with Gordon Wood on the issue; he writes: "In fact, I do not believe that ideas 'cause' human behavior. I am with David Hume in holding that passions, not reason, are the ruling element in all human action" (2011, p. 13). If we believe this, we will recognize the need to educate feelings and sympathies as well as minds, and we will note that some people who are excellent critical thinkers remain unmotivated to act on what they see quite clearly and, worse, that some proficient thinkers actually use their critical ability to do evil.

Despite all its weaknesses, the classical view has had great influence on American education, particularly in its impact on character education.

CHARACTER EDUCATION

Until the second half of the 20th century, character education was more or less the standard approach to moral education in America's public schools (Brown, Corrigan, & Higgins-D'Alessandro, 2012; Nucci & Narvaez, 2008). To be sure, doubts had been raised earlier in the century about its effectiveness. An influential study in the late 1920s concluded that children who experienced character education were inclined to be good when adults were watching them but not so good when adults left them alone (Hartshorne & May, 1928–1930). However, no powerful alternative was available until Lawrence Kohlberg introduced the idea of cognitive stages of moral development in the 1960s. Kohlberg dismissed character education programs as a "bag of virtues" approach, and we'll discuss his model in the next section on reason as source of moral conduct.

Here we should pause to note an error made repeatedly in education—adopting ideas or methods "whole hog" and then discarding them entirely when they fail to be panaceas. A far more intelligent response, one promoted by critical thinking, is to ask: What is useful here? For whom? Under what circumstances? How do the elements to be retained contribute to our overall aim to educate better people?

In that spirit, let us examine character education for both faults and useful possibilities. The basic idea of character education is to build character through instruction on the virtues. In the early 20th century, the Character Development League sponsored curriculum materials, *Character Lessons*, for use in public schools (White, 1909). The classical emphasis on the close connection between knowledge and virtue is evident throughout this work. One might argue that the League ignored the warning of Socrates that virtue cannot be taught directly, but despite his own reservations, Socrates did acknowledge that teaching has *something* to contribute to the development of virtue. In agreement with this counsel, we might find something to question in the League's recommendations and something to admire.

First, as the Hartshorne and May study confirmed, it does seem to be a mistake to teach the virtues directly as specific learning objectives. *Character Lessons* presents lessons on 31 virtues, starting with obedience and including self-control, sympathy, ambition, determination, and patriotism, each carefully linked to the next. Patriotism, for example, is described in the outline as the "application of the foregoing Traits in relation to the State," but in the section devoted to its discussion, we read: "Patriotism is love of one's country, which prompts obedience and loyalty to its government" (White, 1909, p. 90). One might hope that the virtue of patriotism would be qualified by the other 30 virtues, but there is no indication of this in the definition or, for that matter, in the elaboration of patriotism as a virtue. With the horrifying experience of 20th-century examples of patriotism behind us, we may properly be concerned with the League's emphasis on respect for authority. Today, we might want to suggest that the "loyalty" of patriotism should be directed toward the approved principles of our government, not simply the government. In agreement with Socrates, we advise critical self-examination directed not only at our individual lives but also at our collective political lives.

It should also be noted that character education has been heavily directed at elementary education (Davidson, Lickona, & Khmelkov, 2008). Because the work discussed previously was designed for grades 1–8, it is perhaps understandable that little is said about the application of critical thinking to the virtues, but it is important for elementary school teachers today to keep in mind that they are preparing students to be thoughtful citizens. Is there a way to introduce students to the sort of thinking that will enable them, at the proper time, to criticize authority and not simply obey it? And what is that time? When and how should such criticism be encouraged?

One reason that critical thinking is avoided at every level of public schooling, not just elementary school, is that it necessarily involves controversies. At a time when Protestant Christianity dominated public education and the great majority of the population had no formal education beyond elementary school, it was perhaps easier to legislate what constituted virtue and character. The basic moral message was to obey authority—parents, teachers, government, God—and there was little encouragement to challenge these authorities or even to examine the relations among them. Today, however, the need has arisen to discuss and critique the virtues themselves. When, for example, might honesty not be considered a virtue? How about ambition? Or patriotism? It is not that a program in character education cannot address moral ambiguities, but so far no adequate program has been developed to do so.

That said, we should still recognize some strengths in the character education tradition. One is the use of exemplars in guiding moral thought and action. We often ask ourselves what a greatly admired person, a person of fine character, might do in the situation we face. It has become popular today, for example, for young people to ask—sometimes in a joking manner—"What would Jesus do?" When we can't ask a trusted mentor directly for advice, we spend some serious time considering the possibilities. Another strength of character education is the use of biography and other forms of literature. Stories invite interest, and biographical stories can be inspirational. Further, their use promotes the integration of disciplines and supports a paramount aim of education—the search for meaning. A plan to follow up on elementary school character education with suggestions for a high school program applying critical thinking to the virtues might be useful.

REASON

As we saw in the brief summary provided by Berlin, one enormously influential school of moral thought names reason—rational self-direction—as the source of individual and political moral conduct. This view follows the classical tradition in equating virtue and knowledge and insists on the universality of the human capacity to reason on moral matters.

Immanuel Kant, one of philosophy's all-time great thinkers, argued that moral conduct should be defined as obedience to the principles identified by moral reason. A given act should be judged moral if and only if it is the product of dutiful application of the relevant principle. Kant insisted that the consequences of an act—however desirable or undesirable they might be—have nothing to do with its moral evaluation. This approach, positing *duty* as the fundamental element in moral life, is known as *deontology*, and it contrasts sharply with theories such as utilitarianism that point to consequences as the basis for evaluating moral decisions and conduct.

If this were a course in moral philosophy, we would have to spend a great deal of time on Kant and his deontological views. From an intellectual standpoint, it would certainly not be a waste of time, and some critics actually recommend that all teachers be required to take such courses. But, as we will remind readers several times, the huge, formidable amount of knowledge required by teachers is probably best presented in the context of education, not in courses sharply separated and treated in the various specialized disciplines. This should not be interpreted to mean that teacher candidates should not take courses in the philosophy department; that would be a ridiculous recommendation. It is to remind us that student teachers may not see any useful connection between a sophisticated treatment of moral theory and moral education, and it is that connection that should be foremost in planning the curriculum for teacher education.

Kant's deontology makes the prohibition of lying absolute, and a discussion of this view should be fascinating for high school students. Is there any moral justification for telling a lie? What is a "white lie"? Should we tell the truth to our enemies? (See Bok, 1979; Noddings, 2015a, 2015b). In general, is it possible to maintain all of our principles simultaneously, or must we sometimes reluctantly sacrifice one to advance another? Berlin is again helpful here in criticizing the philosophical tradition that puts such heavy weight on moral reasoning and duty to those principles discovered in the process of reasoning:

> Principles are not less sacred because their duration cannot be guaranteed. Indeed, the very desire for guarantees that our values are eternal and secure in some objective heaven is perhaps only a craving for the certainties of childhood or the absolute values of our primitive past. (1969, p. 172)

Berlin agrees that we should, wherever and whenever possible, stand staunchly for our avowed principles yet recognize their relative validity: "To demand more than this is perhaps a deep and incurable metaphysical need; but to allow it to determine one's practice is a symptom of an equally deep, and more dangerous moral and political immaturity" (p. 172).

If we were conducting a discussion with high school students today, we would surely have to consider the moral/political debate that raged recently over the Senate Report on the activities of the Central Intelligence Agency (CIA). This is a perfect—if deeply troubling—example of debate over moral principles. One side holds strongly that it was our duty as a nation to uphold the principle against torture; the other looks at actual and potential consequences and concludes that our duty to preserve the safety of our nation comes first. Teachers supervising this discussion should provide enough background in moral philosophy to give some weight to both positions. They should insist on logical and considerate argument. Although teachers should express their own opinion if asked, they should not try to lead students to the conclusion they themselves have reached. Notice that this advice is itself open to challenge. There are teachers and teacher educators who will insist—perhaps in the character education tradition—that students *should* be led to the morally right conclusion. But, except in those few cases that are morally, inarguably clear, we must allow both sides to be heard. Otherwise, we will have to continue our too-longstanding practice of avoiding deeply controversial issues. We might close the discussion with the quote from Berlin, reminding students that sometimes, regrettably, we must sacrifice one principle to preserve another. Is this such a case?

In addition to the wonderful topics of discussion generated by an introduction to deontology, teachers should be aware that an influential program of moral education was based on moral reasoning. Kohlberg put forward a cognitive moral development approach in the 1960s and 1970s. The idea was heavily influenced by the stage theory of cognitive development advanced by Jean Piaget (1954, 1970). For several decades, Piaget was one of the most prominent names in psychology. Today, although Piaget is still recognized as one of the fathers of constructivism, his work is not so widely read, and there is far less discussion of his stage theory.

Kohlberg posited six stages, two in each of three large categories: preconventional, conventional, and postconventional. Teachers should understand that, although many psychologists are classified as developmentalists, not all accept stage theory; that is, they may agree that certain traits and capacities develop from natural tendencies over time, but they do not claim that these developments arrange themselves in well-defined stages. Kohlberg's stages are well defined, and one cannot attain stage 4 without going through stage 3. The influence of reason as the basis for morality is clear throughout. Consider the conventional level's two stages:

Stage 3. The Interpersonal Concordance or "Good Boy-Nice Girl" Orientation

Good behavior is that which pleases or helps others and is approved by them . . . . Behavior is frequently judged by intention—the judgment "he means well" becomes important for the first time. One earns approval by being "nice."

Stage 4. Society Maintaining Orientation

There is an orientation toward authority, fixed rules, and the maintenance of the social order. Right behavior consists of doing one's duty, showing respect for authority, and maintaining the given social order for its own sake. (Kohlberg, 1981, p. 18)

Notice that stage 3 recognizes feelings, but stage 4, supposedly a higher stage, emphasizes reason and duty. Kohlberg claimed, on the basis of his empirical studies, that the average woman attains to stage 3 on his scale, and the average man to stage 4. He found that very few people reach stage 5, the Social Contract Orientation, and stage 6, Universal Ethical Principles Orientation, is speculatively ideal. The entire scheme claims reason as the source of moral obligation.

Carol Gilligan (1982) challenged not only the empirical results of Kohlberg's studies but the whole scheme. It is not the case, she argued, that girls somehow lag behind boys in moral development. Their moral thinking is different; it is not so tied to reason and rules:

Thus women not only define themselves in a context of human relationship but also judge themselves in terms of their ability to care. . . . But while women have thus taken care of men, men have, in their theories of psychological development, as in their economic arrangements, tended to assume or devalue that care. (1982, p. 17)

Even today, work traditionally done by women is economically devalued, and women's success in the male-defined public world is judged largely by how well they do in comparison with men.

We can now see at least three good reasons for spending a bit of time on Kohlberg's program. First, it is a striking example of a theoretical scheme based solidly on the primacy of reason as the source of morality. Second, its discussion (and that of Piaget's work) should remind teachers that educational ideas can be enormously influential at a given time and yet fade away rather swiftly. Recognizing this, teachers should be continually encouraged to examine purportedly new ideas critically. Third, the critique of reason-based theories such as Kohlberg's opened the door for care ethics, an approach that puts more emphasis on feeling than on reason as the source of moral motivation.

Before moving on to a discussion of feelings-based approaches to moral theory, we should remind readers that the reason-based approach is by no means dead. The work of John Rawls (1971, 1993) on political philosophy is built solidly on principles of the social contract, a contract described by Kant, Rousseau, and Locke: "They are the principles that free and rational persons concerned to further their own interests would accept in an initial position of equality as defining the fundamental terms of their association" (Rawls, 1971, p. 11). The idea—one that students might find both challenging and fascinating—is to consider how rational beings, stripped of all knowledge about their own likely individual, economic, and political status, would reason and argue to establish the rules of justice for their proposed society.

If we did not know what position we would hold in the proposed society, what sort of rules would we suggest? Would we be inclined, as Rawls suggests we would be, to ensure that the least favored would be adequately provided for under our rules? Can students imagine that some people would shrug off the possibility that they might find themselves in the least-favored class and therefore be less than enthusiastic about Rawls's proposed scheme of justice? Why might people behave this way? What besides reason influences our moral decisions?

PASSIONS AND FEELING

We must use reason to ascertain and make judgments about facts, and reason is clearly necessary to apply logic and come to conclusions. However, we can use reason toward questionable ends, and we do not always act, even on the morally admirable ends we discern; they may not motivate us. We are motivated by feelings. We admire, Hume said, "benevolence and humanity, friendship and gratitude, natural affection and public spirit, or whatever proceeds from a tender sympathy with others, and a generous concern for our kind and species" (1983/1751, p. 18). Sympathy—feeling for another's pain, fear, or need—moves us to action. "Reason," Hume wrote, "being cool and disengaged, is no motive to action, and directs only the impulse received from appetite or inclination, by showing us the means of attaining happiness or avoiding misery" (p. 88).

Now, obviously, Hume is not dismissing virtue, character, or reason from moral life. They all contribute vitally to our moral conduct, but we *act* on our passions. This suggests strongly that the task of teachers and parents is to educate the hearts and feelings of our children, not simply their minds. In discussing moral education, psychologists today often emphasize *empathy*, defined by Martin Hoffman as "the involvement of psychological processes that make a person have feelings that are more congruent with another's situation than with his own situation" (2000, p. 30). Children must be reminded to notice, understand, and respond appropriately to the feelings of others. Whether we use "sympathy" or "empathy" in this context, we are referring to what is felt, or should be felt, by the moral agent.

In the last three decades, interest has grown in care ethics, a moral theory rooted in the experience of women (Gilligan, 1982; Noddings, 2013/1984), one that shares with Hume an emphasis on feeling as that which motivates moral conduct. (For a sampling of recent work on care ethics, see Engster, 2007; Groenhout, 2004; Ruddick, 1989; Slote, 2007; Tronto, 1993.) Care ethics differs from classical virtue ethics, deontology, and utilitarianism in several respects. First, it is a relational ethic; it notes and describes the roles of both carer and cared-for. It is not just the carer as moral agent who contributes to moral action; the cared-for contributes substantially to maintenance of the relation by responding to the efforts at care. Second, in contrast to contemporary ethics of reason and justice, it is needs-based, not rights-based. Moral agents as carers listen to expressed needs, feel something as a result, and respond sensitively—not always positively—to the need expressed. Even when a carer cannot meet the expressed need, she responds in a way meant to preserve the caring relation. There are times when a carer does not have the resources to satisfy the need, and there are times—often in parenting and teaching—when she wants to discourage the expressed need and move the cared-for toward something thought to be better for all involved. Further, "carer" and "cared-for" are not permanent designations. In adult relationships, members regularly change roles, each acting sometimes as carer, sometimes as cared-for. In both positions, they contribute to the relation.

Although description of the caring relation is rooted in female experience, its relevance is not confined to family and small community life. Virginia Held comments:

> The ethics of care calls for the transformation of the different segments of society, with caring values and cooperation replacing the hierarchies and dominations of gender, class, race, and ethnicity. It recommends families characterized by mutual care; educational, health care, and child care institutions well supported and developed; economies focused on actually meeting needs rather than enriching the powerful; military-industrial power under social constraints and decided by women as well as men in diplomatic and political institutions, military services, and defense industries. . . . Bringing up new persons in caring relations that would be as admirable as possible would be seen as society's most important goal. (2006, p. 160)

When we move beyond person-to-person situations, however, we must consider the difference between caring-for (as described in care ethics) and caring-about, or concern that can be found in all moral theories. Care ethics is certainly not alone in seeking the social improvements listed by Held. Its special contribution is located in its description of how these goods should be accomplished. It is careful to point out that, in moving from the general concern of caring-about, we must ensure that the conditions thereby created establish and maintain support for caring-for (Noddings, 2002a). Too often, guided by ethics of rights and justice, we base our interventions on *assumed* needs and highly generalized principles; we fail to consult the recipients of our care and respond to their *expressed* needs. This attitude has long dominated pedagogical thinking, and today it is perhaps stronger than ever. Those in charge, who clearly "care about," prescribe what the curriculum will cover, how it will be taught, and how students will prove they have learned it. The care approach, as a relational ethic, recognizes the centrality of relations and works through these relations to make life better for all those involved.

RELATED POLITICAL CONSIDERATIONS

The school of thought that placed reason at the center of moral philosophy quite naturally led to political philosophies of rights and justice and documents proclaiming the rights of citizens are treasured. As citizens, we pledge our allegiance to them. In the current Common Core State Standards for English Language Arts (ELA), special emphasis is placed on reading and understanding many of these documents. Although the emphasis itself is praiseworthy, far too little attention is given to the context in which these documents were produced. Without considerable study of that context, it is unlikely that students will achieve a real understanding of the documents. It is not enough to analyze the formal structure, learn the definition of terms, and consider the stated purpose of a document. To understand the importance of these documents, students need to know something about the times in which they were written, the events that motivated them, and the lives of their writers. The Common Core standards do not provide helpful advice on these essential matters.

The documents we treasure are, for the most part, designed to prohibit injury, ensure freedom, and promote equality. Careful thinkers should see immediately that two of these goals—freedom and equality—might often conflict with each other. (Remember Berlin's warning on this.) Well-informed citizens should be on the watch for such conflicts and be prepared to engage in a continual dialogue focused on advancing both aims and, where possible, reducing the conflict between them.

In line with the earlier discussion in this chapter about the sources of morality, we should spend some time in considering the place of these documents in the history of citizenship. Were they causes of great changes, or were they proud claims of achievements already accomplished? This is an important question because too often it is supposed that a document itself can prevent injury or ensure freedom. Elaine Scarry (2014), for example, in her impressive study of thermonuclear armament, seems to suggest that the U.S. Constitution, properly understood, can prevent nuclear destruction. If she is correct in most of her argument, the Constitution may indeed *prohibit* nuclear warfare, but obviously it has not prevented it, and it cannot *prevent* it. The very least required of the government and its citizens is that they agree that the Constitution does indeed prohibit such warfare. Then they must act on that recognition.

But as we found cause to question the primacy of reason as a source of morality, so might we question the power of documents to govern our personal and communal lives. Bad people ignore and violate the rules laid down in a document; good people dissatisfied with its provisions will work to change it. If achieving the common good were simply a matter of reasoning our way to a logically defensible position, we would solve the world's political problems by starting with something like Rawls's "original condition" (1971, 1993) and, through faultless logic, produce a plan for ideal citizenship. But, as we saw earlier, there are passions involved in our moral decisions. Certainly, passions motivated the Magna Carta, the Declaration of Independence, the Constitution, and the Civil Rights Act, and clearly passions are involved in the interpretation and implementation of such documents. It is not enough to *know* what should be done. We must act cooperatively in consonance with what we think we know.

The idea here is to get students thinking about concepts such as fairness, equality, and freedom; about injury, lawlessness, and competition; and about compassion, cooperation, and connectedness. Where does patriotism fit into all of this? Character education has traditionally described patriotism in terms of loyalty to one's country and government. It has put considerable emphasis on obedience to authority. Should students be encouraged to question authority? We turn to that topic next.

CHAPTER 2

Authority

Most thoughtful people today probably agree that rational members of any group should not accept the group's authority without question. Indeed, many groups—religious, national, local, international—have improved over the years as a result of questions raised by their members. What should schools do to encourage such thoughtful questioning of authority, and at what age should students be invited to join in the process? We will return to this topic in some depth in later chapters, especially in one on patriotism, but we will get a start here by exploring what might be accomplished in elementary schools by way of class meetings, the provision of choice, and conversation. We will also suggest several topics that should be introduced for discussion at the middle and high school levels.

CHILDHOOD AND CHOICE

All children hear the words "Mind Mommy," "Mind Daddy," and "Mind your teacher" from an early age, and rightly so. Because we care about the health, safety, and moral growth of our children, we try to start them on the right paths. But our long-term objective is to develop morally sensitive, rationally independent, critical citizens. How do we move beyond the "mind your mommy" stage?

One promising possibility is to provide youngsters with reasonable choices. Assuming there is no compelling health-related problem, young children may safely be allowed to choose the flavor of ice cream they would like, their play things for the moment, the pants they will wear today. Thoughtful parents provide a reasonable set of options, and children are invited to choose among them. The children cannot go wrong, because their parents have laid out only acceptable possibilities. This sounds so obviously right that it must be trivial, but it is not. It is fundamentally important. The idea of choice is so important that some discussion of it appears in virtually all books on child care and early education. (See, for example, Comer, 2004; Neill, 1960; Noddings, 2002a, 2002b, 2013, 2015a; Paley, 2004; Spock, 2001.)

Choices allowed in early childhood establish an expectation that reasonable choice will be encouraged throughout the school years. Alfie Kohn addresses the issue directly: "When someone finally gets around to compiling a list of the ten most astonishing discoveries about education, here is one finding that won't be on it: students learn most avidly and have their best ideas when they get to choose which questions they will explore" (1999, p. 150). The capacity to make wise choices is not only facilitative in school learning; it provides the very backbone of a healthy civil society. Choice is so fundamental in childrearing, education, and civic participation that we are likely to take it for granted, and yet it is the foundation of democratic life.

Closely connected to choice is the topic of conversation. Patterns of family conversation are closely correlated with children's success in school. Some parents converse regularly with their children, and some just talk *at* their children. In the latter case, it is not that parents do not love their children; most of them do. They are stuck in a pattern that has been handed down within families and communities (Heath, 1983). In this tradition, parents instruct, compliment, and scold, but they do not converse with their children. They seem to hold a belief that grown-ups talk and children listen. Children are taught to do as they are told, and not many opportunities for choice arise. We know that such children are often severely deprived of both vocabulary and the skills of conversation.

Discussing the importance of learning the skills of conversation, James Comer describes the family interactions through which he and his siblings became social beings and successful students. At dinner table and after-dinner discussions, both questions and opinions were encouraged: "Thinking, expression, and personal control were practiced in these activities" (Comer, 2004, p. 59). It is skills of this sort that make it possible for students, in due time, to question authority rationally. Without such skills, the unhappy alternatives are either to obey authority without question or to flaunt and disobey it. In the first case, we risk raising citizens who will support a morally deficient government; in the second, we contribute to unfulfilled lives and growth in the prison population.

Because we care about our children and their growth, we sometimes exercise too much control over their choices. Consider a case that has arisen in a school with which we consult. It has a strong commitment to conversation, student choice, and ecological sensitivity. The children grow some of their own food in a rooftop garden. At lunch, enjoyed family-style, the children fill their plates with their own choices from an attractive array of nutritious foods. Now this exemplary school has been challenged by government officials because it does not ensure that each lunch plate is filled (presumably by an appointed adult) with exactly the prescribed amount of each prescribed food. The school officials have pointed out that all of the foods from which the children choose are nutritious; there can be no bad choices. Further, allowing children to choose their food has reduced waste dramatically. In schools where adults make the choices, children simply throw away the foods they would not have chosen. Granted, in our model school where children choose what they will eat, there may occasionally be a perceived lack of balance—say, all greens one day, all fruit another. But even this is not harmful, and it can be corrected by continuing conversation. In an understandable commitment to ensuring that children get what they need, we sometimes undermine the capacity to do what is most needed—learning to make rational choices for themselves. Such choice is the foundation of a healthy civil society.

Of course, many other factors contribute to the success of students and to their growth as rational, competent citizens, but early participation in conversation and choice stands out. Parenting that encourages genuine conversation and well-guided choice is obviously at the heart of early childhood education, and yet we stubbornly refuse to teach parenting in our high schools. We often argue that American education is intended to reduce inequalities and eliminate social classes, but we resist teaching the skills and attitudes that might be most powerful in doing this. We will return to this topic in Chapter 6 in discussions on gender.

PARTICIPATORY DEMOCRACY IN SCHOOLS

Schools can help to prepare thoughtful citizens by involving students in various age-appropriate forms of democratic decisions. When problems arise in a school or class, students should—where possible—be involved in their analysis and recommendations for solution. Suppose, for example, that someone has complained about noise in the halls when students are moving about. Too often today, a solution is imposed by administrators or faculty, and that solution usually involves rules and punishments. Many schools have sought—and more than a few have achieved—silent halls. Why should this be an acceptable solution to "too much noise"? What might the kids suggest? While they are talking about reducing the noise level, they may also be encouraged to discuss courtesy, collegial conversation, and community life in general. Education is more than instruction in the "3 Rs." It is practice in democratic living, preparation for a full life in shared activity.

No one has described the essence of democracy better than John Dewey:

> A democracy is more than a form of government; it is primarily a mode of associated living, of conjoint communicated experience. The extension in space of the number of individuals who participate in an interest so that each has to refer his own action to that of others, and to consider the action of others to give point and direction to his own, is equivalent to the breaking down of those barriers of class, race, and national territory which kept men from perceiving the full import of their activity. (1916, p. 87)

Democracy, then, is not merely a form of governance in which people use free speech to express opinions, vote, win arguments, and nonviolently defeat opponents. It is, rather, a way of life that involves shared objectives, open communication, and generous self-criticism. For Dewey, and for us, a democratic community is dedicated to continuous self-improvement: "Particularly is it true that a society which not only changes but which has the ideal of such change as will improve it, will have different standards and methods of education from one which aims simply at the perpetuation of its own customs" (1916, p. 81). He continues: "The problem is to extract the desirable traits of forms of community life which actually exist, and employ them to criticize undesirable features and suggest improvement" (p. 83).

As children—say 4th- or 5th-graders—discuss the problem of noise in the halls, they may offer positive comments about friendliness, fun, and the healthy content of hall-talk. Or they may comment critically on verbal bullying and/or bad language. To maintain the positive elements of friendliness and fun, they may suggest ways to eliminate nasty language and reduce pushing, shouting, and other forms of noise making. As the students take some responsibility for their own behavior and that of their classmates, they may have to be reminded to treat miscreants as community members who have erred but are still community members. Kids in charge of discipline may take a punitive attitude toward those who violate the agreements. Authority can take many forms, but legitimate authority must remember that it expresses and supports the community's best efforts at continual improvement. Teachers may then want to steer students away from the temptation to appoint student-officers to maintain the peace and remind them continually that they all have a responsibility to maintain a friendly atmosphere in the halls. Before leaving this topic, we should remind readers that many charter schools today put great emphasis on obedience, silence, even walking a painted line as they move from class to class. This sort of submissive obedience should not be encouraged in a democratic society.

Some teachers interpret recommendations on school democracy to mean that great emphasis should be put on democratic procedures. They may, for example, encourage the election of class officers, appoint a secretary, and supervise the regular conduct of class meetings. Early experience with formal civic life may be useful, but this is not what we are suggesting here. Rather, following Dewey, we are more concerned with the family-like conversations that emphasize shared activity and shared responsibility. This emphasis is beautifully described in Marilyn Watson's work applying attachment theory to classroom relationships. The Introduction to her book is titled "A Classroom Where Everyone Belongs" (2003, p. 1), and the aim is to encourage the full development of both individuals and community. The secure establishment of relations of care and trust, extended to the larger community, may prevent or at least reduce the polarization that so often characterizes the form of democratic life that stresses individual freedom and oppositional speech.

THE DANGERS OF OBEDIENCE

In high school, it is time for students to study the dangers of blind obedience to authority seriously. The most obvious case in recent history is, of course, that of Nazi Germany. Here is an opportunity for teachers to examine closely the classical equation of knowledge with virtue. If it is true that "knowledge is virtue," how could one of the most highly educated nations of the 20th century embrace Nazism? Teachers will have to draw attention to Socrates's warning that true knowledge is not just organized information but, rather, material that has been analyzed and evaluated critically. To qualify as knowledge, a collection of facts must be subjected to analysis guided by moral criticism. Similarly, a constellation of skills must be deemed virtuous or not on the basis of how and why the skills are used.

In the years before World War II, there was a strong surge of national pride in Germany. It was widely believed and proclaimed that "there was something special about Germany, her history, the 'instinctive superiority' of her heroes" (P. Watson, 2010, p. 620). As students discuss the period of Nazi control and its enormous stress on German superiority, their attention might be drawn to the current popularity of "American exceptionalism" in the United States. Interestingly, both the earlier German movement and the current American fascination with national exceptionalism are examples of a form of anti-intellectualism. Although both point with pride at their country's intellectual achievements, the movements themselves are largely promoted by conservative groups that often chide their own intellectuals for failing to support the patriotic claims of exceptionalism. Students should be urged to consider where today's emphasis on American exceptionalism might lead us.

Can students see any signs that our devotion to exceptionalism might already be weakening participatory democracy as described by Dewey? In recent news stories, several American critics have been accused of "not loving America" because they have dared to criticize some decisions and actions taken by our country's leaders. From Dewey's perspective, these critics might be credited with a great love for their country. They do not spend much energy in bragging about its past and insisting that this glorious past be preserved in the present and future. Rather, they want their country to become continually better; they are dedicated to Dewey's ideal of continuous, self-critical change.

The horrible era of German authoritarian dominance should be treated in some depth through interdisciplinary studies. In every high school, active faculty interdisciplinary teams should meet regularly and suggest themes that will be addressed in every subject (Noddings, 2013, 2015a). Think what could be done across the curriculum with a broad and deep exploration of the effects of uncritical obedience to authority.

Looking at the period preceding the Nazi era, students might read and discuss *All Quiet on the Western Front* in both English and social studies class. The enormous power of authority, of both government and teachers as its representatives, pushes uncritical young men into war. The narrator says of the teachers who did this: "For us lads of eighteen they ought to have been mediators and guides to the world of maturity, the world of work, of duty, of culture, of progress—to the future . . . . The idea of authority, which they represented, was associated in our minds with a greater insight and a more humane wisdom" (Remarque, 1982/1929, p. 12). Instead, too many teachers glorified an abominable authority and led their students to violence and death.

In math class, students might read a bit about what happened to Jewish mathematicians before and during World War II. Unfortunately, most high school students go through as many as four years of math without hearing the name of a mathematician. The barbaric attack on German Jews had destructive effects on German mathematics:

In 1934, Bernhard Rust, the Third Reich's education minister, asked David Hilbert, the mathematician, how Göttingen—the home of Gauss, Riemann, and Felix Klein, and a world center of mathematics for 200 years—had suffered after the removal of Jewish mathematicians." Suffered?" Hilbert famously replied, "It hasn't suffered, Minister. It doesn't exist any more!" (P. Watson, 2010, p. 662)

Surely a well-prepared math teacher could tell the story of Gauss and his boyhood precocity in math, say a bit about Riemann and the invention of non-Euclidean geometry, and mention the influence of Hilbert on the rigorous revision of Euclidean geometry. The teacher might also remind students that the intellectual authority of Euclid was so strong over so many years that even great philosophers such as Immanuel Kant could not imagine an alternative geometry. All of this would be part of a conversation about mathematics, Jewish culture, and authority gone badly wrong.

As we explore totalitarianism and the dangers of uncritical obedience, we should draw on the emotional or feeling dimension of morality. Students should be encouraged to read Primo Levi on both the physical suffering of those in Nazi concentration camps and their moral/social deterioration. Levi describes that deterioration among prisoners:

We endured filth, promiscuity, and destitution, suffering much less than we would have suffered from such things in normal life, because our moral yardstick had changed. Furthermore, all of us had stolen: in the kitchen, the factory, the camp, in short, "from the other" . . . Some (few) had fallen so low as to steal bread from their own companions. We had not only forgotten our country and our culture, but also our family, our past, the future we had imagined for ourselves, because, like animals, we were confined to the present moment. (Levi, 1988, p. 75)

It is hard for young people in the United States even to imagine living in such conditions, conditions inflicted by a national government. Levi, in his thoughtful and generous reflections, points out that both victims and perpetrators suffered. Some perpetrators cooperated in inflicting horrors in order to save their own lives—if even for a few months; some actually believed in the political state established by Hitler. In his conclusion, Levi reminds readers that the perpetrators were ordinary individuals:

average human beings, averagely intelligent, averagely wicked: save the exceptions, they were not monsters, they had our faces, but they had been reared badly. They were, for the greater part, diligent followers and functionaries, some fanatically convinced of the Nazi doctrine, many indifferent, or fearful of punishment, or desirous of a good career, or too obedient. (p. 202)

Levi's final words are especially important for students to consider:

Let it be clear that to a greater or lesser degree all were responsible, but it must be just as clear that behind their responsibility stands that great majority of Germans who accepted in the beginning, out of mental laziness, myopic calculation, stupidity, and national pride the "beautiful words" of Corporal Hitler, followed him as luck and lack of scruples favored him, were swept away by his vision, afflicted by deaths, misery and remorse. (p. 203)

We can hardly imagine more powerful words on the dangers of accepting and obeying authority without question.

Some students might read and report on Joachim Fest's *Not I* (2013). Growing up in Nazi Germany, Fest remembers the moral agonies his father suffered. Although his father refused to join the Nazi party and thereby lost his position as a teacher, he could do little else in opposition:

To damn the regime at the garden fence, to listen to the BBC and to pray for those in need: that was nothing at all! "Yes!" he went on. "I keep out of things. Like everyone else! But I now know that under the present conditions there is no separation of good and evil. The air is poisoned. It infects us all!" (Fest, 2013, p. 242)

Like many good Germans, Fest's father felt helpless in the nation's capitulation to Nazism. He had to protect his family, and in doing so he could not actively oppose Hitler, but he never actively supported him and the party. As Fest points out persuasively, in the late 1940s (and perhaps even today), Germans were still struggling to understand what happened to their country: "The question still being asked is how these ideas were capable of driving such an old and civilized nation out of its mind. How was it possible that the leaders of the National Socialist movement were able to overcome the constitutional safeguards with so little resistance?" (Fest, 2013, p. 386).

Certainly, teachers and parents want their young people to respect and obey legitimate authority. They must also help the young to understand that good citizens must be on constant guard to be sure that those in authority are themselves upholding the laws to which we are pledged and that the *authority* faithfully represents the ideals underlying those laws. What should we do when *authority* goes wrong?

CIVIL DISOBEDIENCE

Civil society is usually defined as that enormous collection of voluntary associations that make up a society. It does not include the state, and it does not include families (as particular entities) because membership in them is not voluntary. In a democracy, we are deeply and constantly concerned about the healthy relationship between the state and civil society. A democracy, as Dewey reminded us, is best thought of as "a mode of associated living, of conjoint communicated experience" (1916, p. 87). A democratic state supports both the freedom of individuals and free communication among the groups of civil society. When members or groups of the civil society believe that the state has betrayed its mission to uphold justice, they may—in the interest of preserving or renewing the ideals of law and justice—deliberately break the offending law and accept the resulting punishment for doing so. Or they may break some unrelated law—a traffic law or law on gatherings of some sort—in order to draw attention to their protest. This is civil disobedience, the refusal to obey a law established by the state in order to defend what is seen as the larger law.

In our conversations with various groups and individuals, we have frequently heard troubling misunderstandings about "civil disobedience." Even some teachers seem to think that they are committing civil disobedience when, for example, they assist students in cheating on standardized tests. But such an act is not civil disobedience; it is just breaking the law. If they announced to the world that they were doing this and accepted the punishment decreed by authority, they would indeed be committing civil disobedience. At heart, civil disobedience exhibits the deepest respect for state authority; it is nonviolent, and its aim is to ensure that authority abides by its stated ideals. Henry David Thoreau regarded civil disobedience in cases of authoritarian abuse as a *duty* of good citizens (see Thoreau's *On the Duty of Civil Disobedience*, 1849). The requirement that one who disobeys a law will undergo the punishment for doing so makes it unlikely that people will engage in civil disobedience frivolously. The most prominent example from the last century is the Civil Rights Movement led by Martin Luther King for racial justice. King and many of his colleagues suffered jail time for their heroic efforts as did Mahatma Gandhi and Nelson Mandela.

Civil disobedience should be distinguished from conscientious refusal (Rawls, 1971, p. 368). In the latter case, an objector may not be trying to change a law entirely but merely to assert his or her right to be exempt from it. Some religious groups have, for example, claimed a right to be exempt from reciting the pledge of allegiance. Also, many of those who have resisted the military draft have not argued that the draft is itself unjust but rather that their religious convictions should exempt them from it. We'll say more about pacifism in the Chapter 11 on patriotism. Here, by way of introduction, we will mention a story that should arouse the interest of high school students. The poet Robert Lowell refused the draft in World War II on the grounds that the United States and its allies were employing violent acts on civilians. He went to prison for his refusal to serve. It is said that his cellmate, a notorious gangster, said to him: "I'm in for killing. What are you in for?" Lowell replied, "Oh, I'm in for refusing to kill" (quoted in True, 1995, p. 80).

Students today will be interested in accounts of the civil disobedience during the 1960s directed at unjust voting laws and racial discrimination (Zinn, 1968). Discussion of that era should help students to understand the current widespread protests directed at alleged racial discrimination exercised by police against Blacks. This may be the time, too, to discuss the rampant nastiness on racial, religious, and gender issues that appears so often in today's media. If we treasure freedom of speech, should we not accept some responsibility for its quality?

The health of a democratic civil society depends on the intelligent interaction of that society and the state within which it resides. Volumes, whole libraries, have been written about the topics treated briefly in this chapter. It is not our purpose to discuss them comprehensively. Rather, we hope to emphasize their importance in education, and we have tried to illustrate ways in which teachers might approach them. Choice, we argue, is essential in a participatory democracy, and provision for age-appropriate choice should be made at every level of schooling. Class meetings should be conducted, too, in every grade, and attention should be given to considerate conversation. From the earliest days, students should be encouraged to respect and obey authority, but they should also be invited to reflect on and question that authority. Whenever possible, polite, considerate questioning should be directed at the procedures and practices of the school authority, and students should take increasing responsibility for their school's ethos. To do that effectively, students must become critical thinkers. We turn to that topic next.

CHAPTER 3

Critical Thinking

In the previous chapter, we considered how children might be encouraged to question authority. To do this effectively as adult citizens, students need to develop a capacity for critical thinking. Of course, critical thinking is required for many purposes, not only for questioning authority, and the need for this capacity is widely recognized today; indeed, "critical thinking" now appears worldwide as an important aim of education. In this chapter, we will consider several aspects of critical thinking and argue that, if the capacity is to be used for the common good, it must be guided by moral commitment.

DEVELOPING THE BASICS

Teachers have always told students to "check" their work—to use a critical eye on it before submitting it to the teacher's evaluation. This requires at least a bit of critical thinking. In English classes, students are expected to check their work for spelling, punctuation, grammar, paragraphing, and legibility. In mathematics, they are advised to check computation, the labeling of geometric figures, use of symbols, and whether all steps of their work have been displayed. Given these expectations, it is odd that teachers so seldom ask students to "revise and resubmit." Instead, too often the papers are just graded and returned; it is hoped that students will learn from whatever corrections the teacher has made and, thus, do better with the next assignment. Experience shows, however, that students pay careful attention to the grade and very little to the corrective comments. When our emphasis is on critical thinking, we would do better to recommend that students spend some time to think about and revise their current work.

At every stage of work, critical thinking involves a search for meaning. At the simplest level, we need to know what the words mean if we are to understand a sentence. A mere glance from the critical eye will tell us that "red the was sky" is not a sentence, and even young children can rearrange the words—"the sky was red"—to make a sentence. But if they are presented with "The sky was vermillion," they may have to look up the meaning of *vermillion* in order to understand the sentence. It is a basic aim of early education to help children gain meaning through words and sentences. They learn to match symbols with sounds, to convert sounds to symbols, written words to spoken words and vice versa.

Children must also learn to understand and follow directions, and they should exercise a critical eye to be sure—in math especially—that they have done what was asked of them. There are funny stories to be shared here. In the trial of the Knave of Hearts (in *Alice's Adventures in Wonderland*), the jurors hear three dates mentioned: the 14th of March, the 15th, and the 16th. What do they do with these dates? They "eagerly wrote down all three dates on their slates and then added them up, and reduced the answer to shillings and pence" (M. Gardner, 1963, p. 146). We laugh at this story, but it captures a familiar student practice that teachers see often in math classes. Students will isolate the numbers in a word problem and, instead of attending to what they are asked to do, simply apply the easiest operation on the numbers. Most math teachers have seen students decide to add two numbers in a word problem because the division clearly indicated by the context was thought to be too difficult. Often in multiple-choice tests these wrong answers will be listed among the choices reinforcing rather than correcting the tendency.

We see the beginning of critical thinking, then, in figuring out the meaning of words and checking to see if our responses are consonant with that meaning. Even at this level, some students experience difficulty and abandon the search for meaning. Teachers must offer support, humor, inspiration, and constructive criticism. Constant encouragement must be offered: Use a critical eye on your work! Revise and resubmit! We should also reward the efforts at revision. Students should not be "stuck" with a poor grade if they are willing to improve their work.

Before we extend our discussion of meaning, we should mention that "critical thinking" is almost always directed at language. Indeed, it is sometimes narrowly defined as the correct assessment of statements (Ennis, 1962). Although we will not spend much time on alternatives, we want to remind readers that a critical eye can be turned on objects as well as words and that we should give more attention in our schools to the sort of work done by mechanics, toolmakers, builders, repairers, and artisans. (See Matthew B. Crawford, 2009; also Noddings, 2006.) Even in these activities, however, a need usually arises for verbal analysis, interpretation, communicative adequacy, and defense of results. At every level, critical thinkers ask about the meaning of what they see, hear, try out, evaluate, and recommend.

THE SEARCH FOR MEANING DEEPENS

Today's Common Core State Standards put great emphasis on critical thinking, but they do not say much about how critical thinking is defined or how we should teach it. It is unlikely that anyone today would refer to critical thinking as simply the correct assessment of statements. A few decades ago, philosophers and educational theorists debated whether critical thinking could be taught as a subject in itself or had to be treated in the context of another, well-defined subject (Noddings, 2006, 2015b). While most of us agree that some critical thinking skills can be described in general terms such as "analyzing," "interpreting," or "predicting," we also agree that these skills cannot be exercised without some knowledge of the subject matter under consideration. Suppose, for example, that you were asked to assess the accuracy of this statement: In base 12, $3 \times 6 = 16$. If you know nothing about number bases other than 10 (and have not even considered how that works), you might be stumped and insist that $3 \times 6 = 18$, and that's that. It seems that we have to know something about the subject or context in which a statement appears if we are to discern its meaning and determine its accuracy.

The Common Core standards in English Language Arts, as mentioned previously, put great stress on reading documents; students are now supposed to spend more time reading documents than fiction. How much do students need to know about the context in which a document was written if they are to bring critical thinking to bear on it? Consider, for example, the Declaration of Independence. To understand it, students need to know about the times in which it was written and the people who wrote and signed it. This is a fine opportunity for interdisciplinary work—for English and social studies teachers to work together to bring historical and literary meaning to the reading.

But, if our concern is critical thinking, we need to dig even deeper. Clearly, the signers were competent critical thinkers, and they used that competence to challenge the king and British authority. They laid out their complaints and their solution in specific terms. But let's pause a moment and ask a few questions about the possible meaning of some of their language. We are all familiar with the following paragraph from the Declaration:

> We hold these truths to be self-evident, that all men are created equal, that they are endowed by their Creator with certain unalienable rights, that among these are Life, Liberty, and the Pursuit of Happiness.

What could Jefferson, the main author of the document, have meant when he wrote, "all men are created equal"? And what did he mean by "men"? Jefferson, like many others among the signers, was a slave-holder. He certainly did not mean to imply that Black men were equal to White men or that Black men had an unalienable right to liberty. Could he have meant that all men are *created* equal but that inequality comes almost simultaneously with birth through race, class, and family status? And what did he mean by "men"? For many years, "man" was often defined as "human being," not as "male human being." It was widely accepted, for example, that women belong to the class labeled *mankind*. Did Jefferson intend to include women and Black men in his concept of "men"? Our founders seem to have been referring to a relatively exclusive group when they spoke of "all men" and "equality." Here is a strong opportunity for students to exercise critical thinking on a substantial period of history. What did the document mean when it was written? What does it mean to us today?

When we search for meaning, we often move back and forth between what an author (or speaker) meant and what *we* might mean by the same words. We want to agree or disagree with his or her words; perhaps we want to modify them or add to them. Sometimes, as in formal debate, we want to understand what a person has said in order to formulate an opposing position. We want to understand another's words in order to defeat his or her argument. At other times, we want to elaborate on the initial statement. As an example of elaborating on the initial text, consider Elizabeth Cady Stanton's efforts on behalf of women's suffrage. In 1848, at Seneca Falls, she read her "Declaration of Sentiments" that modified Jefferson's Declaration: "We hold these truths to be self-evident, that all men and women are created equal . . ." (see Oakley, 1972, p. 11). This modification was not quickly or gratefully accepted. The founders achieved the independence they sought from Britain in just a few years, but it was not until 1920, several years after Stanton's death, that women finally gained the right to vote. We should extend the discussion by noting that, although Black men gained the legal right to vote far earlier than women, they were often prevented from doing so, and Blacks even today suffer from a host of inequalities. (See, for example, the account in Coates, 2014.)

Teachers should spend some time on the discussion of both *equality* and *men*. On the latter, students should become aware that writers are now expected to use "his or her" or "they" rather than the earlier, supposedly generic "his" in their references to an unspecified individual's comments or acts. How should we handle this change in our writing? Should "they" become acceptable as a singular, as well as plural, reference? Must we use the clumsy "his or her" and "he or she" in all of our writing?

Teachers are necessarily concerned with the problems of teaching critical thinking, but they should also be concerned with the collegial work of applying critical thinking to their own profession. For teachers today, it is especially important to discuss the meanings of *equality* and *equal*. What do we mean when we assert that all children should receive an equal education? In many school districts today, almost all high school children are placed in academic—college preparatory—courses in the name of equal education or equal opportunity. It seems right to most of us that students should have the right to *choose* the college preparatory program, but some of us have serious questions about forcing or assigning students to such a program. How do we define and interpret "equal opportunity" in education? Some define it as prescribing the same course of study for all students (Hirsch, 1987, 1996). Others object that such uniformity fails to recognize the substantial range of talents and interests of American students. Are we providing equal opportunity for a boy with outstanding mechanical talents when we force him into an academic program that does nothing to advance his real talent and may indeed cause him to feel inadequate because that talent is unrecognized? Are we neglecting the possibility that he may use a powerful critical eye on objects and instruments but not, perhaps, on words? We will return to the topic of equality in Chapter 10 where we will also consider controversies on justice and freedom.

Teachers who are good critical thinkers will find many ideas to challenge in contemporary education. For example, should high school students be assigned to programs (or tracks) or should they be allowed to make a well-guided choice? Should there even be a variety of programs at the high school level? How might we ensure that the choice is indeed "well-guided"? What part of the high school curriculum, if any, should be universally required? How large a role should testing play in today's education? Should that testing be norm-referenced or criterion-referenced? Should teacher tenure be eliminated? Should a plan for teacher advancement within the ranks be devised? Should the role of federal government be reduced? Clearly, we cannot take these matters up in any depth here (see Noddings, 2015a, for discussion of many of them), but teachers should be continually reminded that critical thinking must be applied to their own profession.

Let us return now briefly to some problems that arise in teaching critical thinking. A major task, as we have noted, involves the search for meaning from its beginnings in matching written symbols and spoken words. Next we want students to be able to assess work, their own and that of others, for formal adequacy. At a more advanced level, we guide students in analyzing and evaluating statements for intentions, evidence, consistency, and clarity. The purpose of this thinking is sometimes to express opposition, to defeat another in argumentation. But the Common Core stresses, rightly, a more basic purpose—to understand others. This understanding can, of course, be used to strengthen one's opposition to another's case, but it can also be used to support collegiality and cooperative projects.

Teachers should urge students to use patience and persistence in their search for meaning and understanding. In the study of philosophy, for example, students might be advised to "read and believe" a particular writer for a substantial period of time. This does not mean that everything read should be accepted on authority. Rather, it means that we should establish a reasonable level of understanding before challenging the work at hand. In this approach, *believing* is used as a strategy. Students are often encouraged to raise challenging questions right from the start, but this move may be a mistake. It may prejudice readers against what follows and close the door to understanding what the writer is trying to accomplish. It is reasonable to invite questions at the level of formal understanding (e.g., what does *ontology* mean?), and it is the job of teachers to invite and answer such questions. At the deeper level, however, it is often wiser to assure students that further reading will probably clear things up, and an open, receptive attitude facilitates the sort of understanding that answers questions such as: Why is the writer saying this? What in his/her background promotes this? What is he/she likely to say on a related topic? How important are these lines to the total argument? Why has he/she chosen this language? To whom are the critical comments directed?

The approach suggested here not only promotes deeper, more accurate understanding, it also lays the groundwork for collegial cooperation. When we understand another's position and the arguments that support it, we may find a way to compromise. We know that the writer (or speaker) is unlikely to give way on deeply held beliefs, but she or he may well be open to compromise on some issues and thus pave the way for genuine cooperation.

Achieving the level of understanding discussed here can be hard work. Why should students (or anyone) do it? Why should students try to become critical thinkers? The answer—spoken or unspoken—has traditionally been to win arguments. Too often, emphasis has been on defeating others rather than on working effectively with them. We are not suggesting that this motive should be abandoned entirely. It has, after all, led to progress in almost every field of human endeavor, but it has also caused contention and unnecessary harm. Winning an argument is not in itself a moral good, nor is critical thinking. We should want our critical thinking to be guided by moral commitment.

In science, moral commitment has been built in to the use of critical thinking. Scientists challenge each other's work not simply to win arguments but to promote a deeper search for truth. That means that they must accept questions directed at their own work as well as that of others. Critical thinking should be used in the service of truth and human well-being, and that requires moral commitment.

CRITICAL THINKING AND MORAL COMMITMENT

Critical thinking, we repeat, is not in itself a moral good. There are, after all, bad people who are quite skilled as critical thinkers, and there are bad purposes to which critical thinking has been applied. In fiction, we think of the diabolical professor Moriarty, nemesis of Sherlock Holmes. In today's world, we often hear about educated, proficient critical thinkers in the financial world who use morally questionable—sometimes even illegal—methods to cheat others and gain greater profits. Teachers should remind students that critical thinking should be guided by moral motives. It is one thing to apply critical thinking to our studies in order to achieve higher grades but quite another to employ critical thinking to cheat more effectively. Teachers, too, are susceptible to the temptation to cheat. Recent news accounts have reported the shameful story of widespread cheating on standardized tests by teachers and administrators in the Atlanta public schools. Such events present another case for the application of critical thinking to professional life. Should teachers be rewarded monetarily for higher student test scores?

We can perhaps think of many social and political matters on which we are urged to think critically, but sometimes our thinking may be pointed in the wrong direction. For example, scientists are encouraged to find more humane ways to inflict capital punishment when all of us as citizens should perhaps invoke the results of critical thinking to consider the abolition of capital punishment. Our government is trying to control its use of drones in bombing so as to avoid civilian casualties but, perhaps, it should use critical thinking to consider whether bombing of any sort in populated areas should ever be employed. Many such examples should be considered and discussed.

In most of these discussions, teachers should use pedagogical neutrality; that is, they should not tell students what is right or wrong but encourage them to think on each issue critically and to listen carefully to opposing views. Even the recommendation to use pedagogical neutrality should be addressed critically. Surely, there are issues on which teachers *should* take an official moral stance. Cheating may be one such issue. But on many controversial matters, there is more than one position that can be morally defended. If we do not adopt pedagogical neutrality on these issues, we will not be able to discuss them at all. Consider how we might approach questions involving religion in our schools. Should the political debate over evolution be discussed? Diane Ravitch has suggested that "education authorities must separate teaching about science from teaching about religion. . . . Science classes should teach science, as validated by scholarship, and religion classes should teach religion" (2010, p. 234).

Such an approach ignores the debate entirely. What are students expected to conclude if they are told x in one class and not-x in another with no discussion of the debate? Part of the problem surely lies in our longstanding habit of concentrating our teaching on facts and material said to be facts—material our students are expected to believe and memorize. It would be better, in the interest of developing critical thinking, to teach about science, about religion, and about the various debates both between them and within them. Further, the material comes alive in this approach, and students can see a point of studying it. On many controversial issues, teachers should present all reasonable sides. They should also, of course, elaborate on a consensus if one has emerged, as it has on evolution. They should express their own opinion if asked, but this should not be presented as the official view that everyone must accept. If this approach is handled fairly and sensitively, students should feel free to draw their own conclusions, but they should be encouraged to defend those conclusions logically.

Are there matters on which pedagogical neutrality should not be used? Certainly, there are such matters, although here again opinions may vary. No teacher in America today should encourage a defense of Nazism, racism, slavery, or cruelty. However, which topics should be open for critical discussion is itself a matter for critical examination. Is stealing ever justified? Is cheating ever justified? Can breaking the law be morally justified? Remember here our earlier discussion of civil disobedience. Civil disobedience has been defended as a moral duty when a law is perceived to be unjust.

Critical thinking, we have noted, can be used for bad purposes as well as good. As Jane Roland Martin (1992) warned, it can also produce a well-reasoned conclusion that does not induce a response in action. Critical thinkers may be afflicted by the "bystander syndrome"; that is, they may see what must be done—what is right or wrong—but do nothing. In some situations, we are afraid that we might make things worse by acting—for example, by moving an injured person. But that fear does not justify doing nothing. In the cases that worry Martin, bystanders are good thinkers, but they are simply not motivated to act. Recall our brief discussion in Chapter 1 of David Hume's position on this problem when he argued persuasively that we are moved to action by *feeling*, not by reason alone:

> What is honourable, what is fair, what is becoming, what is noble, what is generous, takes possession of the heart, and animates us to embrace and maintain it. What is intelligible, what is evident, what is probable, what is true, procures only the cool assent of the understanding; and gratifying a speculative curiosity, puts an end to our researches. (1983/1751, p. 15)

If Hume was right—and we believe that he was—we must educate the hearts and feelings as well as the reason of our students. This is another good reason for addressing controversial issues in our classrooms. Students are motivated to think and argue because they have feelings on the matter at hand, and they may be motivated to act further if they are moved by the feelings that accompany the conclusions they reach critically. Too often today, we encourage students to study, learn, and argue just to get good grades, gain admission to a good college, get a good job, and make lots of money. These motives should not be dismissed, but we should want more. We need to expand the horizons of critical thinking to open a vision of moral commitment to a fuller life and more generous society.

THE MEDIA THREAT

Many young people today are influenced heavily by what they see and hear on the Internet, especially social media. Here we want to address briefly a problem that is getting increased attention in the national news. Apparently, young men and women are being solicited by radical Islamic groups urging them to join in a global battle to rid the world of what these groups see as injustice, indecency, and defiance of God. It certainly makes sense to talk with our students in school about these matters and to help them apply critical thinking to the messages and information they are receiving from sources on the Internet. Are the messages consistent, or do they contain logical contradictions? Do they identify genuine moral problems that should be addressed? Are there morally and legally acceptable methods of addressing them, methods available to us as American citizens? Are the invitations (and invocations) of these groups exciting? Is it excitement and adventure that attracts us? Why?

Teachers need to talk with each other and with their curriculum groups about how to approach this problem. What part of the problem can be discussed in each class? What can be done in, for example, math class? Are there students who feel left out in both formal classes and extracurricular activities? What can be done to include them? We have to remember that our job as teachers is not limited to presenting and testing factual material. The mission of education has been to produce better people, and we should not neglect that larger aim.

We suggest that critical conversation may well be a more powerful way to approach this growing threat than heavy-handed moralizing, and simply ignoring the threat—as something to be handled by other agencies—is irresponsible. Critical conversation among our teachers and in our high school classrooms should accomplish at least two important educational goals—to get our students thinking seriously about an important moral/political issue and, just as important, to convince them that they are included as members in a participatory democracy.

We will return to this crucial matter in the next chapter on religion and later chapters on the media and patriotism.

CHAPTER 4

Religion

Of all the topics discussed in this book, possibly none is more controversial than religion. Should religion be taught in our public schools? In most parts of the United States today, a course in world religions is permitted, but the contradictions of belief inherent in religion are usually avoided. Students know, for example, that religion involves the idea of God or gods. Dare we discuss, however, the variety of approaches to the questions: Is there a God? How has this God been described?

Most teachers would not dare to encourage a careful consideration of atheism, and few would give critical attention to the deistic leanings of our Founding Fathers or to the deeply divergent views of religion on slavery. What does it mean to be "spiritual" but not "religious"? What is mysticism? Are prayer and meditation synonymous? How do religions attempt to answer basic philosophical questions such as, why do I exist? Are there ways in which these controversial topics might be included in the school curriculum? And can this be done without resorting to indoctrination?

These topics are so controversial that we doubt they can be included in a standard curriculum. However, they are central to human life. Our suggestion is that they be considered and developed within the 4-year social studies program described in the Introduction and supplemented by relevant discussion in all of the disciplines. Such an arrangement would place both the decision to include and the development of relevant materials in the hands of local educators and citizens. In this arrangement, there would be no specifically defined learning objectives, no tests, and no grades. The overall aim is to develop thoughtful, well-informed citizens for a participatory democracy.

The development of themes on highly controversial topics is properly an interdisciplinary undertaking. Although a particular topic—in this case religion—would not appear as a specific entry in the standard curriculum, related elements might well appear in the basic disciplinary courses. Each of the disciplines should be asked to contribute something essential to the understanding of religion, and we will offer several suggestions along these lines as the chapter develops. Clearly, the preparation of teachers in each of the disciplines will have to be enriched if this program is to succeed.

Let's start with a basic topic central to the study of religion: belief and unbelief.

BELIEF AND UNBELIEF

Many students enter high school with religious beliefs they have never questioned. In some cases, even a speculative thought of unbelief is forbidden by the religious tradition in which they have been raised. It is not the job of teachers to challenge this basic orientation but, rather, to help students understand the range of deeply felt views that differ from their own. Certainly, all students should gain some understanding of atheism, agnosticism, and deism. At the very least, these words should be addressed in a vocabulary lesson. A generous approach to their study might be to start with an account of deep agreement on moral/ethical values between believers and unbelievers, between Christians and atheists. "Intelligent believers and intelligent unbelievers are often closer in thought and spirit than intelligent and unintelligent believers" (Noddings, 1993, p. xiii).

Unfortunately, atheism has been closely associated with communism since the days of the Cold War. Today, many who retain political allegiance to communism are also Christians, and it should be made clear at the start of our discussion that atheism did not arise out of communism. People have always questioned the existence of a deity or deities, and there are careful thinkers who use the word *God* to refer to something other than a sacred being. John Dewey, for example, said:

> But this idea of God, or of the divine, is also connected with all the natural forces and conditions—including men and human association—that promote the growth of the ideal. . . . We are in the presence neither of ideals completely embodied in existence nor yet of ideals that are mere rootless ideals, fantasies, utopias. For there are forces in nature and society that generate and support the ideals. . . . It is this *active* relation between ideal and actual to which I would give the name "God." (1989/1934, p. 34)

Interestingly, there were those who responded to Dewey's *A Common Faith* with relief, believing that he had finally confessed a belief in God. Others—more astute—recognized Dewey's confirmed atheism.

Similarly, the theologian Paul Tillich spoke of a "God above the God of theism" (1952). Because of this contention, Tillich is often thought of as an atheist, but, as in Dewey's case, others hang on to the belief that Tillich was not an atheist. Technically, the label atheist is correctly applied to Tillich; he did not believe in the personal God of theism. Students should understand at the outset that many thoughtful people—Alfred North Whitehead and Ralph Waldo Emerson, for example—have expressed devotion to "the forces of good" even though they deny the existence of God as a being or person.

Thus, perhaps the first thing to make clear in a brief exploration of atheism is that it should not be identified with evil or, for that matter, with any particular political view. Students should be made aware, however, that some reputable thinkers have even linked religion itself more closely to evil than to good. Bertrand Russell, for example, wrote: "I think that anybody who surveys past history in an impartial manner will be driven to the conclusion that religion has caused more suffering than it has prevented" (1963, p. 201). Similarly, John Stuart Mill, a strong advocate for women's rights and an equally strong adversary of slavery, also suggested that religion is a source of moral evil. Speaking of his atheistic father, Mill wrote: "He found it impossible to believe that a world so full of evil was the work of an Author combining infinite power with perfect goodness and righteousness" (2007, p. 58).

But educators must be cautious not to endorse the idea that religion is a source of evil. Our advice is to present atheism as the rejection of belief in a person-God but not as an organized attempt to overthrow religion. We should admit that there are atheists and atheistic organizations that do promote this goal, but our aim as educators is to emphasize the many ideas shared by thoughtful believers and unbelievers. Both want to make the world a better place.

As an example of shared thinking and generous dialogue, we might refer to Martin Gardner, a writer well known for his math columns in *Scientific American* and his critical/appreciative work on Lewis Carroll's *Alice's Adventures in Wonderland* (*The Annotated Alice*, 1963). Gardner begins a chapter in his *The Whys of a Philosophical Scrivener*, "Why I am not an Atheist," with a statement of agreement with Bertrand Russell, an outspoken atheist:

> Whenever I speak of religious faith it will mean a belief, unsupported by logic or science, in both God and an afterlife. Bertrand Russell once defined faith, in a broader way, as a "firm belief in something for which there is no evidence." If "evidence" means the kind of support provided by reason and science, there is no evidence for God and immortality, and Russell's definition seems to me concise and admirable. (1983, p. 209)

Although Gardner dismisses almost everything said about God in the Old Testament, he nevertheless asserts belief in both a personal God and immortality.

There are at least two more words to include in our vocabulary lesson on religion. People who say that there is no way to prove either the existence or nonexistence of God and, therefore, that it is appropriate to reject both belief and unbelief are said to be agnostics. Richard Dawkins (2006), a prominent advocate of atheism, criticizes *agnostics* for their unwillingness to reject theism entirely; he argues that, although we cannot prove that God does not exist, the evidence is overwhelmingly in favor of atheism. However, he may not distinguish carefully enough between those agnostics who are clearly atheistic with respect to a personal God but acknowledge that there may be a creator God (or gods) and those who leave open even the possibility of a personal God. Agnostics who take the first position—that there may indeed be a creator God—are close to deism. They remain undecided on belief in a creator-God.

Deism differs from both atheism and theism. It does not posit a personal God, but it does recognize a supreme intelligence of some sort. The God of deism does not answer prayers or intervene in any way with the daily affairs of human beings. It created the universe and keeps it running smoothly. Some take it to be synonymous with the laws of the universe.

Interestingly, many of America's founders were deists, and students should be made aware that, strictly speaking, the United States was not founded as a Christian nation. Our first presidents—Washington, Adams, Jefferson, and Madison—have been widely recognized as deists, and it has been argued that Jefferson and Madison may have been atheists (Jacoby, 2004; Kruse, 2015). Certainly, students should learn that the phrase "In God We Trust" did not appear on our coins until the Civil War and that "one nation under God" was added to the Pledge of Allegiance in 1954; the Pledge itself was formally adopted only in 1945. Interested students might want to investigate further into the religious revivals, supported in part by the perceived threat of Communism that arose in the 1950s.

RELIGION, SLAVERY, AND WOMEN'S RIGHTS

Edward Baptist writes, "The vast expansion of slavery in the United States happened in tandem with the emergence of evangelical Protestantism" (2014, p. 200). Before 1800, relatively few Americans were regular church-goers, and our founders were adamant in their separation of church and state. However, "by the 1850s, half or more of all white Americans had come to participate regularly in some sort of church" (Baptist, 2014, p. 200). Possibly the main cause of this growth was the felt need of people moving into new geographical territory for connection and some sort of permanency, and since there were few established churches on the frontier, it was natural for them to turn toward itinerant evangelical preachers.

As Baptist and others have pointed out, the tandem growth of slavery and evangelicalism is not easily explained. Evangelical services did adopt some African customs such as physical movement, shouting, and semi-fainting, but they also accepted slavery as a God-ordained practice. The attitudes of evangelicals ranged from a belief that Negroes had no souls to the abolitionist commitment to free the slaves, but Christian support for slavery dominated in both the south and west. Our current history text-books too often underemphasize the role of religion in supporting slavery.

Students need to think and talk about the connection between religion and the maintenance of slavery. The long-lasting effects of slavery and its religious justification are still with us. In many communities today, Black people come under suspicion and police challenges far more often than Whites, and our prison population is heavily Black. The unfair connection between Blacks and crime can be traced back to the days of slavery and its defense by religionists. Ta-Nehisi Coates writes:

> Pro-slavery intellectuals sought to defend the system as "commanded by God" and "approved by Christ." In 1860, *The New York Herald* offered up a dispatch on the doings of runaway slaves residing in Canada. "The criminal calendars would be bare of a prosecution but for the negro prisoners," the report claimed. Deprived of slavery's blessings, Blacks quickly devolved into criminal deviants who plied their trade with "a savage ferocity peculiar to the vicious negro." (2015, p. 69)

Coates ends his article with a powerful reminder that the question of justice for Black people is:

> more urgent than ever. The economic and political marginalization of black people virtually ensured that they would be the ones who would bear the weight of what one of President Nixon's own aides called his "bullshit" crime policy. . . . And should crime rates rise again, there is no reason to believe that black people, black communities, black families will not be fed into the great maw again. Indeed, the experience of mass incarceration, the warehousing and deprivation of whole swaths of our country . . . have only intensified the ancient American dilemma's white-hot-core—the problem of "past unequal treatment," the difficulty of "damages," the question of reparations. (2015, p. 84)

Solution of the problems described by Coates will require the determined collaboration of all components of our society, including those of religion and education. Americans are in the habit of regarding both religion and education as forces of good in our world, and their positive contributions should not be denied. But we must acknowledge that they have also supported evil and injustice. Perhaps the application of astute critical thinking and a moral commitment to act on its conclusions is a necessary first step.

Religion has also contributed to the subordination of women. Elizabeth Cady Stanton drew attention to the need for a transformation in religion even while she crusaded for women's voting rights. Her colleagues feared that she would alienate supporters by tackling traditional Christianity, but she was undeterred:

> Nothing that has ever emanated from the brain of man is too sacred to be revised and corrected. Our National Constitution has been amended fifteen times, our English system of jurisprudence has been essentially modified in the interest

of woman to keep pace with advancing civilization. And now the time has come to amend and modify the canon laws, prayer-books, liturgies and Bibles. . . . Women's imperative duty at this hour is to demand a thorough revision of creeds and codes, Scriptures and constitutions. (quoted in Ward & Burns, 1999, p. 9)

But religious doctrine and sacred documents are not so easily amended. It is difficult to modify the U.S. Constitution, but it is well-nigh impossible to change the Bible. When a work is accepted as "the word of God," any substantive change must be preceded by an understanding that the document in question should be considered the word of God as interpreted by human beings living at a specific time. Such understanding would encourage criticism and revision, but that rarely happens.

Pearl Buck described vividly the suffering of her mother, a conservative pastor's wife in China, as she struggled to find some recognition of her full personhood:

Since those days when I saw all her nature dimmed I have hated Saint Paul with all my heart and so must all true women hate him, I think, because of what he has done in the past to women like Carie, proud free-born women, yet damned by their very womanhood. I rejoice for her sake that his power is gone in these new days. (1936, p. 283)

But, of course, his power was not gone then, and large vestiges of it remain today. Elizabeth Cady Stanton would indulge in a sardonic smile at some of the changes in attitude toward St. Paul. Instead of deploring and condemning his patriarchal comments on women, many scholars have employed their skills to find evidence that Paul was not really the source of these prejudicial views. Someone else said them, and Paul should be cleared of blame (see Daly, 1974). Meanwhile, men continue to dominate in religious matters.

Today's students might notice that, in a way, Stanton's worried colleagues were right. Women have made considerable progress in occupations and public life without shaking the roots of religion. But educators should be concerned that we are often forced to live a contradiction. On the one hand, we are urged to teach critical thinking; on the other, we are discouraged from leading a critical discussion on one of the most controversial subjects—religion. Surely, a deep, thoughtful religious commitment will not be destroyed by critical thinking.

EVOLUTION

Evolution is a case in point. Although there are still parts of the country in which evolution is rejected or ignored in science classes, most well-educated people understand that evolution and religion are not necessarily at odds. Evolution challenges the Biblical creation story, of course, but it does not necessitate a rejection of theism. Students should learn not only about evolution but also about evolutionary scientists who have retained their religious commitments. Simon Conway Morris, an evolutionary paleobiologist, writes in his introduction to a study of evolution and its compatibility with belief in a creator-God:

> If you happen to be a "creation scientist" (or something of that kind) and have read this far, may I politely suggest that you put this book back on the shelf. It will do you no good. Evolution is true, it happens, it is the way the world is, and we too are one of its products. (2003, p. xv)

At the end of his richly informative book, he urges people to "remove their dark glasses" and see that evolution and a view of the Earth as God's creation are not antithetical: "The complexity and beauty of 'Life's Solution' can never cease to astound. None of it presupposes, let alone proves, the existence of God, but all is congruent" (2003, p. 330).

The essential point here is that both believers and unbelievers should reject the derogatory, often nasty, accusations that have sometimes characterized arguments over evolution (see Thomas Frank's 2004 account of the battle waged in Kansas as an example). It is true that evolution and a literal reading of the book of Genesis are incompatible, but it should be part of every young person's education to learn about, analyze, and draw conclusions about such incompatibilities. There is no need to engage in name calling and condemnation. We can learn from accounts we know are metaphorical and admire both their beauty and wisdom without insisting on their literal acceptance.

Perhaps students should be invited (not assigned) to read Martin Gardner's explanation of why he is not an atheist even though he rejects a literal interpretation of most Biblical stories. After expressing personal horror at the stories of Noah, Abraham's willingness to sacrifice his son, and Jephthah's sacrificial murder of his daughter, Gardner remarks: "The Old Testament God, and many who had great 'faith' in him, are alike portrayed in the Bible as monsters of incredible cruelty. A philosophical theist [such as Gardner himself], standing outside any religious tradition, can construct better models of God than Jehovah" (1983, p. 211). Thus, rejecting virtually all of the dogma of Christianity, Gardner nevertheless expresses agreement and admiration for the opening lines of Hebrews 11: "Now faith is the substance of things hoped for, the evidence of things not seen." He confesses faith both in immortality and an unseen God.

Notice that Gardner has read the Bible and obviously appreciates its literary beauty. Richard Dawkins, an outspoken atheist, also recommends that the Bible should be read in our schools as literature. He lists two full crowded pages of Bible-inspired terms and phrases that "occur commonly in literary or conversational English, from great poetry to hackneyed cliché, from proverb to gossip" (2006, p. 341). Familiarity with the Bible is basic to an understanding of our culture, and it provides a starting point for the critical thinking and debate that should be encouraged. Remember that a primary reason for developing our skill in critical thinking is to understand one another.

As with so many topics in the huge area of religion, we have limited our discussion of evolution to what might be addressed in schools that would bring people together and encourage democratic conversation. It is not our purpose to indoctrinate students for or against evolution, although we certainly believe that Conway Morris is right when he says "evolution is true." Our purpose is to encourage critical thinking and the sort of open discussion that should characterize participatory democracy. This discussion should be encouraged whenever the opportunity arises. Certainly it should be a major topic in the ongoing 4-year social studies program. But it should also be addressed in the standard disciplinary courses. Contrary to Ravitch's recommendation that "science classes should teach science . . . and religion classes should teach religion" (2010, p. 234), a real education—an education for critical thinking in a democracy—must encourage discussion of the debates that arise between religion and science and across other areas of study.

Questions about God can be discussed in every discipline. In mathematics, for example, there has been a longstanding and fascinating debate over whether mathematics is discovered or invented. Some mathematicians speak of mathematics as inherent in the mind of God, a wonderful body of truth to be discovered. Others such as G. H. Hardy are militantly atheist, but even they have often referred to a universe of order and beauty. Belief in the origins and universality of mathematics in the mind of God was strongly challenged with the discovery (invention?) of non-Euclidean geometry, but even before that, there were doubts raised about the origins and nature of mathematics.

Teachers might share with students stories about the religious objections of Pythagoreans to eating beans or trampling on bean plants; Newton's attempt to verify Biblical chronology; Leibniz's philosophical work to absolve God of complicity in evil; Laplace's rejection of the "God hypothesis" to explain the solar system; Kronecker's declaration that God created the integers, man all the rest; and—in opposition to Kronecker's constrained structure—Georg Cantor's lovely comment, "The essence of mathematics resides in its freedom" (quoted in Bell, 1965/1937, p. 579).

Students should be guided to see the dramatic differences illustrated in these views of mathematics and all knowledge. There are those who believe in certain, God-given, absolutes with which all knowledge must begin and others who believe that we should start with real problems and work our way backward and forward to find satisfactory solutions. The friendship and collaborative discourse between the mathematician Kurt Godel and the physicist Albert Einstein illustrate this dichotomy:

> For Godel the equations of mathematics, as opposed to the counsels of common sense, would lead us into the promised land of new insights, whereas for Einstein, it was precisely common sense that was the final touchstone for assessing what the mathematicians had to offer. (Yourgrau, 2005, pp. 16–17)

We will return to this basic philosophical difference repeatedly.

FREEDOM, CHOICE, AND COMMITMENT

We generally regard *freedom* as a condition in which we are able to decide for ourselves how we will live and what we will do. Most Americans treasure both personal and national freedom. But we noted earlier that our choices—even when they appear to outsiders as free—are sometimes predetermined by prior moral commitments. It is not unusual in such cases to hear someone say, "I had no choice." Our choices are often constrained by family obligations, earlier promises, or deeply held moral or religious beliefs. Those experiencing these constraints, however, usually do not interpret them as a loss of freedom.

Indeed a deep religious commitment is sometimes felt as an ultimate state of freedom. Monks or nuns, Buddhist as well as Christian, for example, may feel marvelously free from many of the concerns experienced by others. They have made a basic choice that eliminates the need to make a host of everyday choices. There may be no need for them to choose what they will eat or at what time, when they will converse and with whom, how they will dress, how they will spend their days and nights. To most of us, such a restricted life represents an almost total loss of freedom. To those who choose—make a commitment—to this life, the feeling is one of rapturous freedom, to know and to love God, without the constant interruptions of daily life. This sort of commitment, however, should not be made lightly. Most religious organizations require a novitiate or period of intended commitment during which the novice is encouraged to think deeply about his or her commitment.

On a less intensive level, all good parents hope to induce their children to make a commitment to reject lying, stealing, cheating, and all forms of behavior that cause harm to others. At its most effective level, such commitment very nearly eliminates temptation; at least, it should strengthen a resolve to resist temptation. Effective moral commitment, whether it is motivated by religion or by loving parental guidance, removes the sort of anarchic freedom that permits immoral choices and encourages a form of freedom that allows children to pursue a good life.

But this sort of freedom requires constant critical vigilance, not un-questioning obedience. We have already discussed the need to examine authority carefully and, in drastic situations, to consider the possibility—even moral duty—to engage in civil disobedience. Similarly, we have men-tioned the advice of Elizabeth Cady Stanton to challenge and revise many Christian doctrinal statements and stories. In Chapter 11, we will consider how students might be encouraged to apply critical thinking to the topic of patriotism.

On being asked to help students use critical thinking on matters related to religion, teachers must understand that there is a huge difference between supporting religious freedom and leaving students in a state of ignorance that makes it impossible or sinful to think critically on religious topics. Our purpose should not be to indoctrinate but to invite critical and appreciative conversation among students with very different views. We want to encour-age them to understand one another.

Science fiction and fantasy allow the exploration of moral controversies in an abstract, alternative, or hypothetical environment that may act as a metaphor for a current issue that might otherwise be difficult to discuss in a public school classroom. This can be particularly helpful for religious is-sues or issues that could be perceived as touching on religious beliefs. Some authors to consider in this vein include the Taoist-anarchist Ursula LeGuin (*The Telling*), the Christian apologist C. S. Lewis (*Chronicles of Narnia*), and Lois Lowry (*The Giver* and *Number the Stars*). All three of these au-thors deal with issues of attempting to understand or relate to beings that are different or other.

In this chapter, we have explored some ways in which teachers might promote critical thinking on religion. We hope that it is unproblematic to introduce the words *theism, atheism, agnosticism*, and *deism*. In discussing these words, we have suggested that teachers point out—through specific biographical references—the many ideals and understandings shared by be-lievers and unbelievers. A main objective of this discussion is to produce enlightened citizens who are ready to become active citizens in a democracy. To participate effectively in that democracy, we must try to understand our own commitments and those of others.

Well-educated students should know that honest, thoughtful people may differ greatly in their conception of God and spirituality. Typically, Christians believe in a personal God; that is, they believe in God as a person to whom one should listen and to whom one can talk. Secular Christians, deists, and some agnostics, in contrast, may regard "God" as a universal force ensuring order in the universe. Reading (by invitation, not require-ment) some material by C. S. Lewis, Martin Gardner, Bertrand Russell, John Dewey, Miguel de Unamuno, William James, and G. K. Chesterton, students may be amazed at the common human goods sought equally by believers and unbelievers. The idea is to bring people together, not to separate them and elevate one above another. Certainly, all students should learn that both well-educated believers and unbelievers share a belief in evolution and other fundamental scientific truths.

It may be especially useful for students to learn that believers, as well as unbelievers, may reject many of the Biblical stories. Must we believe, for example, that God deliberately destroyed most of humanity in a great flood? Must we believe that God directed Abraham to murder his son, Isaac, or that he killed Aaron's sons because they mishandled sacred spices? What kind of God would do such things? Familiarity with these stories should be part of everyone's literary education, but it should be understood that their interpretation differs dramatically across the range of beliefs.

Finally, students should be made aware that religion, usually thought of as a force for good in the world, has sometimes promoted evil. It should be no secret that religion has often strongly supported slavery and that for centuries (and to some degree even today) has endorsed the subordination of women. Religion, like all other domains of human thought and commitment, should be analyzed and evaluated critically.

CHAPTER 5

Race

In this chapter, we will look at controversial issues involving race in three major categories: facing our nation's history on racial issues, understanding today's racial issues, and race and education.

FACING OUR HISTORY

It is hard for Americans, taught from childhood to have enormous pride in our nation and its principles, to accept the horror of racial discrimination and, especially, of slavery and the central role it has played in our history. In Chapter 11 on patriotism, we will refer again to slavery in a discussion of educated despair, the deep feeling of shame and cynicism that sometimes afflicts students when they become aware of the wrongs committed by their beloved nation. Here we argue that the central importance of slavery in our history must be faced. Failure to face this dismal history colors our present attitudes and makes it even more difficult to bring us together as a nation. Eddie Glaude reminds us of what we risk if we handle this badly: "Disremembering blots out horrible loss, but it also distorts who the characters take themselves to be . . . . It is this sense of the word that strikes me as particularly useful for our current moment. Disremembering is active forgetting" (2016, p. 47).

Students should know that slavery has a long history worldwide. In America, slavery was not initially confined to the South. Eric Foner points out:

> The Dutch dominated the Atlantic slave trade in the early seventeenth century, and they introduced slaves into their North American colony, New Netherland [New York], as a matter of course. The numbers remained small, but in 1650 New Netherland's 500 slaves outnumbered those in Virginia and Maryland. (2015, p. 28)

Still, opposition to slavery was stronger and grew more rapidly in the North than in the South. Students should hear about the American Anti-Slavery Society, the Manumission Society, the Quakers, and the New York Vigilance Committee.

As students study the period before the Civil War, they may be inclined to think of the North as land of the free and the South as a stubborn defender of slavery. They should be reminded that although the South made greater, more direct, use of slaves in the cotton fields, the North reaped profits from shipping, the capture of slaves, and the giant textile industry dependent on cotton. Indeed, slavery was one of the most powerful factors in producing the economic success of the United States (Baptist, 2014; Wood, 2011). Northern residents who were not themselves slaveholders nonetheless profited from the slave trade.

The study of slavery might be occasionally interrupted by accounts of more recent discrimination. It is important for students to understand that the effects of slavery are still with us. We might get a good start on making this connection by looking at some current literature. This might involve whole-class readings or group project readings. Incidentally, much of our writing is inspired by what we read; and we read a lot! Reading is one of our shared mother/daughter passions along with cooking, gardening, and educating. For an introduction to our recent racial history, we turn to Dennis Lehane's *The Given Day*. Set largely in Boston between the two world wars, this historical novel explores the social climate leading up to the 1919 Boston police strike through the intertwined lives of two young men, Luther Laurence who is Black and Denny Coughlin, the son of a self-made Irish immigrant police captain. This book is a wonderful example of a historical novel that brings an era to life through the detailed interaction of fictional and historical characters facing multiple moral dilemmas—some particular to their time and place, others of a more enduring nature.

The issue for this chapter is race and race relations. Some themes that could be explored in an English or social studies class after reading or hearing a report on *The Given Day* include:

- What would/could have happened if Babe Ruth had called out his fellow White major league players for cheating when they joined a Black pick-up baseball game during an unforeseen train stop in rural Ohio?
- When was major league baseball integrated, and who was the first Black major league player? A related free period or after-school activity might be to air the recent movie *42* about this event.
- What role did the "negro" leagues play in developing self-esteem for Black men and providing entertainment for Black audiences?
- When and how did the NAACP get its start, and why were so many of its early leaders White?
- What were the underlying causes of the East St. Louis massacre of 1917, and what might happen in 1921 to the characters who end up in Greenwood, Oklahoma, at the end of the book?

We Americans are going through another interval of racial tension. How should we discuss this tension in our schools? Exploring the incidents of racial violence that occurred between the two world wars would be an excellent way to introduce the topic of recent events and compare and contrast the causes of and resulting reactions to these events. To help understand current events in the context of history, we will continue to discuss slavery and how it has been treated historically. Then we'll move on to address current racial problems and how our schools are addressing them.

Who writes history? Much of what we think of as history consists of stories of great men as told by great men. Winston Churchill is reputed to have said: "History will be kind to me because I intend to write it." Winston was witty and he did write history. History, however, is much more than the study of great men, victorious battles, or the rise and fall of civilizations. The word *history* comes from the Greek *historia* (ιστορια), which means inquiry. History today encompasses "past events as well as the memory, discovery, collection, organization, presentation, and interpretation of information about these events" (Wikipedia). It can be presented through film or other media, written, displayed in museums and monuments, or passed on from one generation to the next through recitation, song, or other traditions. History reflects the culture and philosophy of the era in which it is written or displayed as well as the personal beliefs and preconceptions of the writer or presenter and thus may contain commentary on moral lessons learned or to be learned from past acts. History is about people and their past thoughts and actions. In this regard, we need to remember that human beings are not perfect, that people who have been lionized by history may not have always done the right thing, and that people are shaped by the times in which they live. Recent controversy at Princeton University over President Woodrow Wilson's alleged racism is a good example of this aspect of history. Do we erase Wilson from monuments because he was a racist, or do we recognize that, like all human beings, he was not infallible and hold discussions about these issues? Might our erasure have the undesirable effect of "disremembering"? Historians elucidate past thought and action through their inquiry of the past, but historians and great people alike can also suppress history and erase people and their acts from memory. There are people today, for example, who would like to remove any mention of the holocaust from history books.

Students might like to know that the great adventure stories, *The Count of Monte Cristo* and *The Three Musketeers* by Alexandre Dumas, were inspired by the life of the author's father who was born in Haiti to an aristocratic White father and a Black slave. Napoleon Bonaparte, out of jealousy and suspicion, did his best to erase all memory of the tall good-looking and successful General Alex Dumas. In *The Black Count*, journalist and historian Tom Reiss restores this swashbuckling swordsman to his rightful place in French history (2012). Teachers should explore local resources such as museums, parks, and monuments for examples of underreported minority achievement, the suppression of actions the majority is not proud of, and local myths and legends. Historical inquiry may be made of living people or records of human activity, but the results will always be subject to the interpretation and motivation of the inquirer and hence subject to revision.

When it comes to revision, the history of Florida is a prime example of repeated reexaminations of the past and reinterpretations of facts and myths. I (Brooks) was reminded of this recently when I received a *Special Edition Newsletter of Florida State Parks* describing the various celebrations of Black History Month to be held in the parks in February this year (2016). Of the six events highlighted, three are Civil War reenactment sites, two commemorate the flight to freedom by Black slaves at sites then under Spanish or British rule, and one is a museum exhibit in remembrance of the 20-year operation (1949–1969) of a park at Silver Springs for Blacks only that was down the river from the historic, then for Whites only, attraction that had been in operation since the 1870s. While these sites and the events they attest to may be good topics for study during Black History Month, none of them cast the state of Florida in a good light considering its multiracial diversity. One must be careful when studying past events of which we should not be proud to recognize the good as well and current progress especially so as not to cast our students into despair or a sense of hopelessness.

I recognized one of the Civil War sites as a place I had read about before. Shortly after moving to Florida in 2013, I happened upon the just-published *Finding Florida: The True History of the Sunshine State* by T. D. Allman. In a chapter entitled "Disambiguation," Allman tells the story of the battle of Olustee based on eyewitness accounts and then the history of the manufactured victory that resulted in the existence of the Olustee Battlefield Historic State Park.

> It would be nice to limit an account of the Civil War in Florida to what happened during the Civil War, but the subsequent misrepresentations of what actually happened and the ensuing redefinitions of what it meant have come to disfigure America's understanding of itself even more than the original violence did. Until Americans liberate themselves from the fictional Civil War, they may never transcend their national legacy of slavery, racism, hypocrisy, denial, and dishonesty. (Allman, 2013, p. 223)

In the case of the battle of Olustee, The Daughters of the Confederacy turned an opportunistic assault by Confederate troops on a like-sized Union advance into a Confederate victory to be commemorated as Florida's very first State Historic Monument in 1909. According to one account, "In this battle the Confederates won a complete victory over a much larger force than their own" (Allman, 2013, pp. 232–233). The sad truth is that with 5,200 participants knowledgeable of the local terrain, the Confederates failed to consummate a victory by chasing down the fleeing Union soldiers, who actually numbered 5,500, because in the words of one Confederate field officer, they were too busy "shooting niggers." The "niggers" that were being shot were wounded Black Union soldiers. More than 1,000 Black soldiers fought at Olustee for the Union, including soldiers from the African-American 54th Massachusetts Volunteer Infantry Regiment, the subject of the Academy Award–winning 1989 movie *Glory*.

Now Florida's history is being reinterpreted again, and topics that were ignored or suppressed in the past are being explored. Today the Olustee Battlefield Historic State Park website mentions the participation of the 54th Massachusetts Regiment in the battle, notes that scenes from the movie *Glory* were filmed in the park, and refers to the battle as Florida's largest battle in one of our nation's bloodiest conflicts. It does not mention the shooting of the wounded Black soldiers, but neither does it call the battle a Confederate victory. Last year, the Keys History & Discovery Center in Islamorada hosted a special exhibit of landscape paintings by the Highwaymen, a group of self-taught African-American painters who sold their paintings to tourists along U.S. Highway 1 in the 1950s and 1960s. (See *The Highwaymen: Florida's African-American Landscape Painters* by Gary Monroe.) Currently, the Mel Fisher Maritime Museum in Key West, best known for its exhibits of treasure from the Spanish galleon Atocha, has half of its second floor, as well as a traveling exhibit, dedicated to artifacts from the slave ship Henrietta Marie and to the history of slavery, our next topic for discussion.

In our social studies classes, is our treatment of slavery adequate? Do our students know that most of our first 16 presidents were slaveholders or sympathizers? How should we think about segregation and its effects? These are touchy subjects and are often not well addressed by many textbooks in current use. There are, however, many ways in which these topics can be raised to begin to foster open discussion. In a cross-curricular setting where themes are integrated across the curriculum through careful planning and discussion among participating teachers, these questions can be tackled by many different disciplines. They can also be addressed in special courses devoted to race and race relations. Let's explore both options.

In a cross-curricular context, to supplement traditional history or social studies course work or even the special social/political issues forums we recommended earlier, the topic of slavery can be raised in many different subject areas. In biology, environmental science, or economics courses, teachers could look at the role of the North in the slave trade:

> In preparing a museum devoted to the seventeenth century commercial port of Salem, National Park Service officials carefully checked shipping documents, bracing themselves for an attack, and were relieved to have been unable to uncover any record of slaving on any Salem ship. But they should not take too

much comfort in this. Aside from the fact that much slave trading was done clandestinely, the search for these records misses the important point. Regardless of how many ships actually did or did not carry slaves, or how many New England merchants did or did not buy or sell Africans, the New England merchants of the cod trade were deeply involved in slavery, not only because they supplied the plantation system [with the poorest quality fish to feed the slaves] but also because they facilitated the trade in Africans. In West Africa, slaves could be purchased with cured cod, and to this day there is still a West African market for salt cod and stockfish. (Kurlansky, 1997, p. 82)

New England also made rum for export from molasses made by slaves in the Caribbean:

Felton & Company, a Boston rum maker founded in the early nineteenth century, described the trade with remarkable candor in its 1936 drink guide. "Ship owners developed a cycle of trade involving cargoes of slaves to the West Indies—a cargo of Blackstrap Molasses from those islands to Boston and other New England ports—and finally the shipment of rum to Africa." (Kurlansky, 1997, p. 89)

In short, slaves could be purchased in Africa for cash, cod, or rum.

In a biology or environmental science class, the production of molasses from sugarcane can be raised in the discussion of the origin of various food plants or nonnative and invasive species. In the New York Times bestseller, *The Drunken Botanist*, Amy Stewart tells how hybrid species of sugar, crosses between Chinese and Indian wild stock, traveled well and thrived throughout Asia and Europe. Columbus brought these plants to the Caribbean:

Once it arrived in the New World, sugarcane gave us rum, but it gave us something else, too: slavery. Starting in the early 1500s, European trading ships sailed to West Africa and went from there to sugar plantations in the Caribbean, introducing human cargo to their trading partners and opening one of the most monstrous chapters in our history. There was nothing pleasant about work in sugarcane fields. In blistering heat, the canes had to be cut by hand using enormous knives, pressed in powerful mills, and boiled in ferociously hot kettles. There were snakes and rodents and vermin of all sorts living in the fields. It was dangerous, exhausting, backbreaking work. The only way to get people to do it was to kidnap them and force them to, under penalty of death—which is exactly what happened. Slavery was abhorrent to some Europeans and early Americans: British abolitionists, for instance, refused to take sugar in their tea to protest the way in which it was manufactured. But hardly anyone refused to drink rum. (2013, p. 97)

Slavery came to the American South for the harvesting of cash crops as well, notably tobacco and cotton. Much has been written with the aim of casting the Civil War as a fight for states' rights versus federal intervention, but the key issue was slavery, as is made clear by the written declarations of secession by South Carolina, Mississippi, and Georgia. The Mississippi Declaration of Causes of Secession reads in part (the second paragraph):

> Our position is thoroughly identified with the institution of slavery—the greatest material interest of the world. Its labor supplies the product which constitutes by far the largest and most important portions of commerce of the earth. These products are peculiar to the climate verging on the tropical regions, and by an imperious law of nature, none but the black race can bear exposure to the tropical sun. These products have become necessities of the world, and a blow at slavery is a blow at commerce and civilization. That blow has been long aimed at the institution, and was at the point of reaching its consummation. There was no choice left us but submission to the mandates of abolition, or a dissolution of the Union, whose principles had been subverted to work out our ruin.

These declarations make for interesting reading. South Carolina's declaration deals with legal issues, and references the Declaration of Independence, the Articles of Confederation, and the Constitutions of both the individual states and the United States. Georgia's declaration addresses economic issues and the dependence of northern commercial and manufacturing interests on Federal subsidies and international intervention at the expense of southern agricultural interests through the Walker Tariff Act of 1846. We will say more about the issues raised in the Mississippi and Georgia declarations in Chapter 9 on money, class, and poverty. These declarations would make a great starting point for a history or civics class to foster debate and discussion on moral issues concerned with race as related to the documents drafted by our founding fathers that we rely on to this day for our nation's governance.

We have addressed topics for discussion around slavery and its moral issues that can be raised in science, economics, history, and civics classes, but there is also a wealth of material that can be used in language arts, art and media, or music classes. We will focus on literature here but must briefly mention the possible incorporation in art, media, and music classes of African-American folk arts and crafts from the period of slavery, the evolution of rock and roll and rap from negro spirituals and slave work songs that formed the basis of the blues, and the many movies and documentaries that have been made about slavery and the civil war. The body of literature on slavery can be divided into three categories for study. There is literature about slavery and the slave experience, written by both slaves and others, and then there is literature written by slaves that has nothing to do with slavery but that underscores the basic humanity and individual talents of African-American writers. All would be appropriate for study in English or language arts classes, and a rich discussion could center on comparing and contrasting writings from each category, literary criticism of the works, and the moral issues raised in each. A class on parenting could spend a lesson contrasting the moral lessons of *Aesop's Fables* with the lessons contained in the *Uncle Remus* stories or the African-American folktales about Anansi the spider (a trickster). It might interest students to know that poetry was published by African-born slaves as early as the late 18th century. Phillis Wheatley, named after the ship (The Phillis) that brought her to America from West Africa at the age of 7 and the Wheatley family of Boston who purchased her, began writing poetry at the age of 14 after her master's daughter, Mary, taught her to read not only English but Greek and Latin as well. In 1772 Wheatley had to defend her authorship of her poetry in front of a panel of Boston luminaries that included John Hancock and the governor of Massachusetts. People were reluctant to believe that a Black female slave could have written work such as:

> TWAS mercy brought me from my Pagan land,
> Taught my benighted soul to understand
> That there's a God, that there's a Saviour too:
> Once I redemption neither sought nor knew.
> Some view our sable race with scornful eye,
> "Their colour is a diabolic dye."
> Remember, Christians, Negroes, black as Cain,
> May be refin'd, and join th'angelic train. (Wheatley, 1773)

Another set of contrasts and comparisons could be made between slave narratives and contemporary fiction describing the lives of slaves. Three books come to mind in this latter category, though there are likely many others. Toni Morrison's 1987 Pulitzer Prize-winning novel, *Beloved*, is a ghost story in which an escaped slave, Sethe, is haunted by the daughter she killed to prevent the child from being taken back into slavery. *March*, another Pulitzer Prize winner, published in 2006 by Geraldine Brooks, is a love story between the absent father from Louisa May Alcott's *Little Women* and a slave that he meets while working as a traveling salesman in the South on the eve of the Civil War. Finally, Margaret Wrinkle's 2013 *Wash* tells the story of a Black slave, Wash, whose Tennessee owner rents him out as a "traveling negro" to procreate breeding stock. These stories and the many moral issues they confront can be contrasted with the narratives of slaves, four of the most well-known of which can be found in the 1987 volume edited by Henry Louis Gates, Jr., *The Classic Slave Narratives,* which includes the autobiographical stories of the lives of Olaudah Equiano, Mary Prince, Frederick Douglass, and Harriet Jacobs. The best-selling novel of the 19th century, *Uncle Tom's Cabin*, by the abolitionist Harriet Beecher Stowe would provide an additional contrast to the slave narratives that were written in the same era and the more recent fictional works cited previously.

RACE TODAY

As we come to grips with our racial relations in both history and literature, we should keep in mind Glaude's warning that "disremembering is
active forgetting" (2016, p. 47). All over the country today, especially in the
South, groups are protesting the presence of statues and other tributes to
people and groups once revered but now criticized—even condemned—as
racist. We can hardly imagine a more controversial issue. Students should
be invited to discuss whether the removal of memorials is an appropriate
response to our national confession and remorse or an instance of active forgetting. Is there a way to remember without bestowing honor or acceptance
on the racial injustice we now deeply regret?

Consider first how we might address the racial attitudes of our pre-Civil
War presidents. Most of them were slaveholders or sympathizers. Should
we eliminate memorials to George Washington, Thomas Jefferson, James
Madison, James Monroe, and Andrew Jackson? Most of us would not agree
to such a move. Surely, there are good, morally justified, reasons for remembering these American leaders. We should neither deny their contributions
nor overlook their racism. It is dismayingly clear that people can engage in
both admirable and detestable activities. Somehow, we must recognize and
remember both. Many of our schools and colleges face this problem now.

Peter Galuszka notes that "how far a school can go to remedy possibly
racist symbolism, including statues, buildings and stadiums, is a widespread
dilemma faced by scores of colleges across the country that in some way
have ties to the Southern rebel history or other embarrassing connotations"
(2016, p. 12). But the embarrassing connotations are not limited to the Civil
War era. When there is well-documented evidence of racism, as in the case of
Woodrow Wilson, students and other citizens may clamor for the removal
of all tributes to him. Students might debate the wisdom of this approach.
Did Wilson do nothing to warrant our admiration or gratitude? Is there a
way to remember both the good and the bad, a way that will remind all
of us that we are heavily influenced by the times in which we live and the
problems presented by those times? Waite Rawls suggests, "Memorials are
part of that history. We should erase neither the history nor the memorials"
(quoted in Galuszka, 2016, p. 13). This means adding context and urging
critical thought on current social problems. What might we admire in the
lives of Wilson, Jefferson, and Jackson? What should we deplore? And how
can we make both open for public discussion?

There are many racial issues about which students should learn. Some
of these are not controversial. We know that Blacks suffer (disproportion-
ately) more often than Whites from severe income inequality, discrimination
in housing, and disproportionate incarceration (Desmond, 2016; Glaude,
2016). The facts are not in dispute. Controversy arises when we begin to
argue about what should be done and why.

A major controversy arises when we ask who should be involved in working out solutions to the problems identified, and this controversy is one to which we will return repeatedly. In an earlier chapter, we discussed the importance of conversation and choice in raising intelligent, responsible children. Too often, in working with teenagers, in this time of standardized testing and highly directive teaching, we forget or deny the centrality of conversation and choice (Noddings, 2006, 2015a). Many well-placed people who want to help in the larger society make things worse by taking charge and failing to invite the active participation of those they are "helping." Alicia Garza, for example, cites her disappointment over the attitude of White "helpers" in social justice work: "San Francisco broke my heart over and over. White progressives would actually argue with us about their right to determine what was best for communities they never had to live in" (Cobb, 2016, p. 35). In the article by Jelani Cobb cited here, we read of the frequent breakdowns in social justice programs caused at least in part by failure in communication. Indeed, we hear this complaint again and again whenever inequality is a major problem.

As we talk with our students about this problem—the failure of communication across socioeconomic levels—we should encourage them to think about cooperation and compromise. Later in this book, we will mention the historian Gordon Wood's observation that Americans seem too often to be "all-or-nothing" people. We want to choose one perfect solution that will do the trick instead of exploring all the options and selecting promising bits from all of them to try out. When that solution fails, or seems to fail, we abandon it and seek another "perfect" solution. Students should be encouraged to consider all sides of important issues and to acknowledge possibly good motives in critics with whom they might disagree.

Suppose, for example, that we largely agree with the ends endorsed by Black Lives Matter, and then someone responds with "All lives matter!" How should we react to this? Too often today the reaction is angry; the respondent seems to have missed the point entirely. Voices are raised. The respondent may even be accused of racism, and in some cases, the accusation may be justified. But the result may well be the collapse of a promising organization devoted to social justice. Participants must learn to back off, think critically, listen, and try again.

The exchange just discussed illustrates another important controversial issue. Members of Black Lives Matter want respect and equality *as Blacks*. Of course, their *lives* matter but so does their identity. They seek full citizenship as Blacks—not mere acceptance as though they are no different from a privileged White majority. This means that Blacks should be able to move into any neighborhood they can afford, but it also means that a mostly Black neighborhood should be as secure and prosperous as a typical White one. Integration is certainly a laudable goal but not if it is forced and applauded only as a way to improve the lives of oppressed Blacks. Must

Black people be in the company of Whites in order to improve themselves? Few of us have thought seriously about the possible harms inflicted on Black students by the form school integration has taken. Thoughtful critics have been trying to tell us that Black students transported to White schools suffer the loss of Black teachers as role models, feel cultural disruption, experience a loss of voice, and incur a sense that they are somehow inferior and need help (Milner, Delale-O'Connor, Murray, & Farinde, 2016). Students should be encouraged to explore this very controversial issue and suggest ways in which the dignity of Blacks can be preserved as America moves toward a unified nation. We will address this issue again in the last section of this chapter when we say a bit about historically Black colleges.

Let's return now briefly to a problem identified in the first part of this chapter: what to do with tributes and memorials to people who are now known or suspected to have been racist. To remove their names from public places is to risk what Glaude calls "disremembering." For the sake of those who have suffered under racial discrimination, we should want that suffering to be remembered. But we should also remind ourselves that people—even otherwise good people—can give way to bad ideas that saturate a society at times. And if we remove Woodrow Wilson's name from Princeton University and national monuments, should we also remove that of Thomas Jefferson? Or should we try to recognize the outstanding contributions of Jefferson (Onuf & Gordon-Reed, 2016) while remembering with heavy hearts his life as a slaveholder? Recognizing how enormously difficult such social/moral controversies are should bolster our commitment to make critical thinking a major educational aim. It is not only a just decision that we seek but, every bit as important, a deep understanding of the lives and beliefs of others. Joyce King concludes her article in *Educational Researcher* with a strong endorsement of "critical collaborative inquiry" aimed at such understanding and, thus, better lives for all of us (2016, p. 169).

As this chapter was being written, it was announced that Princeton has decided not to remove Wilson's name or memorials but to emphasize the *positive* contributions he made to both the university and the nation. We worry, however: Will they find a way to tell the full story in their public displays? Discussion of this dilemma might lead to one suffered by many of our southern states. Can they justify retaining celebratory memorials of the Confederacy and those who fought for it? Can we understand the strong feelings on both sides of this issue?

RACE IN TODAY'S SCHOOLS

We begin this section with a continuation of the discussion on integration. We are often reminded that our schools today—despite all the efforts and talk about integration—are more segregated now than they were 40 years ago. Surely, the spirit of equality and common civic interests should drive integration, but too often people think of it as something to be done for the benefit of Black students. Granted the possibly positive effects of racial integration for all races, is there a negative factor to consider? Must Black children be educated with White children in order to learn? We have already mentioned the losses suffered by Black children when they are taken away from their cultural roots. Have we thought about transporting equal numbers of White children to Black schools?

The history of Black education should be part of the education of all Americans. Learning together about the contributions of Historically Black Colleges and Universities (HBCUs) should be enlightening for all students and a source of pride for Black students (Glaude, 2016; Siddle Walker & Snarey, 2004). Such study both recognizes Black people in their fullness as Blacks *and* citizens and underscores the mutual advantages of integrated education. Students should also think critically about the current condition of many Black colleges now suffering financial hardship. Glaude points out that Spelman, Morehouse, Howard, Tuskegee, and Hampton are likely to survive, but many other Black schools may be forced to close (2016, p. 135). It is surely good that Black students may now enroll in traditionally White colleges, but is there no special place for the Black institutions? This is an important issue for critical thinking and discussion.

In a course on Black history or in a biology class, students could read Kenneth Manning's biography of Ernest Everett Just (1883–1941), a pioneering African American biologist and educator. Just experienced every form of education possible for a Black man born in 1883. Until he was 12 years old, he was taught by his mother both at home and in a school she founded as one of the first industrial schools for Blacks in South Carolina. He then went on at age 13 to the Colored Normal, Industrial, Agricultural and Mechanical College (later South Carolina State University, an HBCU), which came into being as a result of the *Plessy v. Ferguson* ruling that schools could be "separate but equal." From this institution he received his Licentiate of Instruction allowing him to teach in *Black* public schools in South Carolina. However, at age 16 he was not ready to teach and still hungry for additional knowledge. He spent the next 4 years at Kimball Union Academy in Meriden, New Hampshire, where he was until his senior year the only Black student. He then moved to Hanover, New Hampshire, and graduated magna cum laude from Dartmouth with many honors. After this he began teaching English at Howard University where by 1910 he had become an associate professor of biology. From 1909 through 1915 he spent his summers as a research assistant at Woods Hole Oceanographic Institute where he completed research that allowed him after a year's residence to receive a PhD from the University of Chicago. By this time he was the head of Howard's Medical School *but was still actively discouraged from even applying for a teaching position at anywhere but a Black institution* (Manning, 1983).

The emphasis on the positive features and contributions of historically Black schools might also reinvigorate our efforts at integration by drawing attention to the benefits gained by all. In many of our "integrated" schools today, Black students tend to self-segregate at lunch tables, playgrounds, and social events. Some of this group clustering may be a result of the way we have distorted the purpose of integration. As students gain greater respect for the group "being helped," self-segregation may be reduced. Then again, we might explore the possible benefits of such clustering. Does it have positive features?

Black pride and solidarity may also have negative features beyond isolation. On the one hand—as we have argued throughout this chapter and others—full recognition of Black lives and identity is both positive and necessary for the well-being of a participatory democracy. On the other hand, we should worry about the angry advocacy of separation expressed by some Black thinkers and writers. Darryl Pinckney (2016) notes that Ta-Nehisi Coates has advised Blacks to resign themselves to the continuing racism of Whites and to build their own proud, separate lives and communities. How do our high school students, both Black and White, respond to this?

Let us turn now, briefly, to the idea of a course devoted solely to the topic of race and racism. Lawrence Blum has taught such a course at the public Cambridge Rindge and Latin School in Cambridge, Massachusetts. He has also written about this course in *High Schools, Race, and America's Future* (2012), providing us with both an in-depth look at the course and its outcomes and a syllabus and reading list. He devotes considerable time in the class to lessons around slavery, but his syllabus is also a good source for other topics for moral discussion on race and racism. The important aspect of this course for our present discussion is the fact that it was taught as an honors course to a carefully selected racially mixed class in a public school. Blum tells us that "when you have a racially mixed class engaging with race as a curricular subject, it is a very special combination" (2012, p. 185):

> When students come to have respectful and engaged conversations with peers of other races, learning to listen and to express themselves across the racial divide, this is a moral step forward, and it is personally enriching as well. Students learn to treat others with respect across divisions that often inhibit people from achieving that respect. They learn to be more accepting, welcoming, and appreciative of differences, rather than hostile, fearful, prejudiced, or resentful of them. This is more than mere tolerance. My students did not merely tolerate one another. Respect and appreciation are core moral attitudes and, especially in the face of potentially divisive differences such as race, they define a higher moral standard than tolerance—one we should look to our schools to help students achieve. (pp. 185–186)

Blum goes on to mention the civic aspects of his curriculum and the relation to critical thinking and moral commitment:

> I have emphasized the critical thinking dimension that we saw in the class's moral discussion and also in assignments such as that on Walker and Jefferson . . . . Critical thinking helps citizens analyze social phenomena and evaluate public issues and policy proposals connected with them. Other civic capacities are also involved, for which both the composition of the class and the curriculum are important. Race remains a major source of disparity in access to education, health, a decent job, a decent income, a home in a good neighborhood, and other aspects of life in the United States. So, if civic engagement aims (among other things) to improve the lot of all U.S. citizens and to create a more just society, understanding racial issues and being able to discuss them intelligently and productively with fellow citizens is an absolute necessity. (2012, p. 186)

This idea of fostering intelligent and productive discussion with fellow citizens through diverse class composition and appropriate curriculum can be applied as well to gender and socioeconomic diversity in the classroom, as we will discuss in later chapters; here we should note that the shared discussions should occur across class and across school programs; they should not be confined to honors classes.

A final, highly controversial issue to be considered here concerns language. Should well-educated Americans learn to respect Black English as we do other foreign languages, or should we insist that all students master standard English? This topic is addressed in several places in this book, but it is especially relevant here. Should we commit ourselves to recognizing and respecting Black English? Can we do this and still encourage all students to learn and to use standard English where it is expected?

When I (Brooks) moved to Pittsburgh, Pennsylvania, I found myself irritated by the local dialect, particularly the use of the word *need* as a helping verb as in, "this *needs* washed." I told my children that "Pittsburghese" was not to be spoken in our house. Later, working in Newark, New Jersey, I found myself irritated by the pronunciation by Black colleagues of the word *ask* as *axe*. Why do such trivial matters bother us, and what do we do about it? Even though I find these vernacular differences offensive to my ear, I have learned to listen through the words and pronunciation for meaning. I am not sure that requiring everyone to speak standard English as opposed to understanding and confronting their own biases is the right or only solution. And yet, in job interviews, classroom participation, and other first encounters, first impressions do matter! My horror of the pronunciation of *ask* as *axe* has been forever changed by my recent reading of a mystery novel, Jeffery Deaver's *The Twelfth Card* (2005). The following excerpt from a conversation between a father and daughter walking through Harlem beautifully highlights the issues:

"When I was inside [in prison]," he explained, "I got my high school diploma and a year of college."

She said nothing.

"I mostly studied reading and words. Maybe won't get me a job but it's what drew me. I always liked books and things, you know that. I'm the one had you reading from jump . . . . I studied Standard. But I studied Vernacular too. [Black English]. And I don't see anything wrong with it."

"You don't speak it," she pointed out sharply.

"I didn't grow *up* speaking it. I didn't grow up speaking French or Mandingo either."

"I'm sick of hearing people say, 'Lemme axe you a question.'"

Her father shrugged. "'Axe' is just an Old-English version of 'ask.' Royalty used to say it. There're *Bible* translations that talk about 'axing' God for mercy. It's not a Black thing, like people say. The combination of saying *s* and *k* next to each other's hard to pronounce. It's easier to transpose. And 'ain't'? Been in the English language since Shakespeare's day."

She laughed. "Try getting a job talking vernacular."

"Well, what if somebody from France or Russia's trying for that same job? Don't you think the boss'd give them a chance, listen to 'em, see if they'd work hard, were smart, even if they spoke different English? Maybe the problem's that the boss is using somebody's language as a reason *not* to hire him." He laughed. "People in New York damn well better be able to speak some Spanish and Chinese in the next few years. Why not Vernacular?"

His logic infuriated her even more.

"I *like* our language, Genie. It sounds natural to me. Makes me feel at home. Look, you've got every right to be mad at me for what I did. But not for who I am or what we came out of. This's home. And you know what you do with your home, don't you? You change what oughta be changed and learn to be proud of what you can't." (2005, pp. 469–470)

There are two important points here. First, the father, Jax, recognizes the differences between what he calls Vernacular and Standard and consciously chooses when to use each. But the second point is a controversial issue worthy of discussion. Why do we perceive the speaker of Vernacular differently from someone speaking ungrammatical English with an Eastern-European accent like the character Gru in the movie *Despicable Me*? I asked my son-in-law what he thinks when he hears someone say *axe* instead of *ask,* and his immediate response was, "They are uneducated or sloppy and too casual and probably African American." We will talk more about cultural/linguistic issues in Chapter on Money, Class, and Poverty.

If we accept the pessimism of Coates and some other Black critics, we might just give up on teaching Black children how to speak and write standard English. But Coates himself has obviously mastered the language and succeeded in the writing profession. In his pessimism, he might argue that his success in writing has not changed the White attitude toward Blacks and Blackness. Students should be invited to consider the possibility that we can work on both sides of this problem. We can work to increase respect for Black English, *and* we can accept an obligation to help all of our students to master standard English. What they do with that mastery should be up to them. Unfortunately, we have to anticipate Coates-like responses to this position: It *should* be "up to them," but it is not. We have a long way to go in ridding ourselves of racism.

CHAPTER 6

Gender and Public Life

In the past few decades, women have made considerable progress in the public world and, although women's salaries still lag behind those of men doing similar work, many women now participate successfully in professional life. But important questions remain: Are we making a mistake by judging gender equality in terms of how well women are doing in the male-defined public world? Should we work toward redefining that world to incorporate the traditional social concerns and moral orientation of women? Can embracing the needs and desires of an increasingly vocal LGBTQ population help us cultivate the best that both book-end gender orientations offer?

The choice of order for the previous chapter and this one is intentional. Black men gained the right to vote and participate fully as citizens in the United States in 1870 with the 15th Amendment to the Constitution, women 50 years later in 1920 with the 19th. In 2008 we elected our first African American president; we still have not elected a female president—in spite of the fact that large portions of the rest of the world have been governed by elected or appointed female heads of government or state. It is easier to list the company we keep with those who haven't: France, most Arab nations, Mexico, and Russia are among the few, though Russia did have Catharine the Great! Why have we not explored the possible differences of approach that might obtain through female leadership? Along with slavery, our founding fathers also played a role in the suppression of female independence and governance. Our guiding documents have no inclusive language to suggest that women are meant to be considered as well in the phrase, "all men are created equal." As intellectually gifted and thoughtful as he was on so many issues, Thomas Jefferson thought little more of women than he did of slaves.

In 1790, Thomas Jefferson bought fifty pounds of maple sugar to sweeten his coffee. This was less a culinary decision than a political one: he'd been pressured by his friend and fellow signer of the declaration of independence, Dr. Benjamin Rush, to advocate for the use of home-grown maple sugar instead of cane sugar, which was dependent on slave labor.

Although he was a slave owner himself, Jefferson nonetheless saw the wisdom behind this idea. He wrote to a friend, British diplomat Benjamin Vaughan, that large swaths of the United States were "covered with the sugar maple, as heavily as can be conceived," and that the harvesting of maple sugar required "no other labor than what the women and girls can bestow ... What a blessing to substitute a sugar which requires only the labor of children, for that which is said to render the slavery of the blacks necessary." (Stewart, 2013, p. 257)

Students should be encouraged to further explore the status of women in the early days of our democracy and the struggle that was required to achieve universal suffrage.

For the purpose of this chapter, when we speak of gender we will be referring to the social and cultural characteristics of males and females often called *masculinity* and *femininity*. We will use the term *sex* to refer to a person's biological presentation or sexual orientation. Terminology and how it is used is itself a controversial issue today. Many colleges and universities today use the Common Application form as part of the admissions process.

> Starting this summer, students who use the Common Application will be asked to state their "sex assigned at birth." There will also be a free-response text field in which applicants may describe their gender identity.
>
> These changes, announced last week by the Common Application's leadership, follow calls from students and advocates to change how the standardized application form asks about gender. Currently, applicants are required to choose "male" or "female."
>
> As society's view of transgender people has shifted in recent years, many colleges have made changes to improve the experience of students whose identities don't conform to conventional notions of male and female gender—or align with what's written on their birth certificates ("Common Application," 2016, p. A20).

When examining the character traits that have been used culturally and socially in the United States to define the terms *masculinity* (snips and snails and puppy-dog tails) and *femininity* (sugar and spice and all things nice), we can immediately see the insufficiency of the binary designations—male or female. The terms are even insufficient to describe the full range of biologic possibilities as chromosomal and other anomalies that fit neither category, while uncommon, do exist. When it comes to sexual preference and orientation, the terms *masculine* and *feminine* create even more confusion. In classroom discussion around the college (or job) application process, students might be asked to consider:

- Why do colleges (employers) ask about gender—to achieve diversity, to plan for accommodations (dormitories, housing, bathrooms)? Does it matter for any other purposes?
- How does a student feel when asked to identify as either male or female if he/she is still questioning (one use of the "Q" in LGBTQ)

his/her identity or feeling strange or indignant (Q also stands for queer) about being asked in the first place? This question should be addressed in very general terms, possibly as part of a more general discussion concerning how students feel about being asked to disclose age, race, financial status, or any other personal history.

- What insights and perspectives might members of the LGBTQ community add to a diversified campus or workplace environment?

To foster discussion of so controversial a topic as gender definition with high school students who are struggling with their own identities may be challenging, but it is certainly appropriate and timely. Here we are not just referring to students coming to grips with puberty and the resultant need to identify their sexual orientation, but the struggle that all students go through in terms of expressing the personality traits that will shape both their values and their future roles in life as parents, providers, and contributing members of society. Consider the athletically inclined "tomboy" who suddenly finds herself less attractive to the boys she longs to date because of her desire to lead or the sensitive young man whose caring for injured animals makes him the subject of ridicule by more "masculine" peers. An exercise that might help to open the discussion would be to have all students anonymously complete a survey that would ask them to list three or four character traits that they associate with each of the terms *masculine* and *feminine*. Further insight might be provided by having each student self-identify as male, female, or neither as part of the survey; but no names should be associated with the data to prevent public declarations they might regret at the time or in the future. A list of traits to select from might be provided to help students get started, but they should not be limited to these choices. The traits listed in the work, *Character Lessons,* referred to in Chapter 1 on Sources of Morality, would make a good starting list. Other traits that might be put on the starting list could come from current definitions of masculinity and femininity found on Wikipedia or in dictionaries, and still others might result from a discussion of traits valued by the students that are missing from the above mentioned lists, such as altruism and cooperation. Tabulating the results on a black or white board with masculine traits on one side and feminine on the other, leaving room in the middle for traits on both lists, might result in something like this:

Masculine	Both	Feminine
Aggressive (10m, 10f)	Ambitious	Gentle (10m, 5f, 2n)
Ambitious (8m, 4f, 1n)	Courageous	Courageous (2m, 6f, 1n)
Courageous (6m, 4f)		Ambitious (2m, 2f, 1n)

In this partial list, eight males, four females, and one neither felt that *ambition* is a masculine trait, while two males, two females, and one neither felt it was feminine, so it also appears in the Both column. *Aggression* appears only in the masculine column, and *gentle* appears only in the feminine column.

The discussion that should follow such a tabulation could include:

- Though it appears in the Both column, 13 students feel that ambition is an important masculine trait, and only 5 feel that it is an important feminine trait. Why do we identify some of these traits as more likely masculine or feminine? Is it due to perceived biological differences or cultural/social influences?
- In comparing a list of the 32 traits (and their definitions) listed in *Character Lessons* in 1909 with lists from current character education programs or sources like Wikipedia and dictionary descriptions of masculine and feminine characteristics, what has changed over time? Why? Our discussion of this topic continues in Chapter 7.
- If students were to individually research a character trait, could they find and report on people of both sexes whose lives served as role models for the trait? To allow some choice while avoiding duplication, you could cut up the lists, put them in a box, and let students draw a trait; allow swaps.
- In 1909 when *Character Lessons* was first published, only 21 of the 272 people listed as exemplars for the traits described were women. Will it be easier today to find female role models? Why? Remember our discussion in Chapter 5 about who writes history. Recent trends in historical fiction are providing new opportunities for students to explore the female (if not feminine) side of many familiar stories. Marion Zimmer Bradley in the *Mists of Avalon* has retold the Arthurian tales from the perspectives of all the many women involved: Morgaine (Morgana le Fay), Morgause, Guinevere, Viviane, and Igraine. Even that "face that launched a thousand ships," Helen of Troy, has finally been allowed to tell her side of the story with the publication in 2015 of *Helen of Sparta* by Amalia Carosella. Phillippa Gregory has written many historical novels about the princesses and queens of England and Scotland from a female perspective that give a fascinating account of the lives of women in the historical times described.
- In thinking about their futures, what character traits do students think would be important for roles as partners and or parents? Are these different from the traits required to pursue a chosen job or career or to be an informed and fully participating citizen?

In a recent edition of the newspaper advice column written by Carolyn Hax, a young woman expressed concern over ambivalent feelings about motherhood (*Asbury Park Press*, May 1, 2016, p. 11E). She said, "It feels like being a 'mom' in our culture is so all-consuming and definitive of who you get to be and how you get to live that I worry about the rest of me and us." In her response, Carolyn writes, "I realize you're talking about the gendered aspect, that a male parent is a man and a female parent is a mom." This response may be in part due to the young woman's closing statement in her plea for advice: "It might not shock you to learn that culture and gender are fields I studied in graduate school, and that yes, my field is slightly-to-quite hostile toward pregnancy/childbearing." Why does a woman educated in the fields of culture and gender feel that her field is hostile toward pregnancy and childbearing? Why, from a "gendered aspect," is a male parent a man and not a father?

How do we educate the whole person to allow competent performance of all these future roles? What role has feminist thought played in the way we celebrate differences or deny their existence? Here we like the juxtaposition of the two French sayings—*Vive la différence* versus *Quelle (what) différence?* We will turn next to the conflicts within feminist thought.

WOMEN'S THOUGHT IN DEFINING OUR WORLD

Virtually all feminists seek equality with men in the public world, but some would prefer to change that world—to transform it through a serious analysis and application of women's traditional thought (Noddings, 2015a). In education, these feminist thinkers would give more attention to home life, housekeeping, and parenting, to peace studies, and to the critical analysis of religion. Everyone recognizes how important home life and parenting are to the development of healthy, happy, and moral adults. Why, then, do we teach almost nothing about these topics in our schools? Students should be encouraged to think about and discuss this vital question. As we have pointed out in other chapters, public education was designed as preparation for public life, and therefore, it was directed primarily at boys. Girls received only the basic elements for literacy. When their education was extended to the college level, it concentrated on the tasks of household management, food handling, child care, and community service; it differed sharply from the liberal arts curriculum provided for males. Gradually, the education of girls for home life was abandoned, and girls were allowed to participate in the education traditionally offered to males.

Why was the transition so entirely one-way? Was there nothing in the traditional education of women that might contribute to a better adult life for men as well as for women? For example, the idea of order could be addressed often and not simply as a factor in housekeeping. Order should be explored for its deeper connotations. What might be the connection between an orderly home life and exploration of order in the natural world?

In the social/political world? A main point here is to emphasize concepts that have deep, humanistic meaning but have too often been reduced to "how to do it" courses designed originally for women. If the transition to full education for both men and women had included a careful analysis of women's thought, a new curriculum might have been constructed—one involving, for example, the careful study of order, conversation, choice, collaboration, sharing, comfort, safety, privacy, and listening. Attention to these concepts would enrich the curriculum not only in language arts and social studies but in science, mathematics, and the arts as well.

At this point, some readers might suggest that we add actual courses on home, child development, community life, and family relations. We advise caution on this. Every new course that has not been part of the traditional male curriculum has been considered second-rate, of low academic prestige, and unworthy of college preparatory credit. The same thing would almost certainly happen to courses designed to treat the concepts identified in women's thought. A wiser move would be to add these ideas and their histories to the existing disciplines and concentrate on interdisciplinary connections. In *How to Bake π*, Eugenia Cheng (2015) has demonstrated the connections between cooking and category theory, "the mathematics of mathematics," quite nicely through the use of recipes and kitchen skills. Women have written powerfully on homemaking and its deeper meanings— Jane Addams, Catherine Beecher, Dorothy Day, Lillian Gilbreth, Charlotte Perkins Gilman, Eva Feder Kittay, Sara Ruddick, and Virginia Woolf, to name but a few. But men too have sometimes considered the deeper meanings attached to the house and home.

Gaston Bachelard (1964) wrote almost poetically on the deep meanings attached to the words *home* and *house*. Exploring the house from cellar to attic, he reminds us of the association of cellars with fear and darkness, of attics with hidden memories, of corners with secrecy, and of doors with both entry into the wider world and escape into the peace and security of home. Surely there is something in this book that could be discussed in every discipline, and the concept of *home* could be a major topic of discussion in interdisciplinary seminars. (For more sources on houses and homes, see Witold Rybczynski, 1986.)

In Chapter 11 on patriotism, we will discuss some feminist thinking on war and peace, but we should note here that not all women are or have been pacifists. Women have often supported war and military action, and those who have publicly opposed war have suffered severe criticism. Consider how Jane Addams was vilified for her public opposition to World War I (Elshtain, 2002; Noddings, 2012) and how the first woman elected to the U.S. Congress, Jeanette Rankin of Montana, lost her position initially for opposing our participation in World War I and permanently after voting against a declaration of war in World War II. Now that women are permitted to enlist in the armed services and even to participate in combat, should we consider this a move in the right direction? Should we celebrate or mourn?

Religion is another area of thought in which women's ideas have been largely ignored in our public schools. Elizabeth Cady Stanton wrote a powerful critique of the Bible (*The Woman's Bible*, 1895) in which she challenged the contention—expressed throughout the Bible—that "woman" is an inferior creature responsible for bringing evil into God's paradise. Her colleagues, including her good friend Susan B. Anthony, feared that this attack on traditional religion would alienate people who might otherwise support the campaign for women's suffrage. Similarly, today some feminists fear that an effort to emphasize women's humanistic thinking might impede the drive for women's equality in the political/economic arena. Should we then keep quiet about the abuse of women in Christian thought and history?

At the very least, students should be made aware of the long association of women with evil promulgated by the male religious tradition. Mary Daly has pointed out:

> The myth [of Eve and the Fall] takes on cosmic proportions since the male's viewpoint is metamorphosed into God's viewpoint. It amounts to a cosmic false naming. It misnames the mystery of evil, casting it into the distorted mold of the myth of feminine evil. In this way images and conceptualizations about evil are thrown out of focus and its deepest dimensions are not really confronted. (1974, p. 35)

In Chapter 4, we noted that students rarely get an opportunity to learn something about atheism, agnosticism, and deism. Now we remind our readers that the huge body of religious literature on women and by women is also largely ignored. That ignorance leaves an enormous hole in thinking about moral life. Paul Ricoeur, for example, once wrote, "Man enters into the ethical world through fear and not through love" (1969, p. 30). But this should be challenged:

> We cannot deny that fear inspires some ethical thinking, but so does love. The desire to be like a loving parent is a powerful impetus toward ethical life, and so is the desire to remain in loving relation. A woman's view has to find new language or at least to modify language as it seeks expression. It should not be articulated as mere opposition, but rather as a positive program for human living. (Noddings, 1989, p. 144)

PROGRESS BY THE NUMBERS

While women have made considerable progress globally in the public world as heads of state and directors of major companies, the numbers in the United States are not impressive for a country that prides itself on world leadership and "greatness." According to data available from the National Science Foundation, in 2013, women made up just 15% of the engineering workforce and 25% in math and computer science (National Science Board, 2016). Women's salaries as a percentage of men's in science and engineering have not changed significantly since 1995, when it was 69.4%. In 2013 it was even lower, 68.8%. Women currently represent about 16% of executive officers at S&P 100 companies and 20% of Congress (Dowd, 2015). Why are these numbers so low? Are these the right measures to gauge women's progress toward equality? What has been done to try to change these numbers or accelerate progress toward more equal representation?

WHY ARE THE NUMBERS SO LOW? WOMEN IN STEM PROFESSIONS

Why do more women not enter STEM (science, technology, engineering, and mathematics) professions? Three important reasons, both related and controversial, are often cited to explain why there aren't more women in these fields: a lack of early encouragement and role models, perceived lack of aptitude and consequent lack of preparation, and stereotype threat.

I (Brooks) am a stereotypical female engineer. My father, several uncles, and grandfather were engineers, and my mom (Noddings) was my high school math teacher. As a member since my student days of the Society of Women Engineers, I had heard that most female engineers are the children of engineering parents. In giving a talk on career paths to the women graduate engineering students at Carnegie Mellon, I had an opportunity to confirm this firsthand. When I asked the group if one or both of their parents were engineers, everyone in the room raised their hand. No exceptions! The lack of role models is often cited as a major reason why young women are not attracted to the STEM professions. With media portrayals of women as homemakers and nurses and of science and engineering jobs as dirty, mechanical, physical, and/or nerdy, is it any wonder that girls who have been raised to be neat, polite, and nurturing might find STEM careers both daunting and unattractive? This was certainly true when Mom and I were in high school and only a little better when my own children were that age. Are things better today? What shows are students watching? Who are their role models? Teachers should encourage discussion of media stereotypes and their impact on course selection and potential career choices. We will talk more about this in the next chapter when we look at the lack of stories by and/or about women in entertainment and media of all forms.

The second area of controversy for young women contemplating STEM careers centers on conflicting studies and messaging around aptitudes for mathematics and spatial visualization. While it is true that boys continue to perform better than girls on the math SAT test, it is also true that the SAT has been shown to be a poor predictor of success at college-level coursework, especially for young women. In addition, it is interesting to note that far more attention is paid to male outperformance in math than to the corresponding fact that girls outperform boys on verbal tests. Some would attribute this attention to the fact that math test scores serve as a better predictor of future income and therefore explain the differences in pay between the sexes (Niederle & Vestlund, 2010). Lawrence Summers, then president of Harvard University, made remarks at a diversity conference sponsored by the National Bureau of Economic Research in January 2005 that inflamed the existing controversy on women's aptitudes as a cause for underrepresentation in tenured positions in science and engineering at top universities.

> On the question of aptitude for science, Summers said this: "It does appear that on many, many different human attributes—height, weight, propensity for criminality, overall IQ, mathematical ability, scientific ability—there is relatively clear evidence that whatever the difference in means—which can be debated—there is a difference in the standard deviation, and variability of a male and a female population. And that is true with respect to attributes that are and are not plausibly, culturally determined. If one supposes, as I think is reasonable, that if one is talking about physicists at a top 25 research university, one is not talking about people who are two standard deviations above the mean. And perhaps it's not even talking about somebody who is three standard deviations above the mean. But it's talking about people who are three and a half, four standard deviations above the mean in the one in 5,000, one in 10,000 class. Even small differences in the standard deviation will translate into very large differences in the available pool substantially out." (Jaschik, 2005, p. 2)

This statement raised such a furor among the academic community internationally that Summers apologized in February saying,

> My January remarks substantially understated the impact of socialization and discrimination, including implicit attitudes—patterns of thought to which all of us are unconsciously subject. The issue of gender difference is far more complex than comes through in my comments, and my remarks about variability went beyond what research has established. (Jaschik, pp. 2–3)

Apology notwithstanding, the lid was off the box for continued debate and in March 2005, Harvard's Mind Brain and Behavior Inter-Faculty Initiative held a spirited debate between Harvard psychology professors Steven Pinker and Elizabeth S. Spelke, titled *The Science of Gender and Science*. This debate focused on whether test-driven indications of male superiority in certain aspects of visual-spatial perception and mathematical ability, as well as interests and motivation, are driven more by biological sex differences (Pinker) or by socialization (Spelke). Both psychologists cited scientific studies and data to support their positions and a video and transcript of

the debate, including the slides presented, are all available online (Pinker &
Spelke, 2005).

One purpose in viewing or discussing this debate with students would
be for teachers to point out the passion of both participants for their
respective positions, the fact that the debate is occurring between a man
and a woman who are *both* high-powered professionals, and the good
nature of the participants who are both quick to point out areas of common agreement. Another purpose would be to explore two controversial
questions:

- If Pinker is right and there are real biologic sex differences that
  impact both capability and motivation for mathematical and
  engineering pursuits, then are we right to push young women to
  pursue equality in these areas beyond an appropriate representation
  with regard to current test differences? If boys outperform girls
  by two to one on the top scores for the SAT, then maybe 50%
  participation by women is unrealistic, but ought there not be at
  least 30% women in these fields rather than 15%?
- If Spelke is right and socialization is the larger, if not only, factor,
  what should be done to change the way we view women's abilities
  and desires to pursue careers in these areas? If there is some element
  of truth to both positions, how would this change what we do?

There are also many studies that show that our third controversial concern, stereotype threat, may have a significant role to play in the performance
of women on tests like the SAT that are perceived to be competitive. An interesting article written by an undergraduate woman at MIT, "Michele G.,
18," appeared on the MIT admissions blog on September 3, 2015, with the
title, "Picture yourself as a stereotypical male." In this article, Michele ex-
plains that stereotype threat

> refers to a theorized mechanism by which people underperform (on tests, com-
> petitions, etc.) in response to awareness of stereotypes about their demographic
> group. It's related to a largely subconscious apprehension about confirming the
> negative stereotype, which hinders cognition, impairs concentration, and under
> some conditions reduces preparation or effort. (MIT Admissions Blog, 2015)

She then goes on to cite many examples of studies that have been done
to support the idea that stereotype threat significantly impacts the performance of girls on standardized tests. Muriel Niederle and Lise Vesterlund
have compiled information on similar studies presenting "results that suggest that the abundant and disturbing evidence of a large gender gap in
mathematics performance at high percentiles [Summers's 3 to 4 standard
deviations above the mean] in part may be explained by the differential

manner in which men and women respond to competitive test-taking environments" (2010, p. 130).

Women drop or opt out of science and engineering careers, particularly from academia, for some of the same reasons that women leave other professions—to start families, to support the career of their spouse, and/or to earn more money. The "good old boy" network, lack of support, pay inequality, and harassment are real, and yet Summers had the audacity to say (on that same day in January 2005) that

> he believed that the most important reason for the gender gap was the same reason fewer women fill top positions in many "high-powered" professions: They are less likely than men to work the long hours expected for advancement in these careers. He noted that the women who are in senior positions are "disproportionately either unmarried or without children." Noting the long hours of work required to move ahead, he said, "it is a fact about our society that that is a level of commitment that a much higher fraction of married men have been historically prepared to make than of married women." (Jaschick, 2005, p. 2)

The controversy here is twofold: Why have men been "historically prepared" to make larger time commitments to their careers than women? And, as Summers noted himself, these differences raise "the question of whether organizations are making appropriate demands on people" (Jaschik, 2005, p. 2). The answer to both questions may largely be addressed by creating a more balanced approach to work/life for everyone and then allowing people to choose their level of personal commitment without incurring penalties for doing so. Two instructive stories on women's levels of commitment as scientists and mothers come to mind.

In an interview published in an educational journal, Hope Jahrens, environmental scientist and author of *Lab Girl*, describes how she was banned from her laboratory during a difficult pregnancy:

> But, I tell you, of all the things that I've been through, getting told I couldn't come to the lab—that was the absolute rock-bottom worst thing. . . . There's no fitting into the male world when you're eight months' pregnant. Male spaces don't tolerate that. (Voosen, 2016, p. B14)

This is a woman who completed her PhD in geobiology at the University of California, Berkeley, has received three Fulbright awards, was named by *Popular Science* in 2005 as one of the "Brilliant 10" young scientists, and by *Time* magazine as one of their "100 Most Influential People." A tenured professor at the University of Hawaii at Manoa in Honolulu, she is definitely one of Lawrence Summers's high-powered people, but she was *not allowed* to choose her *level of commitment* during her pregnancy.

Another exceptional woman scientist, Sylvia Earle, related the following story about her participation in the Tektite II underwater habitat project. Her first foray into popular science writing was in the August 1971 issue of *National Geographic,* an article the editors chose to title "All-Girl Team Tests the Habitat." Earle was 34 at the time; the youngest participant was engineer Peggy Lucas, then a 23-year-old "girl." She goes on to relate how a man she considered a mentor later told her he had opposed her participation in the project because she was a mother (Earle, 1995). Earle is an American marine biologist, explorer, author, and lecturer. She founded an ocean engineering firm and set the women's world record for depth in 1979 in a Jim suit to 1,250 feet beneath the surface. She has been a National Geographic explorer-in-residence since 1998. Earle was the first female chief scientist of the U.S. National Oceanic and Atmospheric Administration and was named by *Time* magazine as its first Hero for the Planet in 1998.

Many women have enough guilty feelings about leaving their children at home to pursue a career without having choices made for them by others, with or without their knowledge. However, the lead author of a working paper published in June 2015 by the Harvard Business School, professor Kathleen McGinn, has the following message for working mothers: "When you go to work, you are helping your children understand that there are lots of opportunities for them." The study showed that

> Daughters of working mothers are more likely to be employed, hold supervisory positions, and earn more money than the daughters of women who don't work outside the home. The researchers also found a statistically significant effect on the sons of working women, who are likely to spend more time caring for family members and doing household chores than are the sons of stay-at-home mothers. (Fisher, 2015, pp. 2–3)

HOW MIGHT WE MEASURE EQUALITY?

The World Economic Forum (WEF), a 45-year-old nonprofit foundation based in Switzerland and dedicated to "improving the state of the world," developed a Global Gender Gap Index in 2006. The index focuses on four areas: economic participation and opportunity, educational attainment, health and survival, and political empowerment. It is designed to measure the percentage attainment against a goal of gender equality in each of these areas. With 142 countries participating in the index for 2014, the United States ranked 20th overall. With the four areas of focus weighted equally, the United States was fourth in the area of economic participation and opportunity but 54th in the area of political empowerment. The score for economic participation says that we are about 83% of the way toward attaining equality in this area, which was measured by five subindexes and heavily weighted (31%) by the subindex on wage equality between women and men for similar work, for which the United States scored only 66%. The data included in the report for 2014 on this index and the conclusions drawn are fascinating in themselves and would make a great subject for discussion in our proposed social studies forum or in a regular social studies or math class. What we want to emphasize here, though, is that all of these measures are looking at the equality of women in today's male-dominated world. Some questions for discussion on this point might include:

- The United States only scored 18% attainment in the area of political empowerment. How might life be different in the United States if we made progress in this area? How is life different in the Scandinavian countries of Iceland, Finland, Norway, Sweden, and Denmark, all in the top seven on this metric? Would attainment of equality on this metric automatically change the other three areas due to a greater emphasis on women's concerns?
- Are there other metrics that could be used that might better reflect women's concerns? As an example, the United Nations began preparing a World Happiness Report in 2012 to help member countries gauge the happiness of their people and to use the results to guide public policy. What is being measured for this report, and how does it differ from the items being measured for the Gender Gap Index? Are some the same? The five Scandinavian countries mentioned previously all ranked in the top eight for happiness along with Switzerland, Canada, and the Netherlands, while the United States ranked 15th.

There is also a Global Peace Index devised by the Institute for Economics and Peace. In 2015, the United States ranked 94th out of 162 countries on this index. The Scandinavian countries were all in the top 20 with Iceland and Denmark ranked first and second. Why does the United States score so poorly on this metric? It should not be surprising to note that we rated only better than Syria, Russia, Israel, and North Korea as least peaceful on the militarization domain. It should also not be surprising that we ranked 118th on the domain "ongoing domestic and international conflict," since this domain includes: number of deaths from external organized conflicts and number, duration, and role in external conflicts, among others. Would greater empowerment of women change the behaviors that cause us to rank poorly on the Global Peace Index?

WHAT HAS BEEN DONE TO FURTHER EQUALITY?

Many people are aware of affirmative action or at least have heard the words. What most people don't know is that as with voting rights, legislation to prevent racial discrimination came before legislation to prevent discrimination against women and culminated in the Civil Rights Act of 1964. Provisions of the Civil Rights Act established the Equal Employment Opportunity Commission and aimed to end discrimination in all firms with 25 or more employees. However, the amendment of Title VII of the Act to prohibit employment discrimination based on sex was seen by some as an attempt

> to derail the bill, but once it was proposed women flocked to support the measure. Then the Equal Employment Opportunity Commission refused to enforce Title VII. [The first case was brought to the commission by airline stewardesses.] One EEOC director called it "a fluke . . . conceived out of wedlock," and even *The New Republic* asked, "Why should such a mischievous joke perpetrated on the floor of the House of Representatives be treated by a responsible administration body with this kind of seriousness?" Infuriated women mobilized, forming the National Organization for Women in 1966. (B. Friedman, 2009, p. 290)

Controversy surrounding affirmative action, whether applied to discrimination based on race or sex, is worthy of classroom time and discussion. Students should be helped to understand the difference between affirmative action and quota systems, the concern that affirmative action leads to reverse discrimination, and the role of affirmative action in creating diversity of thought and ideas in education and the workplace.

The second major legislative milestone for women's equality was achieved six years later with enactment of Title IX of the Education Amendments of 1972. Many people are only familiar with one aspect of Title IX, if they have heard of it at all, and that is the requirement for equal funding and facilities for women's sports. Few realize the possible breadth of application of Title IX, which states "No person in the United States shall, on the basis of sex, be excluded from participation in, be denied the benefits of, or be subjected to discrimination under any education program or activity receiving Federal financial assistance" (Winslow, 2010, p. 1). Title IX was coauthored by Representative Patsy Mink of Hawaii and renamed the Patsy Mink Equal Opportunity Education Act in 2002. It was introduced in Congress by coauthor Birch Bayh, Senator from Indiana. Senator Bayh's remarks on the Senate floor illustrate the intended importance of this Act for women's rights:

> We are all familiar with the stereotype of women as pretty things who go to college to find a husband, go on to graduate school because they want a more interesting husband, and finally marry, have children, and never work again. The desire of many schools not to waste a "man's place" on a woman stems from such stereotyped notions. But the facts absolutely contradict these myths about the "weaker sex" and it is time to change our operating assumptions. . . . (1972, p. 5804)

While the impact of this amendment would be far-reaching, it is not a panacea. It is, however, an important first step in the effort to provide for the women of America something that is rightfully theirs—an equal chance to attend the schools of their choice, to develop the skills they want, and to apply those skills with the knowledge that they will have a fair chance to secure the jobs of their choice with equal pay for equal work. (1972, p. 5808)

While sports was not explicitly mentioned in the original statute, sports became its banner headline when Billie Jean King defeated former Wimbledon champion Bobbie Riggs in what was dubbed the "Battle of the Sexes." Winslow (2010) notes that "the 1973 match captivated and changed the way women looked at themselves" and cites a quote from King in a later *Newsweek* interview, "I just had to play. Title IX had just passed, and I . . . wanted to change the hearts and minds of people to match the legislation." (p. 2). Winslow also relates:

> In 1971, fewer than 295,000 girls participated in high school varsity athletics, accounting for just 7 percent of all varsity athletes; in 2001, that number leaped to 2.8 million, or 41.5 percent of all varsity athletes, according to the National Coalition for Women and Girls in Education.

In 1966, 16,000 females competed in intercollegiate athletics. By 2012, that number jumped to more than 150,000, accounting for 43 percent of all college athletes.

A recent article in the *New York Times* found that there are lasting benefits for women from Title IX: participation in sports increased education as well as employment opportunities for girls. Furthermore, the athletic participation by girls and women spurred by Title IX was associated with lower obesity rates. No other public health program can claim similar success (pp. 2–3).

Today, Title IX is being invoked to protect women students against sexual violence, to allow pregnant and parenting students to finish high school, and to encourage greater inclusion of women in programs (vocational and STEM related) that will lead to higher wages. The Common Core State Standards for English Language Arts & Literacy in History/Social Studies, Science, and Technical Subjects suggest that junior and senior high school students should be able to:

1. Delineate and evaluate the reasoning in seminal U.S. texts, including the application of constitutional principles and use of legal reasoning (e.g., in U.S. Supreme Court majority opinions and dissents) and the premises, purposes, and arguments in works of public advocacy (e.g., *The Federalist*, presidential addresses).
2. Analyze seventeenth-, eighteenth-, and nineteenth-century foundational U.S. documents of historical and literary significance (including The Declaration

of Independence, the Preamble to the Constitution, the Bill of Rights, and Lincoln's Second Inaugural Address) for their themes, purposes, and rhetorical features. (p. 40)

Perhaps it might be more useful for students to study 20th-century legislative documents like the Civil Rights Act and Title IX that govern the way they will be treated today!

WHY ARE THE NUMBERS SO LOW? WOMEN IN ENTERTAINMENT

Earlier we noted that perhaps the hullabaloo over the male domination of exceptionally high scores on the math SAT might have something to do with a correlation to future high-paying jobs. What is happening today in the entertainment industry certainly supports this idea. We're not talking about science and engineering jobs here, but the high-paying jobs in entertainment. Sandra Bullock and other "A-list" actresses have started asking directors and producers to send them parts that have been rejected by their male peers.

> "I said, 'I want to do what Jim Carrey's doing.' I was looking for something he didn't want."

Consider that sentence: despite being one of the most bankable actresses in the world, Bullock wanted to scoop up the crumbs from Carrey's banquet table. Imagine the parts women merely nominated for Oscars must be offered.

It's not just an issue of character depth; it's one of sheer volume. Among last year's 100 top-grossing films, 12 featured female protagonists. Of all the speaking characters, only 30% were women, according to Martha Lauzen at San Diego State University, who began issuing an annual "Celluloid Ceiling" report in 1998 to lay bare Hollywood's gender gap (Dockterman, 2015, p. 46).

And it's not just the jobs in front of the camera. "The most wildly lop-sided numbers have to do with who is behind the lens. In both 2013 and 2014, women were only 1.9 percent of the directors for the top 100-grossing films" (Dowd, 2015, p. 43). In the research cited earlier by Lauzen, "in 2014, 95 percent of cinematographers, 89 percent of screenwriters, 82 percent of editors, 81 percent of executive producers and 77 percent of producers were men" (Dowd, 2015, p. 43). So it really is about both money and visibility. Here we are talking about underrepresentation of women in an industry, particularly in the high-paying jobs; the next chapter focuses on the lack of women's stories in all forms of entertainment.

CHAPTER 7

Entertainment, Sports, and Media

In this chapter we will explore three broad areas:

- the role of entertainment in defining ourselves and our role models and heroes;
- the contrasting roles of sports as a component of education and as entertainment in hero creation; and
- the role that the digital revolution in media is playing in how we are entertained, informed, and persuaded and how we communicate with each other.

We will explore each of these areas within the context of the controversy between the idea that "the business of America is business," as professed (or prophesized) by Calvin Coolidge in the 1920s, and the contrasting view of his contemporary John Dewey that the real business of America should be democracy. Dewey conceptualizes a democratic "individuality" as a counterbalance to the subversion of America's rugged individualism to a new individualism reduced to an economic relation by corporatization. We owe thanks to Kerry Burch (2012) for this framework as one he identified in *Democratic Transformations: Eight Conflicts in the Negotiation of American Identity* with pedagogical value. Burch quotes from a 1930 work by Dewey identifying an underlying conformity behind the celebration of American "individualism":

Nowhere is the decline of the old-fashioned individual and individualism more marked [than] in leisure life, in amusements and sports. Our colleges only follow the movement of the day when they make athletics an organized business, aroused and conducted under paid directors in the spirit of pure collectivism. The formation of theatre chains is at once the cause and the effect of the destruction of the older independent life of leisure carried on in separate homes. . . . The press is the organ of amusement for a hurried leisure time, and it reflects and carries further the formation of mental collectivism by massed methods. Crime, too, is assuming a new form; it is organized and corporate. (Burch, 2012, pp. 103–104, quoting Dewey)

ENTERTAINMENT

Whether rolling bones for dice or telling stories about the mammoth hunt around the campfire in the cave, entertainment has been part of the human experience from the beginning. Entertainment generally implies an audience—fellow players in a game or viewers/listeners at a performance—thus entailing a social activity that brings people together. Even solo entertaining activities such as reading or playing a video game have their social aspects through book clubs, discussion groups, and online communities of fellow players. But entertainment has changed over time in at least two fairly significant ways. First, entertainment has become an industry through the mass production and distribution of written material, music, and visual performance, particularly in the United States where it has become the embodiment of the saying that the "business of America is business." Second, these same mass distribution techniques have created an opportunity for entertainment to be a vehicle both to sell products and ideas and at the same time to allow people to isolate themselves from differing viewpoints through personalized digital choices. We will talk more about the sale of products and ideas in the final section of the chapter.

We spent a pleasant afternoon recently talking about the ways that entertainment has changed in our respective lifetimes. Spanning four generations from Noddings to her great-grandchildren (Brooks's grandchildren, in particular), there were differences and similarities. We talked about the evolution of drama from attendance at live performances to radio, movies, and television; the importance of reading for all four generations as a source of entertainment, an opportunity to relate to others, and a source of information and knowledge; and the progression of board, card, and paper-and-pencil games like dice baseball to today's online video environment where "there's gotta be an *app* for that," so you can play it on your smart phone. The two changes we have already mentioned came into play in this discussion—the increasing commercialization of all aspects of entertainment and the decreasing opportunities for face-to-face social interaction as a result of the digital revolution.

When I (Brooks) was a child, we played battleship with graph paper and pencils—you each hid your fleet on a marked grid and then tried to find and sink each other's ships by calling out coordinates. My children played the game as a pre-fab plastic board game with plastic pegs for the ships. Now my grandchildren can play it alone or with players anywhere in the world on their iPhones. Both themes are present here. In the paper-and-pencil and plastic game board versions you had to be physically and mentally present to play, and maybe, in the game board version, there could have been ads for other games on the box. In the digital version, it is highly unlikely that you will be in the same physical location as your fellow player(s), if any; you need not be fully mentally present either, as you will likely be multitasking with whatever device you are playing on; and you will be bombarded with advertisements between rounds of play. Have these changes impacted our self-identity formation? In removing face-to-face interaction, is there an attendant loss of empathy? Some recent studies would suggest this is the case. The older or more experienced child no longer has the opportunity to coach the younger by giving hints or affirmations, such as "now you've got it," when the younger makes a good move or to educate on the differences between a submarine and a destroyer. There is no opportunity in digital play for one player to observe that the other is distracted and not at his or her best or losing his or her temper and not being a good sport. Students could be asked to observe this for themselves by having two groups play an online version of a two-person game like battleship or checkers with unidentified opponents in another room and then bringing the groups back together to play the same game face to face. They could count the number and type of social interactions that occur in each version of the game and then discuss as a group how the two experiences differed. Which did they prefer and why?

Older students could combine this experiment with discussion of selected readings on the impact of digital media on identity formation. The works of MIT clinical psychologist and sociologist Sherry Turkle are instructive:

> Turkle finds the roots of the problem in the failure of young people absorbed in their devices to develop fully independent selves, a topic she began to explore in *Alone Together* (2011). In that book, she examined the way interaction with robotic toys and "always on" connections affect adolescent development. She argued that phones and texting disrupt the ability to separate from one's parents, and raise other obstacles to adulthood. Curating a Facebook profile alters the presentation of self. Absorption in a gaming avatar can become a flight from the difficulties of real life. Young people face new anxieties around the loss of privacy and the persistence of online data. (Weisberg, 2016, p. 6)

Students should be asked to consider how digital interaction and social media have shaped their personal views and social interactions. Have their activities in the digital world enlarged their exposure to other points of view, or have these activities allowed them to contract to very narrow "intersectionalities" where they are relating only to others of the same gender, race, and class? We will return to these ideas in Chapter 9 on Money, Class, and Poverty, but for now we would like to point out:

> Within Dewey's framework, authentic democratic individuals will reflect a cluster of associated character traits that are best cultivated when they are socially constituted. These traits—questioning, the capacity to dialogue, to listen, to improvise, to care about the common good and other principles of social justice, to mention a few—spring from individual human potentials, but there is no guarantee that individuals will interact with their social environments in such a

way that these potentials will be stimulated to come to fruition. (Burch, 2012, p. 107)

Does social interaction in a digital environment enhance or diminish one's capability to become an authentic democratic individual?

All forms of entertainment provide us with inspirational role models and potential heroes. But the presented role models in terms of race, gender, and class have largely been determined by two things—who writes history, as discussed in Chapter 5 on race, and who has the money, power, and influence, as discussed in Chapter 6 on gender. We have already seen how women are underrepresented in high-paying jobs in the film industry and that A-list actresses are having male parts rewritten for them as women. Only 11% of writers of top-grossing films are women, and until more women are writing and directing the scripts, the strategy of having rejected male roles rewritten for women will continue. But what about women's stories? Think about all of the Disney movies with female characters, and then realize that until *Frozen* all of the female characters had to be rescued by a guy, some prince or beast. Finally, in *Frozen,* the lead female saves not only herself but her sister too.

For her article in the *New York Times Magazine,* titled "Waiting for the Green Light," Maureen Dowd interviewed more than 100 women and men at all levels of Hollywood. Speaking of how Hollywood treats women's successes as anomalies, Shonda Rhimes, head writer and executive producer of *Grey's Anatomy* for ABC, had this to say:

> "The world of movies is fascinating to me because everyone has amnesia all the time," Rhimes told me. "Every time a female-driven project is made and succeeds, somehow it's a fluke. Instead of just saying 'The Hunger Games' is popular among young women, they say it only made money because Jennifer Lawrence was luminous and amazing. I mean, you go get yours, girl. But seriously, that's ridiculous. There's a very hungry audience of young women dying to see some movies. They came out for 'Titanic' and 'Twilight.' 14-year-old girls going back to see those movies every day. I find it fascinating that this audience is not being respected. In the absence of water, people drink sand. And that is sad. There's such an interest in things being equal and such a weary acceptance that it's not." (Dowd, 2015, p. 45)

This is the same Jennifer Lawrence who found out during the hack of Sony's emails that she had been paid less than her male costars for *American Hustle.* She wrote an essay about this in which she blamed herself for not being a better negotiator. She joked that "Hollywood stars negotiating for a few extra million dollars, a few more lines and a few fewer nude scenes might elicit eye rolls from most. But their success could determine whether popcorn-nibbling pre-teen girls will come to think of themselves as the apple of some man's eye or as an FBI agent, an astronaut or a political consultant" (Dockterman, 2015, p. 47).

I (Brooks) was lucky. When I was in junior high in the 1960s, I wanted to become a marine biologist. I had both Jacques Cousteau *and* Rachel Carson to look up to. If I had wanted to be an astronaut, I would have been out of luck for a female role model, at least in the United States. An American woman, Sally Ride, though born the year before me, did not make it into space until 1983—20 years after the first Soviet woman, 22 years after the first American man, and 8 years after I had graduated from college with a degree in mathematics. Try finding role models for women in mathematics! Again, lucky me—my mom was my high school math teacher.

We talked one afternoon about available role models for women in the literature we read while growing up; both in terms of women writers and women's stories. Aside from the usual, Jane Austen and the Brontes, the only one we could both recall reading was Louisa May Alcott, and we're sure that we both read her books long before high school. Her books are still recommended reading for middle school students today. Note, all of the women writers in the last few sentences lived in the 18th and 19th centuries, and it is now the 21st.

In case this seems strange or forgetful on our parts, take a look at the recommended text exemplars for grades 11 and up in Appendix B of the Common Core State Standards for English Language Arts & Literacy in History/Social Studies, Science, and Technical Subjects. In the section called "stories," only 7 of the 19 exemplars were written by women—with the predictable Austen and Bronte (19th century) and a work by Sarah Orne Jewett also published in the 19th century as the only White female representatives. Thanks to enhanced recognition of the need for diversity the seven also include two Black women, Zora Neale Hurston and Toni Morrison; a Cuban-American woman, Cristina Garcia; and the Pulitzer Prize–winning Jhumpa Lahiri, a London-born Indian. While the inclusion of authors of color is both admirable and desirable, were the authors of the standards totally lacking in 20th or even 21st century White women to choose from? Recent Pulitzer winners or nominees include Joyce Carol Oates, Donna Tartt, Geraldine Brooks, and Barbara Kingsolver. Of these, Kingsolver has written many stories (see *Homeland and Other Stories*) and a novel, *Flight Behavior*, with ordinary women as protagonists telling female stories. Of the 19 exemplar "stories," only 7 have major female characters telling a female story, and one of these was Nathaniel Hawthorne's *The Scarlet Letter*. This is the same Nathaniel Hawthorne who in the 1850s "complained to his publisher about the 'damned horde of scribbling women' whose books outsold his own" (Zeisler, 2016, p. 38).

Other categories of exemplars for grades 11 and up show an even greater bias for male authorship and concerns. Female writers are represented by only 1 of 7 drama works, 5 of 15 poetry works, 1 of 13 texts on language arts, 2 of 11 on history/social studies and 0.5 of 10 (a female coauthor) on science, mathematics, and technical studies. It should also be noted that of the nine women represented in the previous list, 3 are Black, 1 is Hispanic, and 1 is Chinese. In case you were counting, 1 of these 10 female authored works, possibly the most important for women, was authored by multiple women—the Declaration of Sentiments written by the attendees of the first women's rights convention at Seneca Falls, New York, in 1848.

Growing up, my (Brooks) daughters and I did have Nancy Drew, girl detective, and Cherry Ames, nurse as detective. Both of these series were written by women for girls, but these as with most mysteries (many written by very capable women writers like Agatha Christie, Ruth Rendell, Dorothy L. Sayers, and P. D. James) have rarely been considered great literature or public school classroom recommendations. As we mention elsewhere in this book, many mysteries as well as science fiction and fantasy stories include informative, controversial, and moral issues that could promote critical thinking, and yet these genres, while of great interest to many young people, are rarely included in lists of recommended reading. The science fiction and fantasy genres also have a good representation of excellent female writers, including Ursula K. LeGuin, James Tiptree, Jr., C. J. Cherryh, Marion Zimmer Bradley, Margaret Atwood, and Mary Doria Russell. These lists of female mystery and science fiction writers are among our favorites and just the ones that came to mind quickly while writing this section; there are many more. Teachers should not feel constrained by the exemplars listed in the Common Core or any other source. Teachers should find out what students enjoy reading and then help them find works appropriate to their age and reading level that will further their understanding of themselves and others.

Finding and reading stories by and/or about women and the experience of women is not enough in itself. Another missing element in the Common Core standards is the idea that the content of what we are reading contains emotional and moral lessons that should be discussed with students. In the trade-off to promote higher test scores, teachers are instead asked to focus on high-quality informational texts and books of increasing complexity; where complexity is defined in highly quantifiable terms by standards like the ATOS readability formula that looks at average sentence length, average word length, word difficulty level, and total number of words in a book or passage. Using the ATOS scores for the top 25 books read by high schoolers in 2010–2011, Renaissance Learning, Inc. found that high school students are reading books at 5th-grade appropriate levels. The ATOS score for *To Kill a Mockingbird* is 5. 5, *The Catcher in the Rye* 4. 7, and the currently popular *Hunger Games* books 5. 3. Most of the fiction books with ATOS scores above 10 were written in the 19th century or earlier and include works by Homer, Shakespeare, Dickens, and Poe ("American High School Students Are Reading," 2012).

Now, we will confess that we did read most of the works listed in this article with the grade-appropriate ATOS scores above 10 while we were in high school, but we read them because we love to read. We love to read because we had teachers and other role models who loved to read and who helped us understand the emotional and moral content of what we were reading.

> It balloons into a broader discussion about the purpose of an English education. English teachers—at least the ones I know—want to churn out thinkers who wield power through language. We want them to love books, but also to survive. We want them to read a lease in 10 years and know what they're getting into. We also want to turn out good citizens who practice in the streets and at the office what they identify as moral and good in class, people who do not cheat, manipulate, abuse, and unfairly judge others. English teachers, it seems, are in a good position to impose some degree of emotional and moral rigor on the curriculum. (Simmons, 2016, pp. 6–7)

Simmons ends his article, titled "Literature's Emotional Lessons," with this statement: "After all, one only has to live on a violent, beleaguered planet and watch the news to know we are troubled. And one may only have to read fiction to understand that solutions can spring as readily from love and empathy as logic" (p. 7). Where better to find solutions that spring from love and empathy than stories by women, like *To Kill a Mockingbird*, or about the female experience, as in *Little Women*?

SPORTS

It was during the Roaring Twenties and the Coolidge prosperity that sports also became part of the "business of America." The National Football League (NFL) was founded in 1920; that same year the powerful Commissioner of Baseball replaced the National Commission, and in 1921 the National Collegiate Athletic Association (NCAA), originally founded as a rules-making body, conducted its first national championship. Recall Dewey's lament at the beginning of this chapter for the loss of "individuality" in the new individualism of the "business mind" in sports as in other forms of leisure life and amusements. According to Wikipedia's article on "Sports in the United States":

- Sports in the United States are an important part of the country's culture;
- The four major sports leagues, MLB (baseball), NFL (football), NBA (basketball), and NHL (hockey) are among the most financially lucrative sports leagues in the world generating tens of billions of revenue;

- All four enjoy wide-ranging domestic media coverage; and
- Sports are particularly associated with education in the United States.

We want to concern ourselves here with two intertwined controversial topics—the role of sports in education and the mass-marketed hero worship of today's professional athletes. Physical education to train the body as well as the mind has probably existed since the beginnings of education. Consider the following from Plato's *Republic*:

> *Socrates:* 'Have you noticed,' I asked, 'how a lifelong devotion to physical exercise, to the exclusion of anything else, produces a certain kind of mind? Just as a neglect of it, produces another type? . . . One type tends to be uncivilised and tough, the other soft and over-sensitive.' . . .
>
> *Glaucon:* 'Yes . . . excessive emphasis on athletics produces an excessively uncivilised type, while a purely literary training leaves men indecently soft.' . . .
>
> *Socrates:* 'What I should say therefore is that these two branches of education seem to have been given by some god to men to train these two parts of us—the one to train our philosophic part, the other our energy and initiative. They are not intended the one to train body, the other mind, except incidentally, but to ensure a proper harmony between energy and initiative on the one hand and reason on the other by tuning each to the right pitch.' (Plato, 1987, book 3, part 2, 410c–412a)

Beginning with Massachusetts in 1852 and ending with Mississippi in 1917, the states made schooling mandatory and children's time became divided between school time and free time. By the early 1900s many states had laws in place regulating (but not ending) child labor so there really was *some* free time, but what to do with it? Friedman points to one answer:

> In 1903 New York City's Public School Athletic League for Boys was established, and formal contests between children, organized by adults, emerged as a way to keep boys coming back to activities, clubs and school. Formal competition ensured the boys' continued participation since they wanted to defend their team's record and honor. (2013, p. 3)

These activities, lauded by progressive reformers, were thought to prepare children for the physical labor of industry and thus were largely held for the poor children, many from immigrant families, who lived in our bigger cities. By 1910, 17 other cities had adopted programs similar to New York's. Competitive sports were seen as a way of teaching the "American" values of cooperation, hard work, and respect for authority. These activities were extended to children of the middle class when funding for the essentially free clubs and leagues became scarce during the depression, and at the same time, physical-education professionals became concerned that competition might not be good for young children and that league competitions supported only the best athletes and not all children. As organized youth competition left the school system at the elementary school level in the 1930s, it was replaced by fee-based programs like those at the YMCA and sports programs like Little League Baseball and Pop Warner Football that were not affordable for children from poor families (Friedman, 2013). So we see that competitive sports were commercialized for almost every age group and proficiency between the 1920s and 1930s with an attendant loss of accessibility for the poor and a new status conferred on those who could afford to participate—to "pay to play." Public schools continued to support team sports at the high school level but even here, commercialization arises in the competition for college scholarships and entry into the cadre of professional sports athletes. (Most major league baseball players go directly to the minor leagues and farm teams from high school, while NFL football players are largely recruited from college teams.) Controversial questions to be asked here include:

- Should public education promote (and pay for) competitive team sports?
- In particular, should public schools support football when we know its dangers?
- Has the availability of school-sponsored competitive team sports benefited American students? How?

Teachers should read "The Case Against High-School Sports," published in the *The Atlantic* in October 2013. In this article, Amanda Ripley makes the case that we spend far too much on competitive sports in the United States at the expense of academic subjects:

> In many schools, sports are so entrenched that no one—not even the people in charge—realizes their actual cost. When Marguerite Roza, the author of *Educational Economics*, analyzed the finances of one public high school in the Pacific Northwest, she and her colleagues found that the school was spending $328 a student for math instruction and more than four times that much for cheerleading—$1,348 a cheerleader. "And it is not even a school in a district that prioritizes cheerleading," Roza wrote. "In fact, this district's 'strategic plan' has for the past three years claimed that *math* was the primary focus." (p. 10)

Ripley admits that research on student athletes is mixed but generally suggests that sports do more good than harm for those who play. Remember our discussion in the previous chapter on the benefits to women that accrued from increased funding for women's competitive sports after the passage of

Title IX. "But only 40 percent of seniors participate in high-school athletics, and what's harder to measure is how the overriding emphasis on sports affects everyone who doesn't play" (2013, p. 13).

Even though later starting times have been shown to improve performance for high-school-age students, many schools start the day really early (some before 8 A.M.) to maximize available afternoon daylight hours for sports practice sessions. The additional costs of distractions from academic work are not just limited to the exhausting hours of team and cheerleader practice but include time spent on pep rallies, band practice, and transportation to and from games as well as the time committed by parents and the community.

In the same article, Ripley talks about changes that have been made at Spelman College, Atlanta's historically Black women's college. In 2012 about half of the incoming class of some 530 students were obese and had high blood pressure, Type 2 diabetes, or some other chronic health condition that exercise could mitigate. Spelman was spending almost $1 million each year on athletics for the 4% of the student body that played sports.

> Spelman's president, Beverly Daniel Tatum, found the imbalance difficult to justify. She told me (Ripley) that last year, while watching a Spelman basketball game, "it occurred to me that none of these women were going to play basketball after they graduated. By that I don't mean play professionally—I mean even recreationally. I thought of all the black women I knew, and they did not tend to spend their recreational time playing basketball. So a little voice in my head said, *Well, let's flip it*." (Ripley, 2013, p. 14)

In 2012 it was proposed that the $900,000 once spent for 80 athletes to participate in intercollegiate sports would be put toward a campus-wide health and fitness program after the spring 2013 season. An update in *Inside Higher Ed* reports:

> Spelman calls the initiative "a wellness revolution," and—more than a year after the tennis team played its final match—the revolution is finding its legs, Tatum said. In 2012, the number of students enrolled in fitness classes at the college's wellness center was 278. That number is now more than 1,300. Spelman's undergraduate enrollment is about 2,100 students. (New, 2014, p. 1)

Students, parents, teachers, and school administrators should discuss alternative ways to achieve the benefits of cooperative team play, from learning leadership skills to developing the character traits associated with good sportsmanship. Can intramurals or extracurricular civic leagues fill this role and provide an outlet for those whose talents deserve an opportunity? Finally, what about football?

In Florida where I (Brooks) currently live, as in many other parts of the country, high school football is a big deal. Last year, our local news magazine, *Keys Life Magazine*, ran an interview with twin seniors at our local high school who both played on the high school football team. When asked about the best thing that football taught them, they responded eagerly:

> *Henry:* "It teaches you a lot, teaches you to be responsible, that you always have to help the person next to you. It really formed me into a great, honorable, trustworthy young man. It's great to have the football team, all of those guys to talk to and relate to."
>
> *George:* "It teaches you discipline, it helps you to be a better citizen in the community. It taught us to respect everyone, no matter who they are, football teaches great character." (Hixon, 2015, p. 14)

These two are not your ordinary run-of-the-mill high school football players. They are destined for great things: In their senior year they were enrolled in Physics Honors and 3 AP classes. They are now attending Beloit College in Wisconsin, making the dean's list and still playing football. I talked to their mother recently and asked her if she ever worried about their safety playing football and she said of course, she still does. Football is a violent sport, but the boys are aware of the risks. They have been playing since 5th grade, and they love the sport. We include their comments to show that there are perceptions on both sides of this issue to be considered.

It is also noteworthy that the safety debate is not new. The NCAA was founded after two White House conferences convened by President Theodore Roosevelt in 1905 to encourage reforms in college football practices due to repeated injuries and deaths.

> Football at the time was particularly dangerous and violent. In 1905 alone, at least 18 people died and more than 150 were injured playing football. According to the *Washington Post*, at least 45 football players died from 1900 to October 1905, many from internal injuries, broken necks, concussions or broken backs. (Zezima, 2014, p. 1)

Rules were changed, forward passing entered the game and spread players out more across the field, but helmets were not required until 1939 by the NCAA and 1943 by the NFL. In spite of new evidence of Chronic Traumatic Encephalopathy (CTE) found through autopsy studies of former NFL players, the league still has not mandated "helmet models that have shown in tests to better shield against hits that can cause concussions" (Zezima, 2014, p. 5). However, the NFL is spending money to investigate solutions to the problem.

Students might be encouraged to watch and discuss the film *Concussion* released in 2015 and starring Will Smith as the Nigerian-born Dr. Bennet

Omalu who discovered CTE or to read the book of the same name by Jeanne Marie Laskas. Discussions could even be held in a science class—physics would be appropriate—to talk about the potential technologic innovations for helmets that the NFL is cofunding with GE and Under Armour to the tune of $20 million apiece (Roberts, 2015). Head trauma is not, however, the only safety concern for football players. Johnny Unitas, the "Golden Arm," who played in the first Super Bowl and was National League MVP three times retired partially crippled and in constant great pain. "Like most players, Unitas took a physical beating from football, and he had both knees replaced. His right arm was so injured in a 1968 preseason game against Dallas that in recent years he could not pick up a fork and feed himself with that hand" (Litsky, 2002, p. 2).

We turn now to the heroes created by the multi-billion-dollar sports enterprises. I (Brooks) asked my husband, Don, who his heroes were when he was in high school. He knew I was writing about sports at the moment and immediately replied with the names Roberto Clemente and Johnny Unitas. Don grew up and went to high school in Pittsburgh—home of the Pirates, Steelers, and Penguins. I then asked him why these men were heroes. It turns out that it wasn't just because they were very, very good at their respective sports—some would say among the best ever. In Clemente's case it was because he was also a very good person. So good, in fact, that he has been proposed for sainthood. Clemente, the 1971 World Series MVP, died in a plane crash in 1972 while on his way to personally deliver relief to victims of an earthquake in Nicaragua. Johnny Unitas was a local Pittsburgh boy from a working-class family who made the most of his talent, giving others like him something to aspire to. And isn't that what most hero worship of sports figures should really be about? Or is it something different today with the media coverage and mass marketing of professional sports athletes?

Who are the sports heroes of today's youngsters and why? Why do so many young people wear tee shirts and sweatshirts with the name, number, and team colors of sports figures? How much do they actually know about the person whose name they are wearing? Matt Beardmore, sports journalist, admitted in *Psychology Today's* Time Out! blog that as a child his bedroom was a shrine to Michael Jordan. In his 2013 essay "Is it Safe to Worship Athletes?" he cites the work of two marketing professors, Dr. Jeremy Sierra and Dr. Michael Hyman:

> Hyman and Sierra discussed how fans that are "exposed to celebrities via mass media may descend mentally from the genuine social world to a world of artificial experience," and they cited research that argued that "high-level celebrity worship can lead to anxiety, depression, poor mental health, and negative affect; even low-level celebrity worship can lead to social dysfunction and depression (Maltby et al., 2004), and that "Celebrity worship hinders self-understanding

and interpersonal relations, while creating impressions of foolishness, irrespon-
sibility, and submissiveness" (McCutcheon & Maltby, 2002).

    If all of this is true, and hero worship is truly causing people to lose their
own identity this is a significant issue that needs to be addressed. So what's the
solution? Especially since leagues are going to continue marketing their sports
with their star athletes because players are far more marketable than the league
itself. And kids are going to keep idolizing their favorite sports stars, because,
well, that's just what kids do. (Beardmore, 2013, p. 2)

This is clearly something that needs to be talked about in school—in a
physical education class or social studies or even in math where sports statistics can be used to generate interest in statistics in general. What is a hero,
and is it the same thing as a role model?

> That wise basketball philosopher Charles Barkley once declared, 'I am not a
> role model.' A star with the Phoenix Suns at the time, Barkley was lambasted
> by a large portion of the news media who insisted that high-profile athletes, by
> virtue of their celebrity, should act like paragons of virtue, even if they weren't.
> (Rhoden, 2012, p. 1)

In "Seeing Through the Illusions of the Sports Hero," William Rhoden,
a *New York Times* sports columnist, has defined elements of sports heroism:
emotion, propaganda, hypocrisy, and tragedy. There is the emotion of identifying with a person of recognizable greatness in athletic talent, and then
there is the propaganda of idolizing people for prowess in one area while
ignoring real human frailties inherent in the same person. As for hypocrisy,
what is more hypocritical then a corporate sponsor abandoning one fallen
hero like Lance Armstrong but not others like Tiger Woods or Kobe Bryant,
who are still making money for the company? Finally, there is the tragedy
of our inability to forgive and/or separate the good from the bad. Must Joe
Paterno forever be linked to the horror of Jerry Sandusky, or can we be allowed to remember him with fondness as the coach who cared about the
character of his students and saw them through to graduation? But we must
do this, as we suggested with political racist heroes, *without forgetting* his
moral failings.

> Sport has no enduring worth unless attached to a higher set of values.
>   A few years after Barkley made his comments about role models, Bill Bradley,
> the former senator and Knicks star, wrote a wonderful book, "Values of the Game."
> It focused on basketball, but the values Bradley outlined form the foundation of all
> sports: passion, discipline, selflessness, respect, courage, leadership, responsibility,
> resilience.
>   Given the realities of social media, forgiveness and resilience are far more
> valuable than heroism. (Rhoden, 2012, p. 4)

With this parting echo of the Florida football twins' list of positive traits engendered by participation in team sports, we turn now to the role of the media in shaping our thoughts and values.

MEDIA

When we first contemplated this chapter, I (Brooks) immediately sought out two books that I had read as an undergraduate—Marshall McLuhan's *The Medium is the Massage: An Inventory of Effects* and Alvin Toffler's *Future Shock*. Both are works by futurists that were popular at the time they were written—the late 1960s and early 1970s—and both are as applicable today as then. This may be even more true in McLuhan's case as he contemplated the impact of the Internet nearly 30 years before its existence. McLuhan had coined the phrase the "medium is the message" in an earlier work to describe the idea that the way (medium) in which information is conveyed is as important as the content (message) itself. Think of the real-time, graphic images of the Viet Nam war that appeared in our living rooms on prime time television (for today's viewers it is Iraq and Syria). The use of the word *massage* instead of *message* in the title of his 1967 work was deliberate in that media today "massage" all of our senses:

> All media work us over completely. They are so pervasive in their personal, political, economic, aesthetic, psychological, moral, ethical, and social conse-quences that they leave no part of us untouched, unaffected, unaltered. The medium is the massage. Any understanding of social and cultural change is impossible without a knowledge of the way media work as environments. All media are extensions of some human faculty—psychic or physical. (McLuhan, 1967, p. 26)

For Toffler the acceleration of social and cultural change wrought by the bombardment of information, propaganda, and advertising through media was/is creating a state of disorientation and transience in human-ity that he described as "future shock." Toffler compares human learning to the way in which modern computers use a master program that decides which of many available subsidiary programs to use when analyzing and manipulating data. Through this comparison, he describes the need for an education of the future that will enhance human ability to adapt to rapid change by teaching students "how to learn, unlearn and relearn" (Toffler, 1970, p. 414). He continues:

> Psychologist Herbert Gerjuoy of the Human Resources Research Organization phrases it simply: "The new education must teach the individual how to clas-sify and reclassify information, how to evaluate its veracity, how to change

categories when necessary, how to move from the concrete to the abstract and back, how to look at problems from a new direction—how to teach himself. Tomorrow's illiterate will not be the man who can't read; he will be the man who has not learned how to learn." (p. 414)

This is what critical thinking is all about. The media provide us with the controversial issues to which we must apply critical thinking; but without critical thinking, the media will also dictate the values that we will apply in making moral decisions and commitments related to these controversial issues. Thus, McLuhan's point that we must understand the "environments" of the media and Dewey's concern that the decline of an individualistic philosophy of life with the traits described earlier in this chapter—questioning, improvisation—are related to the growing standardization and mass uniformity of the corporatization of social mind and habit. So, what do we need to know about today's media in order to help our students classify and reclassify information, change categories, and evaluate veracity?

In their book, *It's Even Worse Than It Looks* (2012), Thomas Mann and Norman Ornstein devote a section of a chapter on "The Seeds of Dysfunction" to the "New Media and New Culture." They talk about the changes that have occurred since the 1950s when the majority of Americans relied passively (no channel flipping) on the nightly news shows of the dominant three television networks as their primary source of information. There were also multiple newspapers in most metropolitan areas with distinct party leanings on the editorial pages, but their news pages generally attempted to report objectively and relied on facts that were checked and cross-checked. Compare that to today:

> Adam Thierer of the Progress and Freedom Foundation pointed out in 2010 that there were almost 600 cable television channels, over 2,200 broadcast television stations, more than 13,000 over-the-air radio stations, over 20,000 magazines, and over 276,000 books published annually. As of December 2010, there were 255 million websites, and over 110 million domain names ending in .com, .net, and .org, and there were over 266 million internet users in North America alone. (Mann & Ornstein, 2012, p. 59)

The authors go on to cite additional statistics for 2010 from the same source—26 million blogs, 1 billion videos served up daily by YouTube, 140,000 apps available for Apple products (iPhone, iPod, and iPad)—the effect of all of which is the fragmentation of audiences and attention spans and the attendant changes to business models—more advertising, less fact checking and analysis.

First let's talk about the implications of fragmented audiences and attention spans. For news delivered by the three major cable news networks today, Fox, MSNBC, and CNN, the audience fragmentation is clear.

Fox caters to a conservative audience, MSNBC to the left, and CNN struggles mightily and occasionally succeeds in presenting both sides of an issue by pitting pundits from different sides against each other. Very little is covered by any of the networks to a depth that satisfies, and much is repeated ad nauseam. Audiences become further fragmented when we ask the question, "Who watches television news anyway?" The Pew Research Center (2012) reports the following survey results related to audience fragmentation:

- Just 23% of 18- to 29-year-olds regularly watch cable news channels compared to 33%–34% of those between 30 and 64 and 51% of those over 65.
- Viewership for CNN, with its attempted bipartisanship, has fallen since 2002 from 25% to 16% in 2012, while the audiences of regular viewers for MSNBC (15% to 11%) and Fox (22% to 21%) have remained fairly constant over the same time period.
- Reading printed matter is also in decline, especially for newspapers, even though 51% of Americans say they enjoy reading a lot. Those who read a newspaper yesterday declined from 41% in 2002 to 23% in 2012. In comparison, for books the change was only 4% from 34% in 2002 to 30% in 2012.
- In just 2 years from 2010 to 2012, social networking users increased from 19% to 36% across all ages, and those who "saw any news on social networking sites yesterday" increased from 9% to 19%. This latter change was greatest for those between ages 18 and 24 with an increase from 12% to 34%.
- What you watch or read for your news really depends (i.e., statistically significant differences exist) on your age, sex, level of education, income, and political leanings.

How are we to engage in the business of democracy, to dialogue, to listen, to care about the common good and other principles of social justice as Dewey advises or to "unlearn" and change categories, as Toffler and Gerjuoy put it, if we have no common point of reference? We will talk more about this conversation gap in Chapter 9 on Money, Class, and Poverty.

Students might be requested to spend an evening channel-surfing news programs and then report and discuss over the next several days on these questions: What stories were being reported on by various stations? What spin was placed on the same story as reported by different news services? What, if any, primary sources were used or quoted in the stories? (Do they know what a primary source is?) The discussion might then move to commentary and reporting around the same or similar stories that they may have seen in newspapers and magazines or on social media. Special attention should be paid to the validation of Internet sources in general. Further discussion could focus on where and how factual information can be obtained and what role responsible journalists should play in fact-checking stories. Mann and Ornstein give a terrific example of an email that enjoyed wide circulation about military pensions and congressional privileges in which every one of the "facts" was wrong, including one that was repeated from a Fox news report (2012, pp. 63–66). A module of study on news sources and validation could begin or end with a viewing of the award-winning 2015 movie *Spotlight* about the *Boston Globe*'s reporting on child abuse by Roman Catholic priests in the Boston area—a controversial issue in its own right.

Finally, we return to the idea that the "business of America is business," with a look at advertising. Advertising in America really took off during the Coolidge prosperity of the Roaring Twenties. This is what Calvin Coolidge had to say to a convention of advertisers in 1926:

> When we stop to consider the part which advertising plays in the modern life of production we see that basically it is that of education. It makes new thoughts, new desires and new actions. Advertising creates and changes the foundation of all popular action, public sentiment or public opinion. It is the most potent influence in adopting and changing the habits and modes of life, affecting what we eat, what we wear and the work and play of the whole nation. (quoted in Burch, 2012, p. 101)

Today we have gone from an era of mass-marketed culture and mores to an even more divisive imitation of individualism in that advertising is now personalized. "Back to Google, the liberal class's favorite Internet company: they track your web searches to sell you stuff: they scan your emails to sell you more stuff" (Frank, 2016, p. 204). Now, you no longer have to worry about whether you're wearing the latest fashion because the latest fashion has been custom-made just for you—and everyone else who shares your tastes. There's an app for that, and according to Nir Eyal, a former game designer and professor of "applied consumer technology" at Stanford, that app has been designed to create a "persistent routine" or behavioral loop, to trigger a need and provide the solution to it (Weisberg, 2016). McLuhan predicted the insidious collection and persistence of digital information. Toffler predicted the impact: "The Super-industrial Revolution will consign to the archives of ignorance most of what we now believe about democracy and the future of human choice" (1970, p. 263). Toffler believed that new technologies would move away from "homogenized art, mass produced education and 'mass' culture," and "far from restricting our individuality, will multiply our choices—and our freedom—exponentially" (p. 282). But, he goes on to warn:

> Whether man is prepared to cope with the increased choice of material and cultural wares available to him is, however, a totally different question.

For there comes a time when choice, rather than freeing the individual, becomes so complex, difficult and costly that it turns into its opposite. There comes a time, in short, when choice turns into overchoice and freedom into un-freedom. (pp. 282–283)

As one example of the implication of material choices, the United States and New Zealand are the only significant markets that allow unrestricted direct-to-consumer drug advertising. Is this good or bad? There are arguments pro and con that students should be able to research and debate in a science or social studies class. Shouldn't consumers take responsibility for their own health and be aware of drugs that could help them? Does advertising significantly increase the cost of drugs? What position has the American Medical Association recently taken on this issue and why?

On the issues of cultural wares, a good question for classroom discussion might be: How has advertising affected the way we view social and political movements? In *We Were Feminists Once* (2016), Andi Zeisler gives credence to the notion that feminism as a political movement has been bought and sold as just another consumer choice in a vast market. Opening a chapter of her book with the statement "Granny panties are the new feminism," she refers to a statement in a *New York Times* Styles section article from June 2015, titled "Young Women Say No to Thongs" (p. 59). On the same page she quotes Angela Davis from 1994: "I am remembered as a hairdo. It is humiliating because it reduces a politics of liberation to a politics of fashion." This concept of the subversion of culture and ideas by advertising may seem more difficult for students to tackle, but teachers should give it a try.

I (Brooks) was surprised and pleased at the level of awareness that even 6th-graders have when it comes to being propagandized. I showed two videos to a 6th-grade environmental science class. One was a cartoon produced by an environmental nonprofit that presented a lot of factual information to persuade students to stop buying water in plastic bottles. The other was a short video clip of a scientist in a boat in the middle of a plastic-infested Pacific Ocean gyre showing firsthand the impact of plastics on sea life and birds. I innocently asked at the end of the viewing how the students felt about the two videos. I was wholly unprepared for the terrific discussion that followed. The students disliked the admittedly informative and probably factual anti–bottled-water video as they felt that it was biased and clearly intended to leave them with an agenda—to stop buying bottled water. They felt that the other video of the scientist in the boat allowed them to see for themselves the detriments of plastic pollution and formulate their own moral commitment with regard to water bottle production and disposal.

This discussion on advertising and propaganda leads us to our next two chapters and the controversies surrounding capitalism, socialism, and class in the United States.

CHAPTER 8

Capitalism and Socialism

In this chapter, we will consider the teaching of capitalism and socialism from a perspective developed around two of our main themes—the education of citizens for participatory democracy and the centrality of conversation in accomplishing this goal.

CAPITALISM

Capitalism, simply defined, is an economic system in which the ownership and means of production, distribution, and exchange of wealth are in the hands of individuals or privately owned corporations. Capitalism does not require or support a planned economy; that is, the organization and production of commerce is put into the hands of the market. The market consists of an intimate relation of supply and demand. Capitalism is closely identified with the success of the industrial revolution of the 19th century. The invention and widespread use of machinery moved people from occupations centered on their own properties and small businesses to assembly lines in urban centers. It made possible the accretion of fortunes for successful capitalists, owners of businesses that manufactured and distributed new products. This story has long been a central one in American history classes, and it has not been unusual for students to come away enormously proud of American ingenuity and its devotion to capitalism.

The need for workers also promoted the growth of schooling. At the beginning of the 20th century, fewer than 10% of American children attended high school. By mid-century more than half were graduating from high school, and that number increased to more than 70% by the 1960s. The comprehensive high school—a structure that provided academic, vocational, and general programs—was largely responsible for this impressive increase. But it, like capitalism itself, came under severe criticism, and we will look closely at that criticism in a bit.

Capitalism, like religion, is an enormous topic, and whole libraries have been written about it. Here we suggest some basic concerns that all high school students should think about. First, because it is of paramount interest today and has been a longstanding concern, is the matter of economic inequality—today's growing wealth gap. It has been argued that capitalism benefits everyone—the rising tide that lifts all boats. This claim should not be carelessly brushed aside. Perhaps ordinary life in capitalist societies is better in many ways than it was in preindustrial days. But this is not to say that it could not be made better for large numbers of people, and it certainly cannot be denied that the gap between rich and everyone else is large and growing. Whenever a depression or recession occurs, the criticism of capitalism grows, and powerful arguments are made to modify or replace it. As we will note in the next section on socialism, alternatives to capitalism become stronger at such times.

Today, as in the period of the Great Depression, America is experiencing great worry over the shrinking of its middle class and a widespread stagnation in middle-class wages. The great promise of capitalism that every individual can do well economically and that a nation faithful to capitalistic precepts will lead the world in riches is coming under increased scrutiny. Surely, there is something not quite right when more than 90% of the nation's wealth belongs to fewer than 10% of its people.

Critics express several worries about the current operation of capitalism, but there are also other longstanding concerns. One, pointed out by John Dewey and other social theorists, is the way capitalist theory is described. Like religion, it is cast in terms of original certainty—the "Laws of Nature":

> Economic "laws," that of labor springing from natural wants and leading to the creation of wealth, of present abstinence in behalf of future enjoyment leading to creation of capital effective in piling up still more wealth, the free play of competitive exchange, designated the law of supply and demand, were "natural" laws. (Dewey, 1927, p. 90)

This way of describing capitalist theory makes it appear almost sinful to challenge it. "Individuals" were to enjoy the freedom to compete and to reap the rewards of their hard work. "Capitalist virtues" such as intelligence, diligence, frugality, and foresight were to be admired and cultivated. Everyone, it was said, could succeed, and failure to succeed was often taken to be a sign of poor character.

Dewey was also worried about the capitalist way of defining the individual. He certainly believed in individual growth, pleasure, freedom of thought, and self-development. However, he also strongly believed that the *individual* is not a preformed creation but, rather, a socially formed product: "Individuals will always be the center and consummation of experience, but what the individual actually *is* in his life experience depends upon the nature and movement of associated life" (1939, p. 91). Thus, the quality of individual lives depends on the quality of relationships in associated living. We are not born as individuals; we *become* individuals.

Many critics of capitalism have commented on an apparent contradiction in the capitalist way of treating the individual. Despite its great emphasis on individual virtues, it has had little to say about the loss of individuality induced by assembly-line practices installed by the efficient new industries. A philosophy that made the virtuous worker almost sacred also allowed that worker to spend long hours doing repetitive, almost machine-like work. Charlie Chaplin's film *Modern Times* depicted the workers' total loss of individuality on an assembly-line in the 1920s; it is still cited as both a reminder of malaise felt then and a prediction of things to come for the mass of humanity.

Thus, when we look at the ideals and effects of capitalism, we are struck by the stark contradictions. On the one hand, it was announced that anyone who worked hard and intelligently could become rich; this is, of course, the long-treasured American dream. The evidence, it was said, was all around us, and the American economy was moving toward becoming the highest in the world. On the other hand, many people were stuck in boring, low-paid jobs, and they were blamed for their own lack of success. They had missed out on the American dream, but that dream was still alive for the virtuous worker. Significant alternative economic and political ideas were being discussed, but average, everyday workers were made to feel ungrateful, certainly unpatriotic, if they considered them seriously.

Describing these contradictions, Scott Nearing, a lifelong socialist, wrote of the 20th century:

> After the turn of the century the United States became a happy hunting ground for the ambitious, greedy, power-hungry few. But in the process, the North American mass culture made notable contributions to the sum total of economic productivity and scientific and technical advance. . . . I have been living in a technically advanced, fabulously rich country, run by a power-drunk oligarchy, rushing themselves, their dupes and victims into a cul de sac from which there is no escape and in which, if they remain, they, their associates, and possibly the planet earth may be denuded and rendered lifeless for ages to come. (2000, p. 299)

Nearing was also a prominent advocate of the "back to the land" movement, and students might enjoy reading accounts of the farming and home building in which he and his wife engaged (Nearing & Nearing, 1970, 1979). Today their plea to cherish the natural environment and preserve the Earth has been taken up by many environmentalists. However, a good topic for debate in this context might be to contrast the pragmatic realities of "back to the land" environmentalism with the decoupling philosophy of the *Ecomodernist Manifesto* (Asafu-Adjaye et al., 2015).

Published in April 2015, the manifesto presents a new way to look at humanity's interactions with the natural world. Acknowledging that many scientists believe that the Earth has entered a new geologic age, the Anthropocene, shaped by humans and their actions, *An Ecomodernist Manifesto* describes a philosophy that its protagonists feel will create a "good" or even "great" Anthropocene:

> A good Anthropocene demands that humans use their growing social, economic, and technologic powers to make life better for people, stabilize the climate, and protect the natural world.
>
> In this we affirm one long-standing environmental ideal, that humanity must shrink its impacts on the environment and make more room for nature, while we reject another, that human societies must harmonize with nature to avoid economic and ecological collapse. These two ideals can no longer be reconciled. Natural systems will not as a general rule, be protected or enhanced by the expansion of humankind's dependence upon them for sustenance and well-being. (Asafu-Adjaye et al., 2015, pp. 2–3)

The mentioned ideal of harmonizing with nature to avoid economic and ecological collapse seems to represent for the ecomodernists the various attempts at returning to past "simpler" lifestyles that they feel actually impose a higher burden on natural resources through direct dependence on natural systems and resources. They feel that "decoupling of human welfare from environmental impacts will require a sustained commitment to technological progress and the continuing evolution of social, economic, and political institutions alongside those changes" (Asafu-Adjaye et al., 2015, p. 29).

Perhaps the most salient legacy of capitalism for today's schools is the steady, indeed increasing, emphasis on the economic benefits of education. We are urged to get children started in preschool on a track that will conduct them through high school, into college, college graduation, and a good-paying job. We can agree that a good job is a desirable outcome, but is there nothing else we should seek from a good education?

It may be helpful for students to hear and think about the contradictions with which educators, policymakers, and parents have grappled over the past century. Introduction of the comprehensive high school made secondary education popular with a wide range of families. Just as we must give capitalism more than a little credit for the economic/industrial success of the United States, we must also appreciate what the comprehensive high school has accomplished in educating the vast majority of our children. This does not mean that it is a perfect model to be sustained without revision. The comprehensive high school was established in recognition of the need to educate all of our children, not just those who are academically oriented. In theory, it recognizes the full range of human talents and interests, and this is its great strength. In practice, however, the new high school was weakened by the semi-religious mindset of capitalism—that "individuals" are born with certain attributes and that the virtues associated with success in a capitalist society should be encouraged and rewarded. Technically, this meant that any child, from any background, could "make it" into the favored academic courses and future financial security.

An alternative way of thinking would, first of all, ask us to recognize, develop, and reward all of the much-needed human talents. Why should a student who is mechanically talented be told that he would do better to study medieval history than the operation of machinery? Tracking, the practice of providing a variety of programs for students with different aptitudes and interests, is in itself an excellent idea, but we have made disastrous decisions in our implementation of that idea. First, of course, is the decision to rank academic studies at the top and place those students who cannot qualify for such work in programs suited to their lower assessed capabilities, not in programs specially designed to cultivate their real abilities. Second, in designing courses for the "lower" tracks, we did exactly that—made them lower in almost all respects. Third, a decision that has hurt all students was to put such emphasis on the economic outcomes of schooling that we have very nearly forgotten that there is more—much more—to education than preparing for a well-paid job.

It should have been possible to design and implement excellent courses in all of the tracks. Instead, heavily influenced by the capitalist notion that the "best" will somehow naturally rise to the top and that many students have already shown their promise or lack of it by high school, we concentrated on the college preparatory program and, too often, provided weak courses for the less-abled (Oakes & Rogers, 2006). To make matters worse, we continued to measure the progress of all students through the same tests. Predictably, the students in the "lower" classes continued to do less well on these tests.

Consider what might have happened if we had expressed respect for the full range of human talents and the vital work required by an industrial and postindustrial society. With such recognition, students with nonacademic talents would be invited to choose the program best suited to their interests, and they could do so proudly. But that is not what happened. We did wake up to some of the dangers and inequities in the comprehensive high school, but our corrections have in several respects made things worse and, in the next section, we will discuss ways in which those efforts went wrong.

Before moving on to that discussion, we should say something about the third bad decision in program planning. Not only was there a built-in prejudice in the ranking of tracks; all tracks were increasingly directed at economic aims. Children were encouraged (and still are) to prepare for college because a college education ensures them of a better-paying job. Worries about schools' concentration on economic outcomes were expressed early on in the 20th century, but the early objections were directed largely at a narrowly defined vocational education that amounted to job training. Dewey objected strenuously to the separation of general and vocational education, arguing that the interests of vocationalists were primarily directed at the promotion of the "industrial regime," not at the educational needs of individuals and the democratic society in which they would take their place as citizens. (See Kliebard, 1999, p. 127.) One could respond, of course, that the industrial regime was the force that led America to economic greatness and that it is, therefore, entirely proper to make its continued success the main aim of education.

Even the *Cardinal Principles of Secondary Education* (1918), which could have been used to promote an expansion of curriculum over the full range of human concerns (health, command of fundamental processes, vocation, worthy use of leisure, worthy home membership, citizenship, and ethical character), was captured and interpreted by the social efficiency movement and aimed at increasing the smooth operation of the capitalist/ industrial nation. (For consideration of an alternative use of the *Cardinal Principles*, see Noddings, 2013.) Surely, all of the aims listed in the *Cardinal Principles* are worth our attention, but if they are reduced to specific, recipe-like objectives, they lose much of their educative power. Critics of the social efficiency movement may have made matters worse by concentrating their criticism on the perceived loss of classical aims instead of exploring the principles for potentially broader, deeper educational goals. In a sense, critics argued, the social efficiency movement reduced all of education to a form of vocational training. Herbert Kliebard has given us a powerful summary of the worries mentioned here:

> If vocational education is to build on its symbolic success and help reduce the injustices inflicted on a neglected segment of the school population as well as re- vivifying education for all, it will not be by concentrating obsessively on rewards to be reaped at some indeterminate point in the future, or by isolating itself from the rest of education, and certainly not by converting the entire educational sys- tem to the narrow end of economic gain. . . . It can succeed only by extending its reach beyond the promise of distant monetary benefits. (1999, p. 235)

Now, at the time of this writing, several troubling reports have appeared in the news. Apparently, there has been a substantial increase in the mortality rate of white middle-age men over the past 15 years; much of this increase can be traced to suicide, drug overdoses, and excessive use of alcohol. Researchers are trying to find the cause of this disturbing increase. Although we do not have a definitive answer at this time, it seems likely that a form of existential despair is at least partly at fault, and this despair is a result of failed expectations. Paul Krugman surmises, "We're looking at people who were raised to believe in the American dream, and are coping badly with its failure to come true" (2015, p. A23).

Evidence of existential despair should motivate educators to press our profession to move away from the pervasive economic emphasis that now dominates education. There is more to life than making money. As a reminder, we do not advocate either celebrating the American dream or condemning it; once again, we warn against indoctrination. However, educators should take some responsibility to introduce students to a world rich in intellectual, social, moral, and artistic possibilities. We should demonstrate by what we do in school that money is not everything.

SOCIALISM

In simple terms, socialism is a system of social organization that puts the ownership and control of production in the hands of the community. It is not communism, which places ownership and control with the state; most current forms of socialism do not endorse state ownership. Clearly, however, we have to discuss what is meant here by "community." Just as mistaken critics identify atheism with communism, there are those who insist that socialism is a form of communism or leads surely to it. Students should be assured at the outset that many of the world's most prosperous nations today may be described as socialist, and they are not communist. A socialist economy is a *planned* economy, and all those who have an interest in a particular enterprise (the relevant community) have a role to play in that planning. The government (state), too, has a role to play as a participant, not as an owner. In a socialist economy, control is not left to market forces.

Interest in socialism was strong in the United States during the first half of the 20th century, triggered at first by the extreme levels of economic inequality following the Gilded Age. Understandably, interest was at its strongest during the years of the Great Depression, but it died away in the 1950s, in part because of the Cold War and the identification of socialism with communism. Today many people are unaware that there was once a flourishing socialist party in the United States. Indeed, the very label "socialist" fell into disrepute. Now we see a renewed flicker of interest in socialism because Bernie Sanders, a self-described democratic socialist, mounted an active campaign in the 2016 presidential Democratic primary election. Again, the current discontent with an enormous and growing disparity between the very rich and everyone else may be supporting a renewed interest in socialism.

Proponents of socialism argue that it reduces the disparity in riches across the population and that it restores a sense of participation in and responsibility for the direction of the community. As we will see, defining that "community" has been and continues to be a major conceptual problem for socialists. At the national level, we have not yet built what Dewey referred to as "the great community." This, Dewey admitted, is a deep intellectual problem: "the search for conditions under which the Great Society may become the Great Community" (1927, p. 147). In essence, for socialists, the problem is to replace capitalism with socialism or, at least, to employ the basic ideas of socialism to modify capitalism, but to do this they must more carefully define what is meant by "community."

In a community, we care for one another. We do not "let the failures fail" and only the successful thrive. That means that all members of the community will be assured of the life-sustaining elements of food, shelter, clothing, safety, and medical care. Because this basic level of sustenance is guaranteed for all community members, it is not to be considered charity, something that some members give and others receive. Students should be encouraged to think critically about this. How do committed capitalists respond to this? What arguments might they present against it? How will such an arrangement be financed?

Members of a democratic community participate in that community. Dewey put it clearly:

> From the standpoint of the individual, it consists in having a responsible share according to capacity in forming and directing the activities of the groups to which one belongs and in participating according to need in the values which the groups sustain. From the standpoint of the groups, it demands liberation of the potentialities of members of a group in harmony with the interests and goods which are common. (1927, p. 147)

One can see from this last sentence that socialists want to remedy one of the most troubling features of industrial capitalism—the reduction of human beings to machine-like parts of industrial production. The idea here is that all workers should have some say in how their enterprise is conducted and for whose benefit. Everyone involved in auto making, for example, should have some voice in how the enterprise is structured, how its product is produced, how its members are treated, and how it connects with the rest of the world. The growth of labor unions was, of course, strongly encouraged by socialism. Today, unions are being destroyed or weakened. Is that because of a renewed enthusiasm for traditional capitalism or because of mistakes and weaknesses in the behavior of unions? We will continue this discussion later.

Socialism puts far less emphasis than capitalism on the individual as economic entity but far more on a broader sense of what it means to be an individual. Nearing, whose work was mentioned earlier, puts it this way:

> By identifying oneself with the interests of another person, of a group (the family or community), or with some purpose, cause, or idea, life is broadened and may be greatly deepened. One does not have to choose "either/or." One can reach out in all these and other directions. The important thing is to identify with some thing or things beyond the self. Actually, each is part of the whole. (2000, p. 301)

The emphasis on associated living reminds us that, as Dewey pointed out, even individualization is a product of associations and commitments. But, like individuals, groups must interact with other groups, and their efficacy and well-being also depend on the health of those interactions. A *community* is formed by the shared aims and activities of its participating groups. If a group pulls away and considers only its own needs and interests, the community to which it might belong is disrupted. Indeed, it may cease to exist as a community. The current malaise of labor unions should be considered. Perhaps they are failing because they are under relentless attack by a society dominated by renewed capitalist interests. Or perhaps they are failing because they have become too much like the very system they were founded to overcome—too hierarchical, too concentrated on money, too little interested in the welfare of other groups. Or perhaps the fault lies in both possibilities. Thus the "search for the Great Community" remains a challenge for socialists. At every level, individuals and groups must be willing to share interests, goods, and tasks.

Some time should be given to explore what seem to be contradictions in everyday views of capitalism and socialism. Capitalism is often associated with rugged individualism—every individual working hard and honestly in competition with all others. Yet its concentration on production, market dominance, and money has contributed to the reduction of masses of individuals to indistinguishable parts of a huge machine. Socialism, with its emphasis on group control, has worked to remind people that money is not the only or even primary interest of full human beings. One of its primary aims is to free people to pursue other interests—to develop their own idiosyncratic talents.

Both systems of thought give attention to *equality*. Capitalists insist that everyone should have an opportunity to succeed where, again, success is defined primarily in terms of money. Equality is described in terms of a fair and equal start, but extreme differences in wealth at the finish line are not only tolerated but greatly admired. Think of all the rags-to-riches and Horatio Alger stories that have long been told in our society. Socialism, in contrast, is often perceived as a leveling system, one that will bring everyone closer to economic equality. But socialism is concerned not only with economic equality. It advocates the freedom of individuals to pursue a wide range of interests without a disabling fear of financial hardship.

WHAT SCHOOLS CAN DO

American schools have always been concerned with the concept of equality. School people, like most Americans, glibly quote a belief stated in the Declaration of Independence that "all men are created equal," but most of us do not believe that people are born with equal aptitudes and abilities. We have stated a belief in equality before the law and in equal opportunity, not in equal outcomes. The comprehensive high school was designed and implemented with the understanding that children have different abilities and, accordingly, should have different preparation for economic life. "Natural" differences justify differences in educational treatment. Both capitalists and socialists might well agree with this, but capitalists put greater emphasis on the "natural" consequences of these differences. Not everyone can profit from the sort of education provided to the academically talented. Right from the start, the programs in the comprehensive high school were understood, if not explicitly described, as differently ranked. The academic program was understood as the best—as in likely to produce the best economic outcome for its graduates—the vocational next, and the general at the bottom.

But thoughtful people have objected to this approach. The most popular line of objection—one that has grown in force over the last half century—argues that "natural" differences can often more accurately be traced to economic differences in homes, neighborhoods, and school facilities. Schools should do their best to overcome these differences and act on the dictum of Robert Maynard Hutchins: "The best education for the best is the best education for all" (quoted in Adler, 1982, p. 6). The slogan "all children can learn" has rung out across the educational world, and we have been advised to get rid of tracking (Oakes & Rogers, 2006). Although there is much to praise in this campaign for justice, there is also much to worry us.

First, the emphasis on college preparation for all has not eliminated the persistent habit of ranking (or valuing) academic programs and subsequent vocations or careers. In the former arrangement, that of the comprehensive high school, the academic program was ranked at the top, vocational and general programs lower. Now, with so many students enrolled in a college preparatory program, courses are labeled "advanced" or "honors" at the top of the academic list and "remedial" at the bottom. Greater emphasis than ever has been placed on grade point averages and test scores. Students are encouraged not simply to plan for college but to plan for and get into the "best" colleges. Children from more well-to-do families not only go to better high schools, many also receive outside tutoring and test preparation. Thus, the traditional capitalist emphasis on competition and money remains.

A second problem with getting rid of tracking is that we never really gave an honest form of tracking a fair chance. We simply assigned students to tracks on the basis of their academic achievement. Students were rarely asked about their interests, and there was little respect offered for nonacademic talents. Earlier, we noted Kliebard's powerful criticism of vocational education and its neglect of matters other than direct job training. There is no reason why vocational education should not be rich in humanistic topics such as the literature of work, homemaking, the history of unions, art and music associated with work, biographies of inventors, the place of work in communities, civic involvement, happiness, and the meaning of the good life. (See Grubb, 1995; Kliebard, 1999; Nearing, 2000.) Vocational education at its best is about more than earning a living. Matthew Crawford remarks:

> You can earn money at something without the money, or what it buys, being the focus of your day. To be capable of sustaining our interest, a job has to have room for progress in excellence. In the best cases, I believe the excellence in question ramifies outward. What I mean is that it points to, or serves, some more comprehensive understanding of the good life. (2009, p. 196)

Why have we not given greater attention to the development of excellent vocational education? We can list several reasons common to the capitalist tradition: lack of respect for physical work, the lower pay-off associated with it, the perceived inferiority of those who lack academic talent, the increasing displacement of human workers by machines. But there is another reason that, in its hypocrisy, should shame us as a community: *Excellent vocational education is expensive.* It is far less costly to pretend that we believe all children should go to college and simply ignore their real, genuine interests and talents. Algebra for all is cheaper than supplying the diversity of courses we should offer if we honestly respect the full range of human talents. We save money by pretending that we are preparing all children equally for college.

If we were to take seriously the task of developing excellent vocational programs for our high schools, it would still be necessary to face a problem identified by socialists. As Dewey warned us, in a Great Community, groups as well as individuals must interact and share at least some common purposes. Schools can help students prepare for this democratic interaction. There should be opportunities for vocational and academic students to interact socially and politically. Humanistic topics would be included in the 4-year set of seminars already suggested. These seminars would include material from literature, art, music, and civics; they would not be tracked and would include students from all of the school's programs. Not only should there be cooperation across the school disciplines to ensure common learnings, but there would be carefully planned opportunities for students from different programs to share their different special interests. Discussions in these seminars would concentrate on social, moral, and political interests suggested by the students and teachers (Noddings, 2015a). Carefully organized, experience in these seminars should help to prevent the worrisome conversation gap that troubles many social critics today (Anderson, 2007; Putnam, 2015). The fear expressed by several such critics is that Americans are losing the capacity to talk to one another across social classes. We have to do something about not only the growing wealth gap but the equally troubling communication gap.

Socialism, as we have noted, requires the participation of individuals in both social/political and occupational groups. Schools might endorse this emphasis on participation by providing students with more opportunities to choose the topics and projects they will study. Without restructuring the entire curriculum around projects, there are many ways in which students might gain a sense of greater participatory control over their own schooling. In mathematics, for example, students might be allowed to choose whether they sign up for advanced, standard, or minimal courses. This would, of course, be done with the generous guidance of teachers and parents, and this, too, would add to the effort to increase participation and cooperation. Students would be encouraged to think about how they might use mathematics in future study and work, how they assess their own capability, and where they want to employ their greatest effort in study. There would be no higher grade or greater credit for completing an advanced course than a minimum one. A plan of this sort would also reduce the rampant competition over grades. Students who choose an advanced course would do so because they expect to study the subject further or simply because they love it, not because they feel that they must show that they are better than others.

If we reject the idea that an equal education means the same education (same curriculum content) for all, we still have to ask seriously about the topics, issues, and skills that should be addressed in all of our programs. We have already suggested that vocational courses should be rich in humanistic material, but that material need not be exactly the same as that in academic courses. We also suggest the need for basic mathematical skills in the areas of probability and statistics as a prerequisite for all students in critical assessment of complex environmental and technological issues. Here we encounter and endorse the need for greater teacher participation in the construction of curriculum. Interdisciplinary preparation and continual debate about topics, methods, and outcomes should promote an invigorating sense of belonging to the educational enterprise.

Most of the suggestions we have made here are consonant with the basic interests of socialism—respect for the full range of human talents, the participation of individuals in the enterprises to which they belong, and the interplay of groups in common interests. But we should also try to maintain the spirit of invention, industry, and energy that has characterized the capitalist orientation. David Shipler reminds us:

> Winston Churchill once remarked that democracy was the worst system ever devised, except for all the others that had been tried from time to time. The same could be said of capitalist free enterprise: It's the worst—except for all the others. It has a ruthlessness about it, a cold competitive spirit that promotes the survival of the fittest and the suffering of the weak. But it also opens opportunity unparalleled by communism, socialism, or any other variant so far attempted. (2004, p. 88)

One need not pit the two approaches against each other as uncompromising enemies. We can learn from each other. Our aim is to strengthen our democracy. In the words of the 13th-century Sufi poet Jalaluddin Rumi: "Out beyond the ideas of wrongdoing and rightdoing there is a field. I'll meet you there" (quoted in Cravens, 2007, p. 133). Here again Dewey gives us an eloquent reminder:

> Regarded as an idea, democracy is not an alternative to other principles of associated life. It is the idea of community itself . . . wherever there is conjoint activity whose consequences are appreciated as good by all singular persons who take part in it, and where the realization of the good is such as to effect an energetic desire and effort to sustain it in being just because it is a good shared by all, there is in so far a community. (1927, p. 149)

CHAPTER 9

Money, Class, and Poverty

In the previous chapter we discussed the differences between capitalism and socialism in terms of both ownership of production and the emphasis on the "rugged individualism" required for success in a capitalist society in contrast with Dewey's democratic individuality. The latter emphasizes the development of identity through social interaction within a community, clearly a socialist concern. In Chapter 7 on Entertainment, Sports, and Media, we saw how all forms of entertainment and media have been caught up in "the business of America is business," to the extent that we must all take a step back and examine the sources, validity, and implied value propositions of everything we read, hear, and see today. We have examined the controversial issues that divide us with regard to religion, race, and gender. Now we will turn to perhaps the most divisive social categorization affecting our ability to talk with and understand each other today and one that has great implications for the maintenance of our democratic institutions—class.

> Most Americans, in fact, are relatively blind to class, having faith in the upward mobility implicit in a supposedly classless society. Politicians can't abide raising the class question in public because it's a taboo subject. Besides, they're far more electable if they can view their constituencies through the lens of gender, age, race, red state or blue state, or other such commonly discussed and socially acceptable identities. Class, however, is the nation's mad aunt, a troubling part of our past safely stashed away in the historical archives. (Sacks, 2007, p. 289)

Discussion of the role of money in social structures leads to a discussion of those social structures and class differences. We will consider here and in the discussions in Chapter 10 on equality how economic differences interact with the "thought differences" mentioned in our earlier chapters to generate a conversation gap. We encourage exploration of suggestions for reducing the economic gap but also ways of increasing the possibilities for cross-class conversation. Should schools, as we have suggested, give more attention to the universal acquisition of Standard English and the use of formal register? Do schools put too much emphasis on the economic aims of education?

MONEY

For any meaningful discussion of class and poverty to take place in our schools, students must first understand the role of money and the difference between money and wealth. Quite simply, money is a way to measure value, and wealth is the abundance of things that have value (e.g., cars, homes, appliances, stocks and bonds). In a basic or minimal math class, students should become acquainted with what, in business terms, are called the three basic financial statements: the income statement, balance sheet, and statement of cash flows. Understanding the temporal nature of each of these statements and what they represent is the first step in helping students understand how to budget and how wealth is accumulated. This would be more useful to all students than algebra, and basic arithmetic skills could be taught around an in-depth study of these statements. This would also fit well with the recommendations of Andrew Hacker, a teacher of political science and mathematics at Queen's College, who says:

> Calculus and higher math have a place, of course, but it's not in most people's everyday lives. What citizens do need is to be comfortable reading graphs and charts and adept at calculating simple figures in their heads. Ours has become a quantitative century, and we must master its language. Decimals and ratios are now as crucial as nouns and verbs. . . . In fact, figuring out the real world— deciphering corporate profits or what a health plan will cost—isn't all that easy. (Hacker, 2016, p. 2)

The statement of cash flows is like a checkbook: It tells the sources and uses of money as it comes in and out of accounts over a period of time— a month, quarter, or year. The income statement could be thought of as a basic budget. Again, it is a period statement and tells the amounts and sources of income and expenses over a period of time. Students could make a simple budget for their own or their family's income and expenses and then track for a period of time how money actually comes and goes. Last but most important for an understanding of wealth is the balance sheet. This statement is point-in-time specific and reports net worth, assets minus liabilities, at the specified time. To become wealthy, the bottom line of the balance sheet must increase over time.

Once students understand these basic principles and the difference between money and wealth, they will begin to better understand what it means that:

- The median net worth for a middle-income household (income between $44,000 and $132,000 per year for a family of four) rose only 2% over the 30 years from 1983 ($94,300) to 2013 ($96,500). This represents a "nest egg," or reserve of only 1 to 2 years' income that is likely composed primarily of equity in a home and not readily available cash.

- The median household net worth for families with less than $44,000 a year in income actually fell during this period from $11,400 to $9,300.
- In contrast, the median net worth of those households with annual income above $132,000 more than doubled in the same period to $639,400, according to data from the Pew Research Center (as reported by Cohen, 2014).
- The share of wealth owned by the top 0.1% in the United States rose from 7% in the late 1970s to 22% in 2012 (data from Saez and Zucman, as reported by Matthews, 2014).

As we mentioned in the previous chapter, statistics like these help explain the popularity that Bernie Sanders experienced as a presidential candidate as well as much of the current political turmoil. "Instead of doing something about brutal inequality, we simply embrace our national ideology, which, besides religion and money, is meritocracy" (Sacks, 2007, p. 288).

In her 1996 book, *A Framework for Understanding Poverty*, Ruby Payne talks about how the different social classes think about money. Those in poverty think of money as something to be spent, while the middle class tries to manage money, and the wealthy conserve and invest it. Thinking about this in terms of financial statements, you might say the poor only have use for a cash flow statement—money comes and goes, and often there are no bank accounts involved. The middle class and the wealthy have both cash flow and steady income, allowing them to plan and budget and use all three financial statements; but for the wealthy, the emphasis is on growing the balance sheet. We must be very careful here not to confuse chickens and eggs. The poor are not poor because they only think about money as something to spend.

Wealth also implies an abundance of resources other than things with easily monetized value. The wealthy, and to some extent the middle class, have access to educational resources; financial, political, and social connections; and sufficient monetary resources to weather periods of unemployment, ill health, or other financial crises. When we talk about things like a "wealth of knowledge," we are also acknowledging another aspect of wealth—personal resources that have been fostered and encouraged, such as skills, talent, confidence, and daring. That final attribute may seem like something that everyone might have regardless of the class they are born into, but a recent study suggests otherwise.

Jennifer Kish-Gephart and Joanna Tochman Campbell (2015) found that CEOs' perceived social class status during childhood had a definite impact on strategic risk taking (daring) later in life. Compared to their middle-class peers, CEOs from upper-class backgrounds were far more likely to see risks as opportunities and take strategic risks. Those from lower-class backgrounds were also more likely to take risks than those from middle-class backgrounds but not as much as their upper-class peers. The explanations offered for the empirical findings are based on prior sociological research indicating that an upper-class childhood increases self-esteem and security, and a lower-class childhood leaves one with the feeling that there is nothing to lose and taking risk may allow you to advance. In contrast, for those from middle-class backgrounds, risks pose a "double threat"—loss of both current status and future opportunity. The authors conclude:

> Despite the appeal of "rags to riches" stories in American discourse, the long-term influence of social class origins on the upwardly mobile in the workplace—especially those who have reached the heights of the socioeconomic hierarchy [CEOs]—has been unclear. By integrating work on social class, imprinting, and upper echelons theorizing, we provide an important initial step toward understanding the effects of the social class background of strategic leaders on firm-level outcomes. Overall, our results demonstrate that early formative experiences with social class matter. We thus strongly encourage future research related to upward mobility and the role of social class in the workplace. (2015, pp. 1631–1632)

Now that we have seen how money relates to wealth and social class and that social class has long-lasting implications—even for those who have made it to the top—we turn next to that topic.

CLASS

In the study on risk taking in the previous section, *social class* is defined as "a person's perceived place in an economic hierarchy" (Kish-Gephart & Campbell, 2015, p. 1615). Here, the economic hierarchy refers to differences in access to resources and social standing relative to others. As discussed in Chapter 8, the accumulation of wealth has long been the American Dream. "Benjamin Franklin did it. Henry Ford did it. And American life is built on the faith that others can do it, too: rise from humble origins to economic heights. 'Movin' on up,' George Jefferson–style, is not only a sitcom song but a civil religion" (DeParle, 2012, p. 1). Before we can talk about upward mobility though, we have to define what "up" means. Does it mean level of education, social status, income, wealth, or a combination of some, if not all, of these? When we watch programs about life in England before World War II, like *Downton Abbey*, class distinctions seem rather obvious. Were these distinctions as obvious in the United States prior to the Civil War and the gilded age that followed? When the writers of the Declaration of Independence used the phrase "all men are created equal," were they contemplating a classless society free of the aristocratic notions of class as a birthright? What about people of color? How do students think class is defined in the United States today?

To help students grapple with the concept of class and how it operates in the United States, they may benefit from a study of other class systems. The Marxist tradition based on relation to production did not account for slaves as members of a class with political standing and ideology; rather, they were fixed capital like a horse or tools would be. Marx did not approve of slavery, but slaves were left out of the proletarian conversation. The Indian caste system was extremely complicated, but somewhat related to occupation; interestingly, the highest caste, the Brahmins, included teachers along with priests and preachers. In particular, it is interesting to look at Spanish/Portuguese colonial traditions that were both race and place based. You could be born into a family of high social status, but if you were born in a colonial outpost, like Mexico or Brazil, you were automatically a notch down the ladder, a creole; being of mixed race, mestizo or mulatto, was also a cause for reclassification downward, and there were names and stations assigned that depended on what and how much was included in the mixture. (See the poems in *Thrall*, 2012, of Natasha Trethewey, Poet Laureate of the United States.)

This denigration of colonials played a large part in instigating the liberation of the Spanish and Portuguese colonies. El Libertador, Simon Bolivar, was born into one of the wealthiest creole families in Venezuela. To liberate Venezuela from Spain, Bolivar found that he had to unite many interests from classes of people formerly oppressed by his own class—slaves, cowboys (llaneros), and Indians. Bolivar freed his own slaves in exchange for military service and formally abolished slavery in the Bolivian constitution in 1826. "It was a bold move at a time when apparently enlightened American statesmen, such as Thomas Jefferson and James Madison, still had hundreds of slaves working their plantations" (Wulf, 2015, p. 154). To gain the support of the "tough and rough-mannered" llaneros and Indians, Bolivar learned to become an expert horseman.

> As a creole and a city-dweller, Bolivar was not someone they would have chosen as their leader but he won their respect. Though extremely thin—at five feet six inches Bolivar weighed only 130 pounds—he displayed an endurance and strength in the saddle that gained him the nickname 'Iron Ass.' (Wulf, 2015, p. 155)

Thomas Jefferson in a letter to Alexander von Humboldt, a close friend of Bolivar's, followed the revolutions in Latin America with interest and "bombarded Humboldt with questions: If the revolutionaries succeeded what kind of government would they establish, he asked, and how equal would their society be? Would despotism prevail?" (Wulf, 2015, p. 148).

Analogous to the knock-down received by creoles and mestizos in the Spanish and Portuguese empires is a similar treatment, often unacknowledged, of people of color in this country, and not just in the past. Ta-Nehisi Coates points out that "Black families making $100,000 typically live in the kinds of neighborhoods inhabited by white families making $30,000" (Coates, 2014, p. 60). In his *Atlantic* article, "The Case for Reparations," Coates presents clear evidence for continued discriminatory practices, well beyond slavery and the failures of reconstruction that have contributed to the isolation and marginalization of Blacks within our society today. Students might be interested to learn something about the ongoing struggle for reparations by Blacks in this country and the comparison that could be made to the reparations received by Israel from West Germany after the holocaust. "Until America reckons with the moral debt it has accrued—and the practical damage it has done—to generations of black Americans, it will fail to live up to its own ideals" (Coates, 2014, p. 55). Coates argues that a meaningful study and discussion of reparations at the national level would go a long way to raising our consciousness of the issues, even if no money is ever paid.

Eddie Glaude in *Democracy in Black* expresses a similar sentiment:

We have to release democracy from the burden of American exceptionalism. To do this, we have to tell the stories of those who put forward a more expansive conception of American democracy. This will involve confronting the ugly side of our history, recalling the heroic and representative efforts of countless men and women who gave everything to achieve our country, and sacrificing the comfort of national innocence and the willful blindness that comes with it.

This will require a radical reordering of value. Changing our stories is a way of changing what matters. I am not suggesting that we discard the cherished notions of success and self-reliance. But a revolution of value should change what constitutes success and individual initiative. The value of human beings should never be diminished in the pursuit of profit or in the name of some ideology. (Glaude, 2016, p. 203)

Finally, when we talked about the need for improving vocational education in Chapter 8, we hinted at a larger structural problem within U.S. society today—a lack of respect for those who engage in physical labor. No matter how much we automate and innovate, we will still need people to collect the garbage and recycling that are the by-products of success; people to clean, paint, and maintain houses (plumbers, carpenters, electricians, and appliance repairmen); people to dry-clean laundry; people to garden and landscape; people to care for the young and the elderly (orderlies, nurses and day care workers); and people to run what is left of our manufacturing processes no matter how automated they become (welders and machinists). Respect for these services needs to include a living wage.

In discussing what modern technology has actually done for us, the eco-logically minded economist E. F. Schumacher had this to say:

> The question of what technology actually does for us is therefore worthy of investigation. It obviously greatly reduces some kinds of work while it increases other kinds. The type of work which modern technology is most successful in reducing or even eliminating is skillful, productive work of human hands, in touch with real materials of one kind or another. In an advanced industrial society, such work has become exceedingly rare, and to make a decent living by doing such work has become virtually impossible. A great deal of the modern neurosis may be due to this very fact; for the human being, defined by Thomas Aquinas as a being with brains and hands, enjoys nothing more than to be creatively, usefully, productively engaged with both his hands and his brains. (Schumacher, 1973/1989, p. 158)

How did this disdain for blue-collar work come about in the United States? Thomas Frank in *Listen, Liberal* catalogues the rise of a professional class of "knowledge workers" and experts to the detriment of representation by the Democratic Party of working-class interests:

> As a political ideology, professionalism carries enormous potential for mischief. For starters, it is obviously and inherently undemocratic, prioritizing the views of experts over those of the public. That is tolerable to a certain degree—no one really objects to rules mandating that only trained pilots fly jetliners, for example. But what happens when an entire category of experts stops thinking of itself as "social trustees"? What happens when they abuse their monopoly power? What happens when they start looking mainly after their own interests, which is to say, start acting as a class? (Frank, 2016, pp. 24–25)

Frank charges that this is what has happened to the Democratic Party—that it now represents, primarily, the narrow interests of a highly educated professional class. These neo-liberals in their desire to "help" the down-trodden have ceased to listen and see the real needs of those around them and are now prone to blaming the victim—if they only tried harder, got more education. The total distrust of experts has just recently manifested in "Brexit," where the majority in the United Kingdom voted to leave the European Union, largely because they were tired of the "experts."

In an article in *The New Yorker*, "The Big Uneasy," on today's student activism on liberal-arts campuses, author Nathan Heller interviews a number of students at the progressive and liberal Oberlin College in Ohio who are engaged activists in the identity politics of oppressed groups. One student he interviews says that she "plans on returning to my community, I don't want to assimilate into middle-class values. I'm going *home*, back to the 'hood of Chicago, to be exactly who I was before I came to Oberlin"

(Heller, 2016, pp. 20–21). Students should be asked if they see the inherent contradictions in this statement. Does this student really think that she can ever be exactly who she was before she went to college? How would she ever have known that she doesn't want to assimilate into middle-class values without having been exposed to those values? What middle-class values has she found offensive? What would she change, if she could? Listening to her answers and those of our students responding on her behalf may be more important than asking the questions. We need to actively engage in conversation in order to solve our problems and stop assuming that we "experts" have all the solutions.

In commenting on Heller's essay, the columnist David Brooks found that:

> The identity politics the students have produced inverts the values of the meritocracy. The meritocracy is striving toward excellence; identity politics is deeply egalitarian. The meritocracy measures you by how much you've accomplished; identity politics measures you by how much you've been oppressed. In the meritocracy your right to be heard is earned through long learning and quality insight; in identity politics your right to be heard is earned by your experience of discrimination. The meritocracy places tremendous emphasis on individual agency; identity politics argues that agency is limited within a system of oppression. (Brooks, 2016, p. 2)

He goes on to say: "The meritocracy has become amoral. We ask students to work harder and harder while providing them with less and less of an idea of how they might find purpose in all that work" (p. 3).

This again raises two questions: Does everyone have to go to college in order to find both meaningfully gainful and personally rewarding employment? And, is the sole purpose of education to lead to economic reward? To quote E. F. Schumacher again, "there is more to life than GDP," referring to gross domestic product (McCrum, 2011, p. 1). On the first question, good vocational education provides only part of the answer. Increased respect for skilled labor must provide the rest. Witness the tribulations of a Minnesota-based vocational program:

> In the past few years, manufacturers west of Minneapolis have been desperate to hire welders, poaching employees from one another. With the Dunwoody College of Technology, the companies started an accelerated training program: one semester to get a job starting at $32,000 a year. Ads aired on the radio, blurbs ran in church bulletins, and recruiters visited high schools and community events. But the response they often got was, I'd rather go to college.
>
> Dunwoody's career and technical education carries—maybe even reinforces—the old stigma that clung to vocational education: something less for the less fortunate, or a consolation prize. "I hear comments like 'My son or

daughter wasn't successful in college, so I sent them to Dunwoody,'" says Rich Wagner, its president. Ironically, he notes, the nonprofit institution enrolls many students who already have a four-year degree but aren't landing a job. The college has a 99-percent placement rate for its graduates, Mr. Wagner says with an average starting salary of $40,000. "How do we get parents to understand that these occupations are viable pathways to the middle class?" he wonders. "The biggest frustration is that there doesn't seem to be a national voice on this." (Carlson, 2016, p. A24)

One of the reasons there may not be a national voice on this is that the truth is hard to come by and may not be what most people want to hear. For starters, $40,000 a year for a family of four is not a lot of money. It may put one on a pathway to the middle class, but it certainly isn't starting there. It is just 165% of the federal poverty level for 2016 and qualifies one for tax credits to help pay for health insurance. Marco Rubio raised tremendous ire among the educated elite in this country when he said during a presidential campaign speech that "Welders make more money than philosophers. We need more welders and less philosophers" (Sola, 2015, p. 1).

The media immediately went into fact-check mode to prove him wrong. They missed the point. This country does need more welders—"you'll certainly find more job openings listed nationally for welders than those demanding philosophy degrees" (Richmond, 2015, p. 3). But, we still need to pay welders a living wage, and even this is not the point we want to focus on.

In a *Forbes* article titled, "Sorry, Rubio, But Philosophers Make 78% More Than Welders," the author showed a graph with data from PayScale that showed a welder with an associate's degree and 20-plus years' experience making $58,500 a year on average compared to a bachelor's in philosophy making on average $97,000 a year after more than 20 years (Sola, 2015). What the graph doesn't tell you is what this average undergraduate philosophy major has spent the last 20 years doing. When my (Brooks) first husband was applying to medical school, he was told that the number one major accepted at that time to Baylor University's medical school was philosophy. You get an inkling of the fact that undergraduate philosophy majors don't become philosophers by noting that the graph also shows that after 20-plus years, a person with a master's degree in philosophy is earning on average $81,900 a year. Does that make you wonder why the author didn't show what a PhD would net? The other information the graph does not convey is the cost of each of these degrees and the cost of being out of the job market for the additional years of schooling. But that's still not the point we are trying to make.

The point we are trying to focus on is that the purpose of education should be to foster the critical thinking skills required to be a competent, productive, and happy citizen. The *New York Times* published in its politics newsletter, *First Draft*, an article titled "Philosophers (and Welders) React to

Marco Rubio's Debate Comments" (Rappeport, 2015). The article includes statements from Cheshire Calhoun, a philosophy professor at Arizona State University and chairwoman of the American Philosophical Association, and the welding philosopher, Matthew Crawford:

> Ms. Calhoun notes that philosophy is not about toga-wearing thinkers who stroke big beards these days. Rather, she says, the degree denotes skills in critical thinking and writing that are valuable in a variety of fields that can pay extremely well. (p. 2)
>
> Matthew B. Crawford earned his Ph.D. in political philosophy from the University of Chicago but failed to find a job as an academic and ultimately landed a position at a think tank. Unhappy with the work, he quit and became a mechanic in Virginia, using online tutorials to learn how to weld and make motorcycle parts.
>
> He has also continued to write and has published books about his career transition. One of his books, "Shop Class as Soulcraft," is devoted to debunking the notion that manual trades are mindless. "The division between knowledge work and manual work is kind of dubious, because there is so much thinking that goes on in skilled trades," Mr. Crawford said. (p. 3)

And that is the point we are after. It is also a partial answer to the question about the aim of education, other than to produce economic reward. Shouldn't education, at any level, lead to an appreciation of the things that bring happiness and meaning to a life well lived—a sense of purpose for ourselves and others; the satisfaction of a job well done, whether it is fixing a broken motorcycle or writing a book; an appreciation for nature and our place in it, for the beauty of a well-set table with tasty and colorful food and a vase of flowers? But, what about those for whom there is no food, never mind a table to set? We turn next to poverty.

POVERTY

Recent studies have found that upward economic mobility in the United States has *not* declined in the last half-century, but it is lower today in the United States than in Canada and much of Western Europe. It is also lower today than it was pre-1920 (DeParle, 2012; Leonhardt, 2014). Political arguments by both parties that upward mobility in the United States has declined in recent years are wrong in an absolute sense, but right when we compare ourselves to comparable countries like Canada where the ability to escape from the bottom 10th of incomes is higher than in the United States.

> By emphasizing the influence of family background, the studies not only challenge American identity but speak to the debate about inequality. While liberals

often complain that the United States has unusually large income gaps, many conservatives have argued that the system is fair because mobility is especially high, too: everyone can climb the ladder. Now the evidence suggests that America is not only less equal, but also less mobile.

John Bridgeland, a former aide to President George W. Bush who helped start Opportunity Nation, an effort to seek policy solutions, said he was "shocked" by the international comparisons. "Republicans will not feel compelled to talk about income inequality," Mr. Bridgeland said. "But they will feel a need to talk about a lack of mobility—a lack of access to the American Dream." (DeParle, 2012, p. 3 of 9)

Students may well ask—so what can we do about poverty, particularly the type of poverty that Ruby Payne calls "generational poverty"? Some people fall into "situational poverty" due to a particular event or issue—the loss of a job, divorce, an addictive habit, or serious illness. In many cases, with perseverance and the skills and confidence that come from starting someplace higher up, existing safety nets like unemployment payments or Medicaid will be sufficient for recovery.

Generational poverty is defined as having been in poverty for at least two generations. . . . One of the key indicators of whether it is generational or situational poverty is the prevailing attitude. Often the attitude in generational poverty is that society owes one a living. In situational poverty the attitude is often one of pride and a refusal to accept charity. (Payne, 1996, p. 49)

Again, lest we fall into the trap of blaming the victim, we need to understand where the sense of entitlement in generational poverty comes from. For some groups our democratic political system has failed them. We will talk about and listen to some of these groups next.

One place to start is to listen to what people in generational poverty say they need. Who should know better? Let's start with the newly emancipated slaves at the end of the Civil War in the United States.

As Sherman's army scorched and burned its way across Georgia, thousands of slaves descended on the Union lines. By the time Sherman reached Savannah, tens of thousands had descended upon the Union columns. By the time Sherman's army reached Savannah, a huge refugee problem had emerged (estimated at 150,000). The refugee crisis prompted the Secretary of War Edwin Stanton to travel to Savannah for a meeting with Sherman. Importantly, Stanton also requested a meeting with the representatives of the Black leadership in order to ask the newly freed "what they wanted for themselves." There were 20 representatives from local black churches at what has been called the Colloquy in Savannah, held on January 12, 1865. The delegation appointed Garrison Frazier as their spokesman, a 67-year-old preacher who had been free for eight years. When asked what he understood by slavery and what the President's Emancipation Proclamation meant, Frazier said:

Slavery is receiving by irresistible power the work of another man, and not by his consent. The freedom, as I understand it, promised by the proclamation, is taking us from under the yoke of bondage and placing us where we could reap the fruit of our own labor and take care of ourselves, and assist the government in maintaining our own freedom.

Stanton then asked how they planned to "take care of themselves" and maintain their freedom to which Frazier responded:

The best way we can take care of ourselves is to have land, and turn it in and till it by our own labor. . . . We want to be placed on land until we are able to buy it and make it our own. (Burch, 2012, pp. 57–58)

The freed slaves were not asking for formal citizenship or the right to vote, or to be given the land—they were willing to pay for it eventually. The Colloquy in Savannah resulted in Field Order 15, which would grant freed slaves 40 acres and an army surplus mule. In March 1865, Congress established a bureau of freedmen to facilitate the transition from slavery to freedom. By June 1865, 40,000 freedmen were settled on some 400,000 acres. By October 1865, following Lincoln's murder, it was all over. The lands were taken back by then-President Andrew Johnson, an avowed white supremacist (Burch, 2012). Thus reconstruction failed the newly freed slaves, and a path was laid for a potential future of generational poverty. The American Indians are another group with a legacy of generational poverty caused in large part by broken government promises.

Reconstruction didn't work well for much of the South—not just the slaves. Remember our discussion of the secession declarations of the Southern states whose landholders found slavery to be the only way to compete in a world where government subsidies and international interventions like the Walker Tariff favored Northern interests. Cotton played a large role in the maintenance of class divisions both north and south of the Mason-Dixon Line and across the Atlantic as well. It still plays a large role, as we shall see when we talk about globalization at the end of this chapter. The Industrial Revolution in Britain was spurred on by the growth of spinning and weaving mills and the movement of textile manufacture from home and workshop to factories, creating a new working class. By the time of the Civil War, cotton production in the U.S. South amounted to two-thirds of world production and half the value of U.S. exports. The demand for raw cotton in Britain meant that production in the U.S. South had to continue (Rivoli, 2009/2015).

After the Civil War, without slavery, the Deep South solved the labor market problem for cotton growing through the institution of sharecropping, and yet another group of people were put on the path to generational poverty. Public policies were instituted to insulate cotton growers from the risks of free market labor. Crop lien laws changed the status of sharecroppers from tenants with a percentage ownership of the crop to laborers who were paid wages in crops. Cotton growers also opposed public schooling for Blacks and poor Whites, which kept the balance of power in favor of the landowners.

> Moreover, the contractual arrangement between sharecropper and landowner left the sharecropper with little hope of climbing out of subsistence. The sharecropper's dream—to own land—was thwarted by a cycle of perpetual debt whereby the sharecropper's share of each harvest was barely enough to settle the year's debts, and by exclusion from external capital markets. A remark reportedly made by Louis XIV of France is apt: "Credit supports agriculture as a cord supports the hanged." (Rivoli, 2009/2015, p. 20)

Access to credit will come up again when we look at micro-credit as one solution for global poverty. The plight and ignorance of the White illiterate sharecropper is told both poignantly and with humor in Erskine Caldwell's *Tobacco Road*. The story of the Lester family set in depression-era rural Georgia is one that we will see repeat itself over decades and around the globe as the children of those who work the land without adequate remuneration leave their farms for an only marginally better existence in urban textile mills and factories; several of the Lester girls migrate to the low-wage Augusta mills.

Lack of educational opportunity, however, undid the Deep South when the cotton boll weevil began to ravage the crop in the early 1900s.

> Government extension programs were mobilized to spread advice to farmers on how to combat the weevil and save their crops. The news and advice reached the large farms and the educated farmers, but often passed by the illiterate sharecroppers, black and white, who had to fend for themselves. In 1921, approximately 30 percent of the cotton crop—predominantly that produced by small sharecroppers—was lost to the weevil. Many were pushed off the land. (Rivoli, 2009/2015, p. 21)

In her book *The Travels of a T-Shirt in the Global Economy*, Pietra Rivoli goes on to describe two more poverty-inducing iterations in the production of cotton in the United States: the rise of "company towns" in Texas, an idea borrowed from the North ("I owe my soul to the company store") and the importation of Mexican labor to harvest cotton and other crops that began with the shortage of men on the farm in World War II. The *Bracero* program, which started as a wartime emergency measure in 1942, was extended at the behest of farm interests until 1964, by which time 90% of the cotton harvest was fully mechanized, displacing yet again another group of workers, this time of Mexican origin.

Whether displaced from productive land or gainful employment by broken government promises (40 acres and a mule for freedmen and almost every single treaty with the American Indians), deliberately discriminatory practices (see Coates's "The Case for Reparations" or Matthew Desmond's *Evicted*), or technological innovations (mechanical harvesters, long-wall mining equipment, and robotic assembly lines), is it any wonder that a sense of entitlement exists among those in generational poverty? The aim in studying these issues is not for students to despair at either the enormity of the problem (approximately 20% of U.S. children live in households with income below the federal poverty guidelines) or the darkness revealed by a closer study of American history. What we do want is for students to apply critical thinking and moral commitment to these issues and to be able to discuss these issues across class boundaries to help identify a wide range of solutions that will carry us forward to a brighter future for all.

When the poor are asked what they need, so far we have heard these answers: productive land (the freed slaves) and access to credit and education (sharecroppers). Desmond (2016) would add stable homes for the urban poor, millions of whom face eviction each year due to discriminatory or usurious business practices and failed government policies and initiatives:

> All this suffering is shameful and unnecessary. Because it is unnecessary there is hope. These problems are neither intractable nor eternal. A different kind of society is possible, and powerful solutions are within our collective reach.
>
> But those solutions depend on how we answer a single question: do we believe that the right to a decent home is part of what it means to be an American?
>
> The United States was founded on the noble idea that people have "certain unalienable Rights, that among these are Life, Liberty and the pursuit of Happiness." Each of these three unalienable rights—so essential to the American character that the founders saw them as God-given—requires a stable home. (Desmond, 2016, p. 299)

In his article for *The New York Times*, "Harder for Americans to Rise from Lower Rungs," Jason DeParle writes that "The causes of America's mobility problem are a topic of dispute—starting with the debates over poverty" (2012, p. 5). He lists the following controversial issues as contributing factors:

- a thinner safety net than other rich countries, leaving more children vulnerable;
- the likelihood of growing up in a single-mother household;
- high rates of incarceration;
- the income gap—for poor Americans, the floor from which they start is lower;

- the pay tilt toward educated workers and the fact that the educated and affluent have access to better schools and arrive in them better prepared to learn;
- the relative lack of union representation in the United States in comparison to other nations, potentially lowering wages for the least skilled;
- health problems like obesity and diabetes that can limit education and employment; and
- "the sheer magnitude of the gaps between rich and the rest—the theme of the Occupy Wall Street protests, which emphasize the power of the privileged to protect their interests. Countries with less equality generally have less mobility." (p. 6 of 9)

Many of these are topics that we have covered in this chapter. All are topics that could be addressed in the cross-class, cross-curricular social studies forum we recommend. Many of these issues have remedies to be sought in legal, social, and political venues—where better to begin the conversations that will lead to solutions than in our classrooms with the young people who will need to enact them through their votes and actions? But, what if the problem is bigger than the United States? What if the problem is global in proportion?

GLOBAL ECONOMIC AND ENVIRONMENTAL ISSUES

Think globally, act locally, and be prepared to call for global action.

Income disparities and poverty are problems that must be addressed on both the local and global levels from both local and global perspectives. There seem to be two camps in the world today proposing solutions to the problems of a globalized world economy and growing inequality from perspectives that seem to be irreconcilably different. We contend that the application of critical thinking with moral commitment to these problems, through active discussion of the pertinent controversial issues, will highlight the necessity of embracing the best features of all possible solutions and *not* a one or the other approach. The two camps in question could be described as capitalist versus socialist, Republican versus Democrat, conservative versus liberal, or any of several other dichotomies that divide the world into mutually exclusive camps. Therein lies the rub—almost all of these so-called divisions in reality represent spectrums of thought and perspective that through discussion and cooperation could collectively come to better solutions than either bookend alone.

Ignoring for the moment the existence of evil in the world by which we mean the greed of people who exploit every opportunity to advance themselves at the expense of others, we will examine two movements that seem to be coming from very different perspectives with respect to the impacts of globalization. These movements could perhaps be characterized as capitalist versus socialist although this distinction is not always clear. On the one hand are the "Davos" people for whom globalization is a welcome process by which the rising tide of capitalism will lift all boats, and on the other are the followers of the economist E. F. Schumacher, an avowed but open-minded socialist.

The Davos camp are the expert associates of the 1,000 top global corporations that comprise the World Economic Forum (WEF), devisers of the Gender Gap Index discussed in Chapter 6 and sponsors of the WEF summit held annually in Davos, Switzerland. The following mission statement can be found on the WEF website (www.weforum.org): "The World Economic Forum, committed to improving the state of the world, is the International Organization for Public-Private Cooperation."

For critics, "Davos man," a name coined by U.S. political scientist Samuel Huntington, "is shorthand for the globe-trotting elite, disconnected from their home countries after spending too much time in the club-class lounge. Others just wonder if it is all a big waste of time" (Rankin, 2015, p. 1). Major critics of the WEF, including the Transnational Institute and the Occupy movement, are concerned primarily with social justice and the question of whether the world's wealthy elites (the 0.1 percenters) can represent the best interests of everyone in the world. Transparency is another point of contention: Much of the international negotiation to further the aims of capitalism goes on behind closed doors at Davos. Learning about what these powerful organizations stand for and how they can be motivated to listen to concerns about growing inequality in the world is an important first step to discussing the issues.

In contrast to the WEF is the work of the New Economics Foundation (NEF), a member organization of the Schumacher Circle of organizations that promote the thoughts and ideas of the author of *Small is Beautiful* (Schumacher, 1973/1989). The NEF came into being after sponsoring the first TOES (The Other Economic Summit) meetings in the 1980s as a challenge to the right of the leaders of the G7 countries to speak for the economic future of the planet. The NEF is the producer of the Happy Planet Index, which measures the well-being of a country's citizens in comparison to its carbon footprint. (not to be confused with the partially GDP-based World Happiness Index discussed in Chapter 6). A country scores high on the Happy Planet Index if its citizens are happy and long-lived in spite of using less of the world's resources than others. Costa Rica has had the highest (best) score the last two times the index was calculated. Students in science or math classes can calculate their own personal carbon footprint and Happy Planet Index.

George Monbiot, a columnist for *The Guardian*, has been a speaker at NEF-convened events. Mark Lynas of the Ecomodernists discussed in

Chapter 8 was in the past a member of the WEF Global Agenda Council on Decarbonizing Energy. We will concentrate the rest of this discussion on global environmental issues and contrast the thoughts of Lynas and Monbiot as somewhat representative of the two camps we have discussed previously. But first, a short word on micro-credit and peer-to-peer lending as a tool for lifting people out of poverty. This is another controversial issue with both local and global applications and implications. Does it work? Has it empowered women? Has it been coopted by for-profit enterprises out of greed? Has it created a new class of debtors? A study of this single tool for alleviating poverty could comprise an entire semester's worth of cross-curricular activity.

Let us return to the environmental movement where the phrase "think globally, act locally" originated. We all want to know what we can do as individuals to save our planet, a clearly global issue—so that we *can* act locally. Most of us will never have the opportunity to act at a global level. What we all do have, though, is the ability to vote and express our thoughts and concerns to our leaders. They can, in turn, work together through organizations like the United Nations, the NEF, and the WEF, among many others, to influence global corporations and policymakers to do what is right and necessary to solve problems that are global in scale like pollution of the oceans and natural resource conservation and allocation. Actions taken by world governments in the 1970s and 1980s to decrease the use of chlorofluorocarbons (CFCs) in aerosol sprays to protect the ozone layer are a good example of effective global action.

Social and economic justice and saving our planet must go hand in hand. Monbiot and Lynas would both agree with this statement, but they pose different solutions for achieving the same ends. The *Ecomodernist Manifesto*, discussed in Chapter 8, proposes the use of technology as a force for good to both increase general well-being and decrease the human impact on the environment through increased urbanization and large-scale farming. "Cities both drive and symbolize the decoupling of humanity from nature, performing far better than rural economies in providing efficiently for material needs while reducing environmental impacts" (Monbiot, 2015, p. 6 of 8, quoting from the *Ecomodernist Manifesto*). E. O. Wilson might agree, in part, with ecomodernism. In his 32nd book, *Half Earth: Our Planet's Fight for Life* (2016), Wilson recommends that the nations of the world set aside half the Earth's surface as a natural reserve. Many of the reasons that he thinks this could be done easily, as presented in an interview with *The New York Times* (Dreifus, 2016), sound like statements from the *Ecomodernist Manifesto*.

We saw this perception of moving to urban centers as upward mobility earlier when we talked about cotton and the people who left the farms in the Rural South to work in textile mills. It continues today in the "race to the bottom" by corporations seeking the least costly venue in which to operate (less regulation, lower labor costs). Do the people who make this transition benefit, and if so, how? Monbiot, an advocate for small farms among other proposals, would caution that this benefit is not always shared:

> In many other parts of the developing world, rural depopulation has resulted not in a smooth transition to the formal urban economy, but in a highly precarious existence on the economic margins, and a reliance on the informal economy, much of which remains connected to family businesses in the countryside. What the ecomodernists describe as "relieving agricultural workers of a lifetime of hard physical labour" is experienced by millions as underemployment and desperate insecurity. (2015, p. 5 of 8)

However, in speaking of young women working in the garment industry in Shanghai, Rivoli relates:

> He Yuan Zhi agrees with her sisters in time. Yuan Zhi has worked as a cutter at Shanghai Brightness for eight years. It was a good job for a girl from the farm, and it is even better now, she believes, as after several pay raises her pay in 2007 was nearly $300 per month. Yuan Zhi came to Shanghai from the mountainous area of Jiangxi province, because of the lack of opportunity at home in the village. She told me that she misses only two things about her home village: One is the spectacular scenery, and the other is her son, who is back in Jiangxi in the care of his grandparents. Everything else about life in Shanghai, she says, is better than that in the village. I have heard this sentiment, "My life is better now," from innumerable garment workers in China. Each had a story, it seemed, of the drudgery of farm life. (2009/2015, p. 111)

This vignette supports both Lynas and Monbiot's viewpoints—the garment workers feel they are better off for the freedoms they enjoy having moved to the city, but at the same time they are relying on support from home—in Yuan Zhi's case for child care. The key item here is choice. As we discussed earlier in listening to what people living in poverty want, more than anything, they want some control over their own destinies.

Monbiot and Lynas may disagree on how to save the planet, but they both actively engage in the debate through their published viewpoints, and most importantly, they are willing to talk to each other. Both were members at some point in time of organizations that were vehemently opposed to the use of nuclear power to generate electricity. Both have revised their thoughts in this area.

Whether we believe in capitalism or socialism, we must come to understand the basic principles of economic thought and the evolution of these principles over time. Three very different books have helped me (Brooks) understand these principles and the controversies they engender. I have already mentioned two of them: Rivoli's *The Travels of a T-Shirt in the Global*

Economy and Schumacher's *Small is Beautiful: Economics as if People Mattered*. Schumacher, in particular, cautions us to be open-minded. In a letter to his Oxford friend David Astor, he wrote, "My intense interest in socialism is a new departure. . . . What my final opinion will be I don't know, but I am pretty sure that my nature does not allow me to embrace wholeheartedly as 'final' any political creed or system, any 'ism,' or any panacea" (as quoted in McCrum, 2011, p. 4). We also have advocated the careful examination of panaceas.

The third economics book is Todd Buchholz's *New Ideas from Dead Economists*. We close this chapter and move on to Equality, Justice, and Freedom with a few thoughts from Buchholz:

> One problem may not be solved by markets or shrewd governments, though. Can human beings keep up with the pace of new inventions that make traditional jobs and roles obsolete? Can human beings educate themselves fast enough to handle the computer and post-computer age? Most probably can. But as society grows more complex, more and more will fall through the various safety nets—those with psychological, physical, and intelligence handicaps will falter. The world is materially easier but psychologically more difficult to live in today than two hundred years ago. Life in the twentieth century city is as tough on the human spirit as life on the farm ever was. It's quite easy to lose one's footing in the modern world, to be whirled around a factory and spat out a homeless waif, like Charlie Chaplin in *Modern Times*. (1989/2007, pp. 312–313)

CHAPTER 10

Equality, Justice, and Freedom

As we begin a discussion of yet another enormous set of concepts, readers should keep in mind that it is our intention to help teachers address those ideas that may be controversial or poorly understood by students yet essential for effective participation in democratic life. In what ways are people "equal"? What does justice require on issues of equality? And how can we help students to embrace the democratic concept of freedom?

EQUALITY

We have already noted that most people—even writers of the Declaration of Independence—do not believe that all men are created equal in all ways. They may hold a religious belief that all men are "equal in the eyes of God," and that belief is reflected in the human endorsement that all people should be treated as equals before the law. But are there ways in which people are created equal, and how should our understanding of this equality influence what and how we teach?

Surely all human beings are born with certain common needs, often called *course of life* needs: food, water, shelter, adequate clothing, protection from harm, affection (at least in infancy), and some form of connection to other human beings (Braybrooke, 1987). Recognition of the universality of these needs has led most societies to make provision for those who cannot meet these needs on their own. Indeed, most of us believe that justice demands that we do so. We sometimes say that people have a *right* to have these needs met. But we are not born with such a right; it is bestowed on us by an enlightened society.

We might suggest that, in addition to these course of life needs, all people today need some form of education. Are people alike enough that one form of education will suit them all? What of the great differences we see in talents, aptitudes, and interests? Many thoughtful people today insist that it is respect for this variety, these differences, that constitutes the foundation of participatory democracy (Callan, 1997; Fielding & Moss, 2011; Gardner, 1984). If we are to give due recognition to the differences among students, we have to consider two fundamental educational questions:

How can education nurture these differences? What common features should appear in all forms of education designed to accommodate the variety?

We have already endorsed the idea of multiple programs in our high schools—academic, vocational, arts, and special education—and the comprehensive high school was, in theory, an excellent way to accomplish this. But, as we have seen, the underlying democratic premise—respect for the full range of human talents—was betrayed in its implementation. It treated the academic program as the most valuable and all others as second-class alternatives for those whose interests fall along different lines. The correction of this betrayal pursued in the last 30 years or so—eliminating tracks—might be considered another form of betrayal. It continues to rank students by how well they do in an academic program, not how well they might do in a program suited to their aptitudes and interests.

Students in all programs should be invited to talk about this. Do they believe that they have chosen the program in which they are studying, or do they believe that they have been assigned to it because they did not qualify for the academic program? How much guidance have they received? If they are in a vocational program, are they familiar with the names Scott Nearing, Myles Horton, Rosa Parks, Pete Seeger, John L. Lewis, Eugene Debs, and Paulo Freire? If they are in an academic program, did they choose or were they assigned to the sections in which they find themselves? Do they think they should be allowed to choose an advanced course if they wish to do so?

If we agree that an "equal" education does not necessitate the same curriculum for everyone, we still face the question of which topics, methods, concepts, and skills should appear in all of them. Amy Gutmann points out that the primacy of political education can be used to argue "against tracking, sexist education, racial segregation, and (narrowly) vocational education" (1987, p. 287), but we need not—and we will continue to advise that we *should* not—abolish tracking or vocational education. Her fear is that, "Even when these practices improve the academic achievement of students, they neglect the virtues of citizenship, which can be cultivated by a common education characterized by respect for racial, religious, intellectual and sexual differences among students" (1987, p. 287). But tracking can be modified to advance the political education advocated by Gutmann, and we agree heartily when she reminds readers: "The moral primacy of political education also supports a presumption in favor of more participatory over more disciplinary methods of teaching" (p. 287).

Our advice is to design a variety of truly excellent programs that students can choose from proudly and then find a way—perhaps through our recommended 4-year social studies seminars—to bring students together across these programs to discuss significant political/moral issues. This is one way for schools to work toward a reduction of the conversation gap discussed earlier.

The conversation gap should itself be an important topic for students' discussion. It should be interesting, perhaps even enlightening, to hear how students view social classes and their differences. How do they identify a person as belonging to the lower class, middle class, or upper class? The "classes" are usually thought of in economic terms; sometimes we refer to them as poor, middle class, and wealthy, and sometimes we add a "working class" that falls above the poorest of the poor and at the lower end of the middle class. But a description of social classes involves more than economic level; it involves styles of living, neighborhoods, and ways of speaking. This can be a very controversial topic to discuss openly, and the temptation will be strong for students to deny that they engage in such judgments.

However, with patience and gentle persistence, teachers may get students to discuss the use of language. Language is probably the most important influence on our judgment about social class. If we hear someone say, "He don't know nothin'," most of us conclude—unless the remark is a joke—that the speaker belongs to the lower class. It is hard for any of us to admit this, and yet we know that we do draw such conclusions. If, in a seminar of mixed class students, a student becomes angry and says to another, "So, just because I don't talk like you, I'm lower class!?" how does the teacher handle this? It has to be admitted that we do make these judgments, but it should also be pointed out that *here*, in this classroom, we are working together, respecting each other's ideas, and trying to understand the sources of our disagreements. It should be emphasized that a valuable idea or suggestion may be expressed in nonstandard language.

The very possibility of an exchange like this one should make educators keenly aware of a responsibility too often ignored. We make a great fuss about teaching kids to read and write, but year after year we allow them to graduate from high school without mastering standard English. Most of this work should be accomplished in elementary school, but widespread results tell us that it is not always done. In her argument for the primacy of political education, Gutmann underscores the importance of student participation: "But even when student participation threatens to produce some degree of disorder within schools, it may be defended on democratic grounds for cultivating political skills and social commitments" (1987, p. 287). Not only will conversational participation across social classes in schools contribute to a continuation of communication among adult citizens, but its regular, respectfully guided exchanges should help to remove one of the most glaring signs of class difference—use or nonuse of standard language.

Some students may argue that we should respect street talk and Black English just as we do foreign languages. One way to respond to this is to point out that Black entertainers often make regular use of Black English. They do a fascinating job of code-switching, and students might be encouraged to follow their example. Attention should be drawn, however, to the fact that code switching requires a speaker to be fluent in both languages.

Students might enjoy engaging in classroom discussion demonstrating code switching. Mastery of standard English should be regarded as part of the educational aim to provide equal opportunity; the deliberate choice of such mastery as an educational aim should not be thought of as disrespect for those who use nonstandard English.

We still face the challenging question of what the variety of programs should have in common beyond the mastery of standard language. Often, when this question is raised, people begin to identify certain historical events, prominent persons, scientific concepts, mathematical procedures, and artistic personalities as essential to every curriculum. This is far too big a topic to be addressed here, but it should be a central issue for discussion within each discipline. Even there it can quickly get out of hand. At one lively meeting of math teachers, for example, the participants started with sensible suggestions on essential concepts such as variation, the basic laws of operations, and linear equations. Then the discussion became more heated, and one teacher exclaimed, "It is disgraceful that so many college graduates don't know the difference between a definite and an indefinite integral!" This sort of thing should not be left entirely to disciplinary specialists.

Here we will provide some general ideas that should guide decisions in and across all disciplinary lines. First, if we are serious about educating for citizenship in a participatory democracy, there should be provision for student talk in every course. The job of students is not simply to listen but to respond, suggest, wonder, and question, and this sharing should go on at both whole class and small group levels. Effective participation in public affairs requires gathering and assessing information, engaging in genuine dialogue, willingness to compromise, and attention to potentially deep philosophical differences.

Second, at the school level, provision should be made for cross-program projects. We have already suggested that students should participate in four years of cross-program seminars on social, moral, and political issues. There should also be opportunities to work together on various community projects.

Third, an interdisciplinary approach should be adopted by teachers of every discipline. We cannot—probably *should* not—provide exactly the same curriculum for every student in mathematics or English, but we can be sure that all courses will include material that connects the subject with other subjects in the curriculum: biographical accounts, philosophical disputes, political debates, crucial historical events, related literature in fiction and poetry, connections to the arts, and scientific battles.

Our high school programs will be *equal* to the extent that they share a common respect for the full range of human talents and prepare all students for meaningful lives both as individuals and citizens. We will return briefly to a further discussion of equality after the next sections treating justice and freedom.

JUSTICE

Justice is another complex topic. We usually define justice as the use of authority to uphold what is thought to be right or lawful. As John Rawls has put it, "Justice is the first virtue of social institutions, as truth is of systems of thought" (1971, p. 3). Every social institution—government, family, business, church, military, school—may be studied and assessed for its standing on this virtue. The criteria by which an institution is judged on this virtue, however, differ not only across nations and institutional types but also over time.

Students should be made aware that slavery in America was for a long time considered just. It was defended by arguments based on the Bible, on historical accounts, and on widely accepted premises about racial inferiority (Anderson, 2015). Within the practice of slavery, there was a system of "justice"—informal rules forbidding extremes of cruelty. Elizabeth Anderson quotes James Thornwell, a Presbyterian minister who defended the practice of slavery:

> Our savior directs us to do unto others what, in their situations, it would be right and reasonable in us to expect from them. . . . The rule then simply requires, in the case of slavery, that we should treat our slaves as we should feel that we had a right to be treated if we were slaves ourselves. (2015, p. 29)

Notice that this injunction requires humane treatment of slaves, not the abolition of slavery.

It may be hard for today's students to imagine a time in which otherwise good people actually defended the moral rightness of slavery. But there was a time, not that long ago, when the majority of citizens accepted customs forbidding women to vote, own property, or refuse sexual demands of their husbands. Indeed, in defending the practices of slavery, a Southern senator argued in 1860:

> Females are human and rational beings. They may be found of better faculties, and better qualified to exercise political privileges, and to attain the distinctions of society, than many men; yet who complains of the order of society by which they are excluded from them? (quoted in Anderson, 2015, p. 30)

Well, of course, women did complain, but it took a long time to convince American society that women should be admitted to full citizenship, and it was many years after Black men achieved the vote that voting rights were finally granted to women. (See Ward & Burns, 1999.) The idea of justice as the authoritative use of just and right laws has been stable, but what is considered to be right and just has changed dramatically over time. When change has occurred, it has not happened because of some general moral awakening but because those who have been victimized have spoken up, gathered supporters, and worked vigorously to change the laws.

Changing our notions of what is right and just is practical work. Certainly, moral issues are involved, and sometimes moral objections get things started, but often it is the recognition that a legal practice is simply not working well that arouses opposition, and then moral arguments are employed to move things along. Consider, for example, current attempts to lessen the prison sentences of drug offenders. This movement got under way because our prisons are badly overcrowded, and that recognition together with the cost of supporting so many prisoners will probably bring about change. Moral arguments about the unjustifiable racial differences in sentencing for drug offenses will aid the project.

Similarly, abandonment of the morally questionable practice of capital punishment may be settled or at least strongly supported on practical grounds. It costs more to execute murderers than to imprison them for life. Recognition of the financial cost, coupled with reminders that mistakes cannot be undone, should bolster support for the basic moral admonition that deliberate killing is wrong.

Discussion of justice and practical morality should include careful consideration of retributive justice, the branch of justice that deals with penalties and punishment. The basic idea is that there should be penalties for breaking established laws of the institution governed by them. It is widely believed that such penalties strengthen the laws by reminding citizens that they will suffer punishment if they break those laws. Again, it would surely be preferable to have citizens obey laws because they see such obedience as a moral obligation. Certainly, in the family, we would prefer that children obey the fair rules established by their parents, and many good parents avoid the use of punishment for breaking those rules. A sound lecture and expression of disappointment are quite effective in many families. Even at the societal level, many people avoid breaking the law out of fear of shame more than of legal punishment. Most of us treasure the approval of our fellow citizens. It remains the hope of a healthy community that people will see obedience to law as a moral commitment.

At the high school level, students should be invited to participate in both the making and upholding of their school's rules. Teachers and students should work together to analyze and evaluate those rules. Certainly, it is right to require students to show up for classes and, usually, on time. But, on the practical level, does it make sense to suspend students who cut class or are often late? In some schools, for some students, a suspension provides a legal reason for avoiding classes altogether. On the other hand, the threat of suspension may encourage the timely appearance of many students. What might the students recommend?

Students should be involved, too, in a critical discussion of zero-tolerance rules. Many schools have now given up on this morally and practically questionable practice, and it is to our discredit as educators that we ever endorsed such an idea. Sometimes, after all, a rule is broken by accident or by a temporary emotional breakdown. To apply a standard punishment without regard for particular circumstances is not only unsympathetic but often unjust. Indeed, it might justifiably be considered irrational.

It would be worthwhile even today for teachers to reread and discuss the work of Lawrence Kohlberg on "just community schools" (Kuhmerker, 1991) and on moral development (Kohlberg, 1981). The purpose of this reading is not to adopt that program or any other in complete detail. Such adoptions rarely work out, and many useful ideas are simply cast aside along with the discarded programs. The idea that we have been advocating throughout this book is to gather information, analyze, discuss, try out, and evaluate. Faculty and students working together should experiment responsibly on ways to establish and maintain their schools democratically. How, for example, should we handle noisy halls, students who make nasty remarks, and actions that damage school property?

Consider the widespread problem of cheating. Usually, that violation results in a severe reduction of the cheater's grade, and that may be fair. A confirmed act of cheating merits a severe penalty—a zero on the paper or test at hand. But, thinking practically, we should also want cheaters to master the material on which they cheated. Perhaps we should insist that the cheater retake the test or rewrite the paper and, in preparation, work with and help fellow students who failed honestly. Again, the idea is to encourage the development of moral consciousness and to show that we as teachers really care that the tested material be learned. Our collective objective is to teach and learn worthwhile material, not simply to give and receive grades. In addition, our deeper aim is to produce better people—citizens adequately prepared for a place in participatory democracy.

FREEDOM

In Chapter 4 on religion, we noted that some people find freedom from worldly demands by devoting themselves to a religious idea or organization. They give up the freedom that most of us seek and instead find a form of sacred freedom, a realm of devotion in which they are relieved of many ordinary decisions.

Now we need to consider another anomaly in the world of human freedom. Some people are afraid of freedom. Paulo Freire counsels: "The 'fear of freedom' which afflicts the oppressed, a fear which may equally well lead them to desire the role of oppressor or bind them to the role of oppressed, should be examined" (1970, p. 31). Freire's point should be addressed by thoughtful teachers. Might it be that teachers—whole school systems—maintain and even increase this fear? Freire continues: "One of the basic elements of the relationship between oppressor and oppressed is *prescription"* (p. 31). Education, by its very nature, requires at least some prescription, but perhaps an overly prescriptive education undermines the very autonomy we claim as one of our aims.

A. S. Neill definitively condemned authoritarian prescription in education. His opinion is extreme but well worth consideration:

> I believe that to impose anything by authority is wrong. The child should not do anything until he comes to the opinion—his own opinion—that it should be done. The curse of humanity is the external compulsion, whether it comes from the Pope or the state or the teacher or the parent. It is fascism in toto. (1960, p. 114)

Neill's statement does not rule out the prescription of curriculum material. Algebra, with some variations, is a prescribed study within mathematics. It is the decision to *study* algebra that, Neill advises, must come from the student. Teachers and students must work together—talk together, tackle common projects, participate in running their classes together—to decide what will be studied and how. Is it possible to employ this advice in our public schools? Can we come close? Remember that we can learn something important from a program or suggestion without adopting it completely.

One great danger in using heavily prescriptive methods in education is that we may contribute to the acceptance of oppression. Freire, in describing a pedagogy of the oppressed, warns that such a pedagogy "must be forged *with*, not *for*, the oppressed (whether individuals or peoples) in the incessant struggle to regain their humanity" (1970, p. 33). As educators, we want to support and develop that humanity right from the start.

It is instructive to look at political liberation movements to see how things can go wrong. When liberators, such as Simon Bolivar mentioned previously, who are honestly motivated to liberate an oppressed people start work with the oppressed, their relationship often reveals both sympathy and hostility. Michael Walzer describes the two attitudes:

> Sympathy, because the liberators don't just resent the foreign rulers . . . they really want to improve the lives of the men and women with whom they identify: *their* people (the possessive pronoun is important). Hostility, because at the same time the liberators hate what they take to be the backwardness, ignorance, passivity, and submissiveness of those same people. (2015, p. 68)

George Orwell (1958/1937)—whose work on class differences will be revisited in the final section of this chapter—also noted this ambivalence. Orwell commented on his own class snobbishness and that of his fellow socialists. He and his well-meaning colleagues were not about to drop their "aitches," slurp their soup, or mishandle their silverware. Liberators battle both the oppression of the poor and their own persistent snobbishness.

In such situations, the oppressed are not approached as partners in the project of liberation but, rather, as subjects to be studied and reformed. The point was made earlier in the discussion of Elizabeth Anderson's critique (Chapter 4) of how we so often fail to invite the participation of those we hope to help. Instead of working and talking *with* them, we study them and tell them what to do. We fail to recognize their capacity to communicate and our own failure to do so:

> Communicative competence is a shared good of the communicators. It is not a private possession that one party has and the other lacks. If A and B are not communicating effectively due to cultural differences, then both lack cultural capital with respect to each other. . . . When elites are overwhelmingly drawn from segregated advantaged groups, they share their deficits in cultural capital. (2007, p. 604)

As teachers, we face another significant problem in helping students to understand the nature of freedom in a participatory democracy. Not only must we revise our vision of the liberator in our work with students who are disadvantaged and might even be described as oppressed, we must also help all students understand what drives some people to fear freedom. A perceived lack of self-confidence can drive a person to seek success and acceptance through participation in some cause of which he can become a part. Eric Hoffer notes, "The less justified a man is in claiming excellence for his own self, the more ready is he to claim excellence for his nation, his religion, his race or his holy cause" (1951, p. 23). Sometimes our efforts to help all students succeed at the tasks we set for them fail, and there are cases where students do not even see the point of succeeding at the work we have laid out for them. Hoffer continues, "When our individual interests and projects do not seem worth living for, we are in desperate need of something apart from us to live for" (1951, p. 24). Thus some young people are attracted to questionable, even dangerous, movements that promise them acceptance, group success, and excitement. They are afraid of the individual freedom promised by life in a democracy that promotes both cooperation and competition. It is because the fear of freedom and the allure of great causes are both so powerful that responsible religious organizations insist on lengthy novitiates to ensure that declared devotees fully understand the purposes and demands of the life to which they are pledging themselves.

If we want students to embrace the democratic idea of freedom, we should provide them with many opportunities to make responsible choices. Trapped in a school culture that seems to support only one set of aptitudes, they may develop a real fear of the "freedom" promised by a faulty education.

REVISITING EQUALITY

In our earlier discussion of equality, we made several recommendations that might improve the students' sense of belonging. One of those ideas is to encourage student talk, choice, and participation. Now we want to revisit this recommendation. There is a growing pile of evidence that communication across social classes has become less common, and in fact, a social/cultural class gap is growing. Teachers must find a way to discuss this problem.

Almost all high school students today get to read something by George Orwell—usually *Animal Farm* or *Nineteen Eighty-Four*, but they rarely are led to read and discuss *The Road to Wigan Pier*, a classic work of journalism. In it, Orwell presents an open, critical discussion of his own early class snobbishness. He tells us:

> To get rid of class-distinctions you have got to start by understanding how one class appears when seen through the eyes of another. It is useless to say that the middle classes are "snobbish" and leave it at that. (1958/1937, p. 131)

Writing in the mid-20th century, Orwell noted that class prejudice had been reduced, "but undoubtedly the essential feeling is still there," and then he added something that could have appeared in today's American newspapers: "The notion that the working class have been absurdly pampered, hopelessly demoralized by doles, old age pensions, free education, etc., is still widely held; it has merely been a little shaken, perhaps, by the recent recognition that unemployment does exist" (pp. 132–133).

Orwell encouraged us to understand and even poke fun at our own class snobbishness and how those of us in the economic middle class hang on for dear life to our educated patterns of speech. In England, in Orwell's time, an educated worker—even one fallen on hard times financially—would not think of adopting "aitchless" language. And he warns us: "It is quite easy to imagine a middle class crushed down to the worst depths of poverty and still remaining bitterly anti-working class in sentiment; this being, of course, a ready-made Fascist Party" (p. 226). Are there signs of such dangers in today's American society? Because we believe that such class "feeling" remains and is likely to persist, we have recommended that our schools put great emphasis on the universal learning and adoption of standard language. It is almost certainly easier to teach everyone the accepted standards of speech than to try to change the class feelings that accompany differences in speech.

Even if we believe that Orwell's words exaggerate the current class differences in America, we might take the time to share and discuss them with our students. The aim is to strengthen our participatory democracy, to increase the sense and feeling of belonging even as we treasure our differences.

CHAPTER 11

Patriotism

What sort of controversies might arise as we discuss patriotism in our classes? Some people would argue that devotion to one's country is an unqualified good—a virtue that should be embraced by every citizen. A toast proposed by the naval officer Stephen Decatur is often quoted on this devotion: "Our country: In her intercourse with foreign nations may she always be in the right; but our country right or wrong." How much attention should be given to issues of what is right? To what degree does military power determine what is right? Why have some thoughtful citizens advised us to moderate our enthusiasm for military domination? These are all questions to be explored with our students.

Americans often comment approvingly—even brag about—America's "greatness." What does it mean for a country to be great? Is greatness to be measured in terms of power? If our country should slide a bit on the scale of greatness, should our pride and devotion be lessened? Might the pursuit of greatness reduce our commitment to rightness? In this time of global awareness and instant connection, should we consider softening our national patriotism and begin thinking seriously about loyalty and devotion to the Earth? Are global and national patriotism incompatible? These are among the questions to be considered in this chapter.

PRELIMINARY TEACHER TALK

Of all the topics treated in this book, patriotism may be the most difficult to address critically. Public schools, since their inception, have been charged with the duty to instill patriotism in our future citizens. Indeed, right from the days of the founders, the primary aim of education was held to be the production of patriotism through a homogenization of diverse people, a bringing together, that would create and support a national identity. Children were to be immersed and deeply impressed by a heroic past and led to embrace an unshakable commitment to America. As we have noted, a similar attitude has been taken by many citizens toward religion, and attempts to restore God to our schools and public life continue. But the insistence on education for patriotism has never really been effectively challenged. Should it be? Perhaps, we will argue, that depends on how we define patriotism.

Before attempting anything along these lines, teachers should be aware that—in many parts of the country—there is strong opposition to teaching material that criticizes the conduct of the United States on the world scene. There is even resistance to a full discussion of how our country has gone wrong in internal matters concerning race, gender, and class. Teachers must, then, be aware of the opposition they may incur. Resistance to any critical discussion of how America has gone wrong has always been powerful, and textbooks addressing these matters have sometimes been banned (Evans, 2007).

There has always been strong support for what is sometimes called "sentimental patriotism" (Galston, 1991), the sort long promoted in our schools. To encourage an attitude of critical analysis in the study of patriotism is to invite "educated despair." So much has gone wrong, so many violations of our own avowed beliefs have been committed that a critical examination of them might well induce cynicism and alienation. A powerful argument might be made, then, for sticking with a traditional form of sentimental (feeling) patriotism.

It might be useful for teachers who want, nevertheless, to introduce critical reason into political life to read Eamonn Callan's *Creating Citizens* (1997). Callan suggests that critical reason should be supplemented with "emotional generosity" and "historical imagination." (We might be reminded here that this approach could also be used in deciding what to do with the various memorial tributes to those we now recognize as racists.) Looking at our country's moral and social failures, we might make an effort to ask what pushed our people (what they were feeling) to behave as they did and what they might have done instead. As we study faulty political traditions, we should ask, "What is best in this tradition?" and what might encourage that best to become dominant? Callan puts it this way:

> Emotional generosity and the imagination are central to the kind of historical sensibility I want to affirm because without them one cannot adequately answer the question "what is the best of this tradition?" . . . Looking to the past without the easy consolations of sentimentality means confronting a story in which evil may loom larger than good, and the good that is perceptible is not instantiated in anyone or anything in pristine radiance. (Callan, 1997, p. 119)

The danger that we (and Callan) want to avoid is that by encouraging critical thinking on our national history and public life, we may induce apathy, disgust, or alienation. Teachers should be aware of these possibilities. As we noted in Chapter 3 on critical thinking and will re-emphasize in Chapter 12 on moral commitment, we need to educate both minds and hearts. A critical mind should direct our actions, but committed feeling is what motivates us to act.

Let's start our critical examination of patriotism with a topic that has always held an important place in patriotic feelings.

THE MILITARY AND PATRIOTIC FEELING

Military symbolism has long held a prominent place in American patriotism: flags flying, uniformed people marching, bands playing, wreaths laid, statues erected, battles celebrated. Our national anthem, "The Star-Spangled Banner," speaks of rockets' red glare, bombs, and a perilous fight. In contrast, "America the Beautiful," often mentioned as an alternative anthem, speaks of purple mountains, amber waves of grain, and a fruited plain; it pledges us to self-control and asks God to crown our good with brotherhood from sea to shining sea. These are very different symbols of patriotism. Need we choose one, or can we honor both?

This has been—and continues to be—an important question for pacifists, and even those less absolutely against war express concern that the traditional prominence of military ceremonies and symbolism tends to portray a nation's greatness in terms of its military might. Without engaging in indoctrination either for or against military displays, schools should be conscientious in presenting both sides of this important controversial issue.

Virginia Woolf wrote powerfully about possible ways to prevent war. In *Three Guineas*, she asked: "What sort of education will teach the young to hate war?" (1966/1938, p. 22). Addressing the attitude a woman should take in relation to war and the military, she advised:

> She will bind herself to take no share in patriotic demonstrations; to assent to no form of national self-praise; to make no part of any claque or audience that encourages war; to absent herself from military displays, tournaments, tattoos, prize-givings and all such ceremonies as encourage the desire to impose "our" civilization or "our" dominion upon other people.... That the daughters of educated men should give their brothers neither the white feather of cowardice nor the red feather of courage, but no feather at all. (p. 109)

Woolf, appalled by the horror and destruction of World War I, urged women to turn their eyes away from the strutting and bragging of war, to exhibit indifference to the whole world of "manly" arts. Part of her anger, however, was directed at the way women were treated in the "great" societies of England and America. This is how an intelligent woman might explain her indifference to patriotic displays:

> Our country throughout the greater part of its history has treated me as a slave; it has denied me education or any share in its possessions. "Our" country still

ceases to be mine if I marry a foreigner. Therefore if you insist upon fighting to protect me, or "our" country, let it be understood . . . that you are fighting to gratify a sex instinct which I cannot share, to procure benefits which I have not shared and probably will not share. (p. 108)

Woolf wrote this as World War II was just getting started. What might she say today as women are now accepted into the military? Would she see the acceptance of women into combat roles as something to be celebrated or deplored? How might her arguments change? Students should also be made aware of Woolf's strong criticism of economic inequality and the centrality of monetary profits in war-making. Could a similar argument be made today? We know that the United States today spends as much (or more) on its military as the rest of the world combined, and still there are politicians exhorting us to spend even more on it.

In her devastating critique, Woolf told us what *not* to do. To discourage enthusiasm for war, we should turn an indifferent eye on everything associated with the military—just as we might ignore a small boy rampaging about to get attention; ignored, he usually quits and turns to something else. But Woolf told us little about the positive measures we should take. Although she deplored the exclusion of women from high places in education, politics, and business, she saw no way for women to attain inclusion except by joining the "procession of educated men" and embracing the values that bring both personal success and the acceptance of war. We agree with Woolf that the conversation must change—she challenged us directly with the question "how can we enter the professions and yet remain civilized human beings; human beings, that is, who wish to prevent war?" (1966/1938, p. 75).

As a start, without dismissing the cherished stories of national heroes so enjoyed by elementary school children over the years, we might give more time and thought at the high school level to the evils of war and to pacifism. Students should hear, for example, about the work of Jane Addams in developing the International League for Peace and Freedom and her courageous opposition to World War I. Much admired for her charitable and educational efforts at Hull House, Addams nevertheless suffered strong criticism—almost ostracism—for her outspoken opposition to the war. In the high school text on my home library shelf, Addams is mentioned briefly several times for her founding of Hull House and the Women's Peace Party, but none of these efforts are brought together in a substantial discussion of her life and work for which she was awarded the Nobel Peace Prize in 1931. That she suffered greatly from the nasty public attacks of war enthusiasts during and after the war is not even mentioned. "Nothing she has done at Hull House, and none of the earlier celebrations of America's greatest woman and foremost public citizen, shielded her from its attack" (Elshtain, 2002, p. 217). Students might also be interested to learn that Addams opposed the death penalty, linking the attitude that supports it to war virtues. (This is another important controversial issue that might be discussed.)

In the discussion of Addams's opposition to war and Woolf's disgust with the military patriotism that supports it, we see an opening to critique sentimental patriotism and begin a dialogue about the need for critical reason on the topic. But first, perhaps, we have to face the fact that *feeling* is a stronger force than critical reason for bringing people together (Callan, 1997), and we have already argued that it is feeling, not reason, that motivates us to act.

Dorothy Day, another important figure in the history of pacifism, noted the ambiguity in messages received from the Catholic Church. On the one hand, the journal she edited, *The Catholic Worker,* was staunchly pacifist; on the other hand, Catholicism and Christianity in general often supported wars, and the Catholic Church sometimes canonized warriors. Day remained a loyal Catholic, but she lamented, "It is a matter of grief to me that most of those who are Catholic Workers are not pacifists" (Day, 1952, p. 272). This illustrates another facet of the connections between patriotism (or loyalty to an institution) and the warrior tradition. Day was saddened and a bit mystified that readers of *The Catholic Worker*—so patriotic in the feeling sense—did not even realize during the war that the journal favored pacifism. So inflamed were they by patriotic enthusiasm, they did not "see" the journal's pacifism until the war had ended.

Among the stories of pacifism rarely mentioned in our schools is that of Jeannette Rankin, the first woman elected to Congress. In 1917, she voted against the motion to declare war on Germany and, as a result, was not reelected for many years. When she was finally returned to Congress, it was just in time for her to cast the only vote against declaring war on Japan in 1941. That vote ended her congressional career.

Sara Ruddick makes a distinction between pacifism and peacemaking. Peacemakers do not demand an absolute abstention from violence, but like pacifists, they insist on examining and analyzing every incident of violence. In her analysis of maternal thinking, she writes:

> I believe that everyday maternal thinking contrasts as a whole with military thinking. Just-war theories control our perceptions of war, turning our attention from bodies and their fate to abstract causes and rules for achieving them. . . . The analytic fictions of just-war theory require a closure of moral issues final enough to justify killing and "enemies" abstract enough to be killable. . . . Maternal attentive love, restrained and clear-sighted, is ill adapted to intrusive, let alone murderous, judgments of others' lives. . . . If they have made training a work of conscience and proper trust a virtue . . . then mothers have been preparing themselves for patient and conscientious nonviolence, not for the obedience and expressive trust in authority on which military adventures thrive. (1989, p. 130)

Here we can see feeling and critical reason conflict on both sides. Ruddick counterposes the critical reasoning of just-war theorists to the maternal love that condemns warfare. But feeling is also strong in supporting war and violence. Our job as educators is to argue effectively for both humanistic feeling and morally justified critical thinking.

We commented earlier in our discussion of authority and freedom that students should learn how to question authority rationally and nonviolently, and we noted too that obedience to unquestioned authority is sometimes a result of fear of freedom. Attachment to military life is sometimes a product of this fear. There are good reasons, then, for questioning the centrality of militarism in our approach to patriotism. Where should we look?

WHO ARE WE?

Howard Zinn has warned us against an authoritarian approach to patriotism. "Patriotism," he said, "means being true and loyal—not to the government, but to the principles which underlie democracy" (quoted in Westheimer, 2007, p. 176). It is reasonable, then, to think of patriotism as dedication to the good that our nation stands for. This means not only affirming the good already accomplished but also keeping a watchful eye on places where we have gone wrong or might go wrong. A patriot, so defined, does not defend his/her country "right or wrong" but, rather, analyzes, admits, and criticizes its wrongs with the avowed purpose of making things right.

As we think about how we should approach such issues in our schools, we might return to our earlier discussion of equality. We acknowledge that Jefferson and the founders did not believe that all people are created equal in all things. They meant, rather, that all people should have an opportunity to develop and benefit from their individual talents and that all should be treated equally before the law. Recognizing the commitment to equal treatment before the law, students should certainly be encouraged to look at the law historically and consider why Black Lives Matter has become so active. Has it been necessary to change some of our laws? Are Blacks now treated equally before the law? They should be made aware that the United States has one of the highest incarceration rates in the world. Real patriotism, patriotism that celebrates what our nation stands for—liberty, freedom, and the pursuit of happiness for all—should induce active participation in rational, democratic measures to change the conditions that deprive some of our citizens of these promised benefits.

Teachers, especially, should think deeply about the connection between equality and patriotism. Does patriotism require us to insist on equal education for all students? Well, it might depend on what we mean by "equal" in this matter. If we think that "equal" means "same," we would be making a mistake identified by Jane Addams, one of which we should be especially wary in this current age of standardization. "Standardization is a holdover from militarism, Addams asserts" (Elshtain, 2002, p. 203). She was deeply concerned that our attitude toward immigrants and those of different religions was unpatriotic in the deepest sense—that is, that it denied the value of unique talents and differences:

> There is every reason to hope that a cosmopolitan bond will be forged that will substitute for the frayed old bonds of militaristic atavisms. Her ideal of the modern city is one in which solidarity does not depend upon sanctions or a "consciousness of homogeneity but upon a respect for variation, not upon inherited memory but upon trained imagination." (Elshtain, 2002, p. 203)

As we are engaged in writing this book, our country is again experiencing some of the problems Addams warned against. Because we must defend ourselves from attacks by radical Islamic terrorists, some of us endorse measures to keep Muslims from entering our country. Because some want to identify the United States as a Christian nation, there are calls to "return God" to our classrooms and public life. In Chapter 4, we reminded readers that the United States was not founded on Christian principles, that the founders made no mention of God or the Christian religion. Over time, "God" was added to our coins and to the Pledge of Allegiance. Periodically, attempts have been made to "put God back" into our national documents and practices. So far, we have avoided transforming our national documents. We are a "Christian nation" only in the sense that a majority of our population—believers and unbelievers alike—identify with that label.

High school students should be made aware that some efforts to connect state and church have indeed been serious. In 1954, the Senate was urged to consider an amendment to the Constitution declaring, "This Nation devoutly recognizes the authority and law of Jesus Christ, Saviour and Ruler of nations through whom are bestowed the blessings of Almighty God" (quoted in Kruse, 2015, p. 95). The suggested amendment was rejected, but "ceremonial deism" has been quietly accepted at public events. It was and still is entirely acceptable to end governmental speeches with "God bless America" or to invoke God at the start of public meetings. Reviewing these events, Kevin Kruse remarks, "In the end, the 'unwritten constitution' was written into American law and life after all" (2015, p. 105).

But the long-accepted references to God in public life are generally acknowledged as ornamental. We are *not* officially defined as a Christian nation. We use "God" ceremonially, but we do not make such use of "Jesus Christ." This is not to say that the principles for which we stand as a nation are incompatible with Christianity but rather, that it is among our avowed principles to maintain the separation of church and state. *All* religions are protected by our Constitution.

How, then, do we identify ourselves as a nation? Who are we? Gordon Wood points out that many relatively new European states, unlike the United States, "are undergirded by people who had a preexisting sense of their own distinctiveness" (2011, p. 321). But the American case is different:

> In an important sense, we have never been a nation in any traditional meaning of the term. It is the state, the Constitution, the principles of liberty, equality, and free government that make us think of ourselves as a single people. To be an American is not to be someone, but to believe in something. (p. 322)

To believe in a democratic state and to exercise the intellectual and social virtues required to maintain and improve it are the necessary qualities of being American. It is worth discussing with students that the new nation was defined as a *republic*, a form of political organization run by a select group of its people. As noted earlier, a republic by definition calls on its most virtuous citizens to serve as leaders. When the republic becomes a *democracy*, all of its citizens have a role to play and must develop the required virtues. As students think about this, they will realize how important it is that all citizens are appropriately prepared for life in a participatory democracy.

Americans are not, then, defined by race, tribe, religion, or the nationality of our predecessors, and attempts to change the definition—for example, by defining America as a Christian state—might very well undermine the beliefs that made it possible for the founders to invent a nation. Similarly, a loss of the necessary virtues in our citizens might destroy the nation they constructed. Wood reminds us that the Roman republic collapsed because the character of its citizens became corrupted: "Rome fell not because of the invasions of the barbarians from without, but because of decay from within" (2011, p. 325).

The sort of thinking that connects American identity to republican virtuosity is sometimes mentioned as a facet of "American exceptionalism." As a commitment to just government that respects the right of citizens to life, liberty, and the pursuit of happiness, it encourages both devotion to democracy and patriotic pride. At its best, it has made the United States a leader in the political/democratic world, an example for other nation-creators. Indeed, America took responsibility for such leadership throughout the 19th century and usually was among the first nations to recognize new revolutionary governments.

But there is a downside to this acceptance of uninvited political leadership. As the economic and military power of America has grown, fear has also grown that it somehow exercises its power indiscriminately. Should all revolutions be encouraged? As Wood and other historians have pointed out, America's rejection of the Russian Revolution in 1917 created a whole new national attitude toward revolutions. Then, because the United States was so deeply opposed to communism and communist-inspired revolutions, it found itself supporting existing regimes in places such as Vietnam and highly questionable forces such as the Taliban in Afghanistan simply because they resisted communism. We have become keenly aware that not all revolutions are guided by the beliefs we hold for America.

Americans live with something like a belief paradox, and students should be encouraged to think critically about this. On the one hand, we are defined as a nation by our belief in a democratic way of life. On the other hand, some hold religious commitments that they believe underlie our defining beliefs. Notice the three uses of *belief* here. If religious belief really does provide the foundation for our defining national beliefs, then we should acknowledge this in our official documents. That is the argument presented periodically by Christian evangelists. In response, it has been noted that the founders denied the priority of religious beliefs. Their purpose was to create a nation in which individuals would be free to embrace their own religious beliefs without interference from any part of government. Can students find any cases where government was justified in limiting religious belief or the activities based on that belief?

Wood reminds us of another facet of the belief-paradox. We should see what students think of it: "We seem to be very much an all-or-nothing people. It is very difficult for us to maintain a *realpolitik* attitude toward the world" (2011, p. 334). Internally, we endorse the democratic notion that all citizens should be heard—that decisions should be products of deliberative participation. Externally, in the wider world, we seem to cling to the idea of America as the city on the hill, the light of the world, and our political conversation is loaded with references to America's greatness. But how should "greatness" be defined? That is our next topic.

MUST AMERICA BE GREAT?

We should acknowledge at the outset that pride in America's greatness has been a major factor in sentimental patriotism. Will our citizens exhibit the same devotion to their country if they learn of its many mistakes and betrayals of its own principles, or will they suffer the educated despair so well described by Callan (1997)? If, in addition to the cynicism induced by a heavy dose of critical reasoning, they come to believe that America is no longer great, how might their behavior as citizens change? In an election year as this book is underway, several presidential candidates have aroused voter enthusiasm by vowing to "make America great again." What are they promising to achieve?

There was conflict over the idea of national greatness even among the founders. Alexander Hamilton, for example, sought to reproduce a form of European monarchical greatness in the new country—"something noble and magnificent" (quoted in Wood, 2011, p. 257), and this greatness involved a strong military. Although the Federalist vision of greatness and rule by the most virtuous and distinguished was dimmed by the growing emphasis on participatory democracy, the new nation did not reject Hamilton's vision of military might. Military and economic might were to characterize the new American republic as they did the earlier European empires, even though Hamilton's basic political philosophy was largely rejected.

Among the challenges faced by teachers is that of balance. In discussions of U.S. world domination, teachers should discuss the outstanding contributions made by Americans to worldwide communication, transportation, food production, household efficiency, and industrial growth. These accomplishments are rightly seen as sources of pride. Students should be made aware that the century between 1870 and 1970 was a special epoch for the United States, "the nation which has carved out the technological frontier for all developed nations since the Civil War" (Gordon, 2016, p. 3). In its technological leadership, the United States was indeed great.

But students should also be made aware that successful nations—successful individuals—may overemphasize their success and use their position to reduce the rightful power of those they purport to help. Too often, America has tried to force the "blessings" of its way of life on others struggling to find their way. It is one thing to show a way by example, quite another to coerce others into accepting that way. Consider a statement made by Secretary of State Madeleine Albright during the Gulf War: "If we have to use force, it is because we are America; we are the indispensable nation. We should stand tall and we see further than other countries into the future" (quoted in Gardner, 2008, p. 111). Should we stand proudly with Albright on this stance or be embarrassed by such a claim?

Several of today's critics argue for a solid rejection of the emphasis on military and economic greatness and a return to our democratic principles, to a deeper form of greatness. Writing in 2012 of the dangers inherent in our continuing insistence on military strength, Oliver Stone and Peter Kuznick urge:

> What had become apparent was that the real hope for changing the United States—for helping it regain its democratic, egalitarian, and revolutionary soul—lay in U.S. citizens joining with the rebellious masses everywhere to deploy the lessons of history, their history, the people's history, which is no longer untold, and demand creation of a world that represents the interest of the overwhelming majority, not that of the wealthiest, greediest, and most powerful. (2012, p. 615)

What might students have to say on both sides of this big issue? The development of critical reasoning on matters of our nation's place—its greatness—in the world is supplemented by the need for such reasoning on internal citizenship. It is not enough to obey existing law and contribute to charities and community institutions; the good citizens we seek to develop must "question and change established systems and structures when they reproduce patterns of injustice over time" (Westheimer, 2015, p. 39). There is, thus, eloquent support for a form of patriotism defined by critical thinking. Here, too, we must counsel balance. Although we are critical of world history that is largely described in terms of great empires and the exploits of the powerful, we should acknowledge that there are wonderful stories to be told in that history. Students should keep in mind Callan's question—What is best in this tradition?—as they study the rise and fall of great empires. They should also be reminded that critical thinking must be guided by moral commitment if it is to serve the best interests of humanity.

Before leaving this topic, we should say a bit about the linguistic value of exploring the word *great*. The dictionary in our library lists 20 meanings and 9 synonyms of the word, more than enough to sustain a lively conversation. When a popular public figure—perhaps one running for office—promises to "make America great again," thoughtful citizens should press him or her to state clearly what is meant by *great*. As we look at the multiplicity of meanings of the word and the variety of contexts in which it is used, teachers might ask students to select a country from the United Nation's list of almost 200 members—one not among the 10 or 20 most prominent—and study it for signs of greatness. If you lived there, if that were *your* country, how would you describe its greatness? Of what would you be proud? What is the best of its traditions?

GLOBAL PATRIOTISM

An appreciation of the greatness of other nations—what makes their people proud—should be supplemented with an exploration of what might be described as global patriotism. The notion of embracing the whole world as a locus of civic participation has been called *cosmopolitanism*, and it has a long history that has never appealed to people in the way that national patriotism has. Another sense of *cosmopolitan* as belonging to the whole world is often used to describe people whose background and sophistication enable them to feel at home anywhere in the world. But when this term is used to suggest that loyalty is shifted from one's nation to the whole world, critics may construe the shift as traitorous. Indeed, Thomas Paine was widely criticized when he dared to proclaim, "My country is the world; to do good is my religion" (see True, 1995, p. 14). Benjamin Barber (1996) has pointed out that cosmopolitanism has never captivated us emotionally as has national patriotism. Perhaps that is because it does not offer the flags, songs, uniforms, and heroic celebrations that are present at the national level.

But we do now have a special interest that should win our devotion, and this might be called *ecological patriotism*. We have begun to realize that we must actively protect "Earth our home" if life itself is to be preserved. Even here, however, there is controversy. There are those, for example, who refuse to accept the near consensus of scientific opinion that global warming is largely due to human activity that should be controlled. The issue should certainly be discussed in our schools, and students should be led to consider who might suffer economically if the use of carbon fuels is significantly reduced. Are there ways to compensate for this loss?

One way to approach controversies over national vs. global loyalty is to encourage a change in emphasis from devotion to our country as a nation to the physical (natural) place in which it is located. We mentioned earlier a possible change in our choice of national anthem. "America the Beautiful" would draw our attention to our natural environment and how we should protect it. We might also promote deeper, wider study of ways in which to protect the Earth; the welfare of every country depends on the health of our common home. Notice that such a move does not detract from our devotion to our country's principles—who we are—as contrasted with our power to dominate the world.

We also discussed earlier the justified pride American citizens might have in the incredible technical and economic growth achieved in the century 1870–1970 (Gordon, 2016). This enormous growth included dramatic changes in food cleanliness and sanitation. Just as there is controversy today over the role of human activity as a cause of global warming, there was controversy in the late 1800s over the contribution of filthy conditions as a cause of diarrheal diseases, typhoid, tuberculosis, and diphtheria. The cleanup promoted by, among others, the New York's Ladies Protective Health Association (LPHA) did much to reduce the occurrence of these diseases. Could intelligent, persistent activism today help to reduce global warming? In advocating such action, Carl Safina reminds us:

> The right and necessary things are not always decided solely on economic considerations. If ever energy came cheap, slavery was it. Slavery created jobs for slave catchers, a shipping industry built on the slave trade, and a plantation economy that could remain profitable only with slave labor. . . . It was the lynch-pin of the southern plantation economy. But no normal person today would argue that slavery is good for the economy. We've made at least that much progress. (Safina, 2011, p. 295)

Like Gordon, Safina acknowledges the dramatic technological leadership of the United States while simultaneously noting that we lag in important ways:

> The United States ranks behind more than forty countries in its citizens' life expectancy, behind twenty-eight in infant survival. The United States ranks 33rd

out of 34 Western countries in the proportion of its populace who accept evolution (only Turkey ranks lower). (p. 309)

In the final chapter of this book, we will discuss the essential need for moral commitment to guide critical thinking. It might well be the case that, after a careful study of today's climate crisis, students will agree that human activity will have to be moderated and controlled—even if some groups will experience economic losses as a result. Another prominent scientist, Edward O. Wilson, urges religion and science to work together on the crucial task of saving the Earth. Asking himself why he recommends this, he answers:

> Because religion and science are the two most powerful forces in the world today, including especially the United States. If religion and science could be united on the common ground of biological conservation, the problem would soon be solved. If there is any moral precept shared by people of all beliefs, it is that we owe ourselves and future generations a beautiful, rich, and healthful environment. (2006, p. 5)

Looking back on the discussion of religion in Chapter 4, we might also note that Wilson's plea is a lovely example of working across major differences in belief. His book is written as a letter from Wilson himself—a secular humanist—to a southern Baptist pastor. He notes their great differences in belief, but says, "I am confident that if we met and spoke privately of our deepest beliefs, it would be in a spirit of mutual respect and good will" (2006, p. 1). This, of course, is exactly what we are trying to cultivate in educating critical thinking.

CHAPTER 12

Moral Commitment

Critical thinking—an educational aim now promoted almost universally—is not in itself a moral virtue. It is clearly an intellectual virtue but, if it is to contribute to the main educational aim embraced here—to produce "better" people—it must also advance moral ends. Today, most of us are concerned that many well-educated citizens apply critical thinking skills to their own economic and political advantage with little serious consideration about the moral implications of their carefully developed analyses.

In this book, we encourage educators to address controversial issues that demand critical thinking. We have rarely attempted to resolve these issues. Instead, we have suggested ways in which teachers might encourage their students to discuss the issues and to use critical thinking cooperatively to analyze them. We endorse critical thinking for the purpose of understanding, not merely for the purpose of winning arguments. This final chapter will serve in part as a review, but more important, it will underscore the necessity of using moral commitment as a guide to the best critical thinking and then using the outcome of critical analysis to inform moral commitment and action.

Consider our first big topic, the controversial questions involved in teaching children how to relate to authority. Teachers today should apply critical thinking to current school practices that recommend strict rules and absolute obedience. Are such practices likely to produce the citizens needed in a participatory democracy? We have suggested that children be encouraged to make reasonable choices at every stage of development; along with their choices, they should be invited to ask questions about the choices others make. Conversation is imperative in a participatory democracy, and it should be an essential part of every school day. A participatory democracy is not simply an arrangement of governing procedures; it is a mode of associated living that requires both critical thinking and moral commitment to its continual analysis and improvement.

We have spent some time on civil disobedience because the concept is so often misunderstood, and its understanding is fundamental in maintaining the legitimacy of government. Students should learn that an act of civil disobedience is a critically analyzed act that, in publicly disobeying a law, expresses devotion to the larger Law that should disavow the one rejected.

The moral objective of civil disobedience is to restore practice to the true intent of the Law accepted by our society. People who engage in civil disobedience accept the punishment meted out for their disobedience; they want to change what they regard as an unfair law—not simply to defy it in their own interests.

We ask why it is that we teach almost nothing about parenting in our schools. This remains a controversial question today. Certainly, parenting is one of the most important tasks undertaken by adult human beings, so why do we not teach something on it? Social history informs us that "parenting" has been divided for centuries into the roles of men as providers and heads of households and women as caregivers and housekeepers. Education was designed to prepare men for the public world, and women were to learn the work of child care and housekeeping from other women, mostly at home. Further, public education was not supposed to tell people what to do in their private lives. Education that dares to address parenting and home-making might endanger the traditional control of fathers and even pose challenges to some features of religious dogma. It has been widely supposed that schooling prepares people for public life and should not interfere in the private lives of citizens. Thus, the teaching of parenting has been and remains a controversial issue.

In our discussions of parenting, we explore several broad topics: the meaning and need for order, the importance of conversation (and what this means), and the centrality of sharing and learning to make wise choices. The school's role in all of these vital areas is not to prescribe exactly what should be done by parents but rather to invite exploration and to help students acquire knowledge *about* parenting so that they will be encouraged to apply critical thinking to their roles as future parents. We recommend that the discussion be extended to think about the local community and Earth itself as *homes*, places of treasured nurturance, places to be preserved with loving care.

The teaching of religion (Chapter 4) in our public schools has always presented controversial issues. For most of our history, Protestant Christianity controlled the accepted rituals, but gradually participation in these rituals became optional. Public schools today do not teach or preach any one religion, and many schools offer courses in world religions and religious history.

It is odd, then, in this age of newfound religious liberality that so little attention is given to atheism, agnosticism, and deism. Probably many high school students would not even be able to define the terms. Further, it is almost certain that no avowed atheist—however well educated, morally upright, and politically astute—could be elected (or even nominated) for president of the United States. Should we give some attention in our studies of religion to atheism as well as to recognized world religions? Why should this suggestion be controversial? The root of controversy over the teaching of atheism and deism is perhaps intertwined with the controversies about teaching parenting. Many people believe that public schools should not interfere in the private lives of citizens; these people believe that matters of religion, like those of parenting, are matters that should be left to individuals and families. But, if we believe that the primary aim of education is to produce better people, then we must open young minds to the exciting ideas that have been developed in every significant facet of life.

Students should certainly become aware that our nation—according to its founders—was *not* based on Christianity, and many of the founders and early presidents were deists, possibly even atheists. This does not mean that the founding documents of our nation are incompatible with Christianity but simply that they are not specifically built on Christian axioms or principles. Indeed, it could be argued that the religious freedom guaranteed in our written documents is founded on this independence. In addition, in their exploration of our religious history, students should be reminded that Christianity has not always promoted the moral good. It was implicated in both the defense of slavery and the denial of women's political rights.

In addition to several basic lessons in vocabulary and history, we suggest that students should learn about the moral, social, and intellectual commitments shared by many thoughtful believers and nonbelievers. It is a fascinating area of study and one that should help to bring us together as citizens. Recognition that many believers as well as unbelievers accept evolution should also be discussed. Although religious believers and atheists differ fundamentally on the existence of God, they hold many moral commitments in common.

Chapter 4 also makes some introductory comments on freedom, a topic taken up again in Chapter 10, Equality, Justice, and Freedom. Commitment, religious or moral, may set us free from a whole array of temptations. Such commitment allows us to exercise our freedom more wisely over the set of options we have found morally justifiable.

Finally, we should point out that, in discussion of the study of religion in schools, we put great emphasis on interdisciplinary work. Every school subject can and should contribute to the conversation on religion. Differences in how we view eternity, the origins of humanity, the meaning of life, and the nature of morality, of beauty, and of freedom appear in all of the disciplines.

Three main controversies are addressed in our discussions on race in Chapter 5. The first is how far we should go in recounting and analyzing our abominable treatment of Black Americans. Few would question the need to face this awful history honestly; we must. But we also have to prepare for and prevent, if we can, the despair and cynicism that might arise as students become aware of the crimes committed by their own country. It is helpful here to look at religion's opposing roles in supporting and condemning slavery, to acknowledge the positive social and political contributions of prominent slaveholders and, nevertheless, to condemn their participation in maintaining slavery. This approach pushes us to consider a major issue that is controversial today. What should be done with the statues and other memorials commemorating people whose participation in slavery we abhor? Students should be encouraged to discuss this in some depth.

A second vital issue is how to increase diversity and inclusion without losing the richness inherent in group solidarity and pride. Surely, we strive for what we call "unity in diversity." But must Black children be in the presence of Whites in order to learn? Are they automatically left behind if they are not part of integrated schooling? Here we encounter a genuine, deeply touching dilemma. When we study the history of historically Black colleges and universities (HBCUs), we see both intellectual vitality and economic grit. There is, to be sure, financial deprivation within and lack of appropriate respect in the larger world, but there are also wonderful success stories and a tradition of intellectual and moral depth that we should be sad to lose. Oprah Winfrey, Martin Luther King, Jr., Thurgood Marshall, Toni Morrison, Marian Wright Edelman, W. E. B. DuBois, Alice Walker. and George Washington Carver were all educated by and/or taught at an HBCU. What might students suggest as to ways to approach this issue?

Finally in our discussion of race, we have looked at current problems in public education. Where should we address race issues? Should we design courses to treat race specifically? What should be our position on Black English? On this, even the authors of this book disagree to some extent. We agree that our society as a whole should show greater respect for Black English, just as we respect other native languages. But one of us puts greater emphasis on this demand for change in the larger society, while the other recommends that we ensure that all of our students acquire proficiency in standard English. Our respect rings somewhat hollow if we fail to equip all of our students with the linguistic facility demanded in today's society. Can we work successfully on both sides of this issue?

In Chapter 6, we discuss three large areas of concern on the subject of gender. On the first—equal treatment of women in the public world—there is not much disagreement about the goal and principles justifying it. The major difficulty here is how to do it and what stands in the way. On this effort and why progress has been slow, it is useful to study the history of women's rights, and we have suggested some ways to approach this.

On the second, how women's thought and experience might be employed to change the thinking of men and public life, we encounter real controversy even within feminist circles. There are those who oppose efforts to even try to do this because they want to achieve equality for women in the contemporary public world dominated by men. And they fear that any attempt to apply what might be called women's traditional thought will get in the way of this important goal. This fear is similar to the one expressed by Elizabeth Cady Stanton's colleagues when—in the middle of their campaign to secure women's voting rights—Stanton argued for substantial changes in the Bible and religious thought. Her colleagues feared that her comments on the Bible would distract attention from the main goal—women's voting rights. Still, if there are powerful ideas in women's traditional thinking—ideas that might contribute strongly to peace studies and both public and family life—we should at least consider them. Drawing on the work of Virginia Woolf, we return to this important topic in Chapter 11 on Patriotism.

The third area of interest is the gender confusion suffered by many teenagers today. They are surrounded by comments and stories in the news and social media about the lives and experiences of lesbians, gays, bisexuals, and queer and transgender people, and teachers are not always well prepared to address the questions they have. Indeed, they may need help simply in formulating their questions and finding acceptable ways in which to ask them. We want to encourage free conversation, but we also want to protect students against making disclosures they may later regret.

Chapter 8 discusses capitalism and socialism. Not long ago, it was almost impossible to give socialism a fair hearing in our schools. During and after the Cold War, socialism was often equated with communism and widely condemned. Now, due in part to the political popularity of Senator Bernie Sanders, "socialism" has gained a new level of appreciation. At the level of information, students should learn that there was once an active socialist party in the United States, but it faded away during World War II and became anathema in the following Cold War. The first great controversy to debate, then, is the history of socialism in the United States and why we have ignored or even condemned it when so many other advanced countries have embraced it.

A substantial part of Chapter 8 considers how our concentration on capitalism has affected our schools. Why, for example, do we put such emphasis on equality while refusing to provide high-quality programs for children whose interests are largely nonacademic? Must equality be defined as sameness? We return to this important question in Chapter 10. Using capitalist premises, our public education system has concentrated on providing the "best" (same) education for all students—one that would prepare them for the competitive struggle they will face in the economic world. They are advised that hard work will pay off. Using a socialist perspective, greater emphasis would be placed on cooperation, choice, and satisfaction in every facet of life—not only economic or business life.

At the end of the chapter, we suggest that schools should not take an all-or-nothing approach on capitalism and socialism. It should be possible to analyze, evaluate, and retain the best elements of both. We should wish to retain the vitality, inventiveness, industry, and energy that have characterized capitalism and still promote the ideas of respect for a broad range of human talents, participation of individuals in the governance of groups to which they belong, the democratic interplay of those groups, and the welfare of all individuals. Whether and how this can be done is an important topic that requires extended critical thinking.

Several important controversies are addressed in Chapter 9 on Money, Class, and Poverty. Why do we not teach more practical math in our high schools—the mathematics of money, wealth, and financial management? Does everyone need algebra? We should also discuss the meaning of class in America and the growing class divide. It is argued that we should consider renewing respectable forms of genuine vocational education from which students can choose proudly. Students should be encouraged to consider a vocation in which they will find both personal satisfaction and a satisfactory level of compensation.

In Chapter 10, Equality, Justice, and Freedom, we return to topics initiated in earlier chapters. It may seem odd that the most controversial issues emerge from the topic of equality. As a capitalist society, Americans have put great emphasis on equal opportunity. From this view, everyone should have an opportunity to succeed economically. This has led us, in education, to put more and more emphasis on college preparation for all students. We, too, believe that all children should have access to an excellent education. But must that commitment demand that all children should have the *same* education, one concentrated on college preparation? Does equality imply sameness? Perhaps a well-developed sense of justice would direct us to design a variety of educational programs suited to different talents and interests.

If we were to move in this direction, it would be wise to provide opportunities for students from all of the programs to be brought together for conversation and discussion of pressing social issues. Citizens of a participatory democracy must be able to talk with each other—not *at* each other—and such conversation necessitates listening. Many thoughtful social scientists and political critics have commented on the increasing communication gap across social classes in the United States, and this is one matter on which we have made specific recommendations: a 4-year mixed student seminar on social and political issues and a substantial increase in interdisciplinary work. The controversial issue of what equality means in education should be one of central concern.

In addition to its application to the concept of equality, justice should be discussed both from a historical perspective and with respect to current issues. In particular, students should be encouraged to participate in the making of school rules and their enforcement. The active, critical participation of students in this work might well induce educators to get rid of zero-tolerance rules, excessive suspensions, and other top-down methods of maintaining order.

Freedom was an important topic in Chapter 4 on religion. Here we look carefully at the possibility—one raised by Paulo Freire—that the oppressed members of a society may actually suffer a "fear of freedom." This fear seems to arise when well-meaning "liberators" urge the poor and downtrodden to stand up for their rights and claim what is justly theirs. Feeling ill equipped for this task, people hold back in fear. But perhaps the most powerful element in this production of fear is the dominance of the liberators. Too often, with the best intentions, the liberators decide what should be done to improve the conditions of the oppressed; they do not work collaboratively with the people they are trying to help. This is a problem we have noted in several parts of the book. If our moral commitment is to help people, we first need to recognize their personhood and work *with* them.

Chapter 11 presents several issues on patriotism and also gives us an opportunity to extend some of those addressed earlier. The first question is whether to express complete loyalty to our country—"my country right or wrong"—or to cultivate an abiding loyalty to what our country stands for at its best. Obviously, if we choose the latter, we commit ourselves to continuous critical thinking on what constitutes that "best" and how to maintain it. Traditionally, patriotism has too often been expressed through the symbolism of flags, military displays, battle reenactments, and martial music. As a counterbalance, we suggest drawing on the powerful work of Virginia Woolf advising women to separate themselves entirely from this form of patriotism. Some students may react to this rejection of military display with considerable anger. Now that women are allowed to enter the military, should all of us feel better about this orientation in patriotism? Another danger in suggesting that our patriotism might be redirected toward what our nation stands for is the risk that students, newly aware of the wrongs committed by their country, will suffer "educated despair." Teachers will have to approach this subject with great sensitivity.

Students might be less distressed by a suggestion that we think more about our country as a *place* to be preserved and treasured. We might, for example, contrast "The Star-Spangled Banner," which represents the martial approach, with "America the Beautiful" and its emphasis on the physical beauty and cherished brotherhood of our land. More than a few of our citizens have suggested that "America the Beautiful" would make a more suitable national anthem. How do students react to this possibility?

In the same line of thought, if we give our attention to America as our home, we can extend that thought to "Earth-our-home" and encourage the ecological sensitivity required to preserve homes and homelands all over the world. The current urgency for ecological sensitivity may help to achieve balance in our discussion of patriotism. We need not give up memorial celebrations, martial bands, and flag salutes, but we can balance them with thoughtful emphasis on our great ideals and a renewed commitment to the natural places in which we live.

The great purpose sought in this book is to produce proficient critical thinkers who will use that skill toward morally justified ends. Our emphasis has been on the use of critical thinking to *understand*, not simply to win arguments. Philosophers from Cicero to John Stuart Mill have counseled us on the importance of understanding both our own and opposing positions. Mill put the point well:

> What Cicero practiced as the means of forensic success, requires to be imitated by all who study any subject in order to arrive at the truth. He who knows only

his own side of the case, knows little of that. . . . Nor is it enough that he should hear the arguments of adversaries from his own teachers, presented as they state them. . . . He must be able to hear them from persons who actually believe them. (1993/1859, p. 43)

Mill then goes on to emphasize the need for honesty, respect, and the rejection of "intemperate discussion"—sarcasm, invective, attacks on personality, bigotry, and intolerance. He ends his chapter on thought and discussion thus:

This is the real morality of public discussion: and if often violated, I am happy to think that there are many controversialists who to a great extent observe it, and a still greater number who conscientiously strive toward it. (p. 63)

We have another aim, however, for conversation in pursuit of truth. We hope to bring people together—to help them understand each other in the fullness of their humanity. That there is a "real morality" involved in public discussion cannot be denied. That is why we started this book with a review of the sources of moral life and conduct. The first source mentioned, reason, has long been a central concern of education. Most of the educational efforts to teach critical thinking are linked to the effective use of reason, and we certainly endorse this effort. It has, until quite recently, been stressed as a major aim in the teaching of geometry. The work of Euclid, for example, was promoted as an accessible introduction to abstract reasoning and deductive thinking. That emphasis has been tempered in the current teaching of geometry, but the concern with reasoning as critical thinking has become universal across the disciplines. Reason is clearly essential in moral thought and conduct.

Reason, however, is not the only essential factor in moral life. As Hume and other philosophers have argued, it *guides* our action, but it does not *motivate* us to act. *Feeling* motivates us by providing the "I must" that pushes us to act; reason then takes over to direct, to optimize, our action. Recognizing this, schools should give more attention to the education of hearts and to the development of empathy, compassion, and fellow-feeling.

Attention should also be given to the development of character. Although we do not recommend a program of character education as a separate course in moral education, we would not ignore it. As we suggested in several chapters, a strong character can provide us with welcome freedom from questionable temptations and encourage us to pursue worthwhile ends.

If we are serious about developing reason, feeling, and character, we should broaden the curriculum by including more inspiring fiction, biographies, relevant poetry and art, honest accounts of lapses in our country's social and moral life, and inclusive, critical discussion of social, political, and moral life. This sort of thinking and planning should infuse our work in all of the disciplines, and careful consideration should be given to the connections among them.

References

Adler, M. J. (1982). *The paideia proposal*. New York: Macmillan.

Allman, T. D. (2013). *Finding Florida: The true history of the sunshine state*. New York: Atlantic Monthly Press.

American high school students are reading books at 5th-grade-appropriate levels: Report. (2012, March 22). *Huffington Post*. Retrieved from www.huffington-post.com/2012/03/22/top-reading_n_1373680. html

Anderson, E. (2007). Fair opportunity in education: A democratic equality perspective. *Ethics, 117*(4), 595–622.

Anderson, E. (2015). Moral bias and corrective practices: A pragmatist perspective. *Proceedings & Addresses of the American Philosophical Association*, 21–47.

Asafu-Adjaye, J., Blomquist, L., Brand, S., Brook, B., Defries, R., Ellis, E., . . . Teague, P. (2015). *An ecomodernist manifesto*. Retrieved from www.ecomodernism.org

Bachelard, G. (1964). *The poetics of space* (Maria Jolas, Trans.). New York: Orion Press.

Baptist, E. E. (2014). *The half has never been told*. New York: Basic Books.

Barber, B. (1996). Constitutional faith. In J. Cohen (Ed.), *For love of country? Martha C. Nussbaum* (pp. 30–37). Boston, MA: Beacon Press.

Bayh, B. (1972). Comments on Title IX from the Senate floor. 118 Congressional Record, 5804–5808.

Beardmore, M. (2013). Is it safe to worship athletes? *Psychology Today: Time Out!* Retrieved from www.psychologytoday.com/blog/time-out/201310/is-it-safe-worship-athletes

Bell, E. T. (1965/1937). *Men of mathematics*. New York: Simon & Schuster.

Berlin, I. (1969). Two concepts of liberty. *Four essays on liberty* (pp. 118–172). Oxford, England: Oxford University Press.

Blum, L. (2012). *High schools, race, and America's future*. Cambridge, MA: Harvard Education Press.

Bok, S. (1979). *Lying: Moral choice in public and private life*. New York: Vintage.

Braybrooke, D. (1987). *Meeting needs*. Princeton, NJ: Princeton University Press.

Brooks, D. (2016). Inside student radicalism. *New York Times*. Retrieved from mobile.nytimes.com/2016/05/27/opinion/inside-student-radicalism.html

Brown, P. M., Corrigan, M. W., & Higgins-D'Alessandro, A. (Eds.). (2012). *Handbook of prosocial education*, 2 vols. Lanham, MD: Rowman & Littlefield.

Buchholz, T. (1989/2007). *New ideas from dead economists: An introduction to modern economic thought*. New York: Plume.

Buck, P. S. (1936). *The exile*. New York: Triangle.

Burch, K. T. (2012). *Democratic transformations: Eight conflicts in the negotiation of American identity*. New York: Continuum.

Caldwell, E. (1932/1995). *Tobacco road*. Athens: The University of Georgia Press.

Callan, E. (1997). *Creating citizens: Political education and liberal democracy*. Oxford, England: Oxford University Press.

Carlson, S. (2016, May 6). Should everyone go to college? *The Chronicle of Higher Education*, A22–A25.

Cheng, E. (2015). *How to bake π*. New York: Basic.

Coates, T-N. (2014, June). The case for reparations. *Atlantic*, 54–71.

Coates, T-N. (2015, October). The black family in the age of mass incarceration. *The Atlantic Monthly*.

Cobb, J. (2016, March 14). The matter of black lives. *New Yorker*, 34–40.

Cohen, P. (2014). Fueled by recession, U.S. wealth gap is widest in decades, study finds. *New York Times*. Retrieved from www.nytimes.com/2014/12/18/business/economy/us-wealth-gap-widest-in-at-least-30-years-pew-study-says. html?_r=0

Comer, J. P. (2004). *Leave no child behind*. New Haven, CT: Yale University Press.

Common application to change gender-identity options. (2016, May 6). *The Chronicle of Higher Education*, A20.

Conway Morris, S. (2003). *Life's solution: Inevitable humans in a lonely universe*. Cambridge, MA: Cambridge University Press.

Cravens, G. (2007). *Power to save the world: The truth about nuclear energy*. New York: Vintage.

Crawford, M. (2009). *Shop class as soulcraft*. New York: Penguin Press.

Daly, M. (1974). *Beyond God the father*. Boston, MA: Beacon Press.

Davidson, M., Lickona, T., & Khmelkov, V. (2008). Smart & good schools: A new paradigm for high school character education. In L. Nucci & D. Narvaez (Eds.), *Handbook of moral and character education*. New York: Routledge.

Dawkins, R. (2006). *The God delusion*. Boston, MA: Houghton Mifflin.

Day, D. (1952. *The long loneliness*. San Francisco, CA: Harper & Row.

Deaver, J. (2005). *The twelfth card*. New York: Pocket.

DeParle, J. (2012, January 5). Harder for Americans to rise from lower rungs. *New York Times*. Retrieved from www.nytimes.com/2012/01/05/us/harder-for-americans-to-rise-from-lower-rungs.html

Desmond, M. (2016). *Evicted: Poverty and profit in the American city*. New York: Crown.

Dewey, J. (1916). *Democracy and education*. New York: Macmillan.

Dewey, J. (1989/1934). A common faith. In *Later Works* (vol. 9). Carbondale: Southern Illinois University Press.

Dewey, J. (1939). "I believe." In *Later Works* (vol. 14). Carbondale: Southern Illinois University Press.

Dockterman, E. (2015, November 2). Women flip the script. *Time*, 44–47.

Dowd, M. (2015, November 22). Waiting for the green light. *New York Times Magazine*, 40–47, 60–61.

Dreifus, C. (2016, March 11). A plea, while there's still time. *New York Times*, D5.

Earle, S. (1995). *Sea change*. New York: Random House.

Elshtain, J. B. (2002). *Jane Addams and the dream of American democracy*. New York: Basic.

Engster, D. (2007). *The heart of justice: Care ethics and political theory*. Oxford, England: Oxford University Press.

Ennis, R. (1962). A concept of critical thinking. *Harvard Educational Review, 32*(1), 83–111.

Evans, R. W. (2007). *This happened in America: Harold Rugg and the censure of social studies*. Charlotte, NC: Information Age.

Fest, J. (2013). *Not I: Memoirs of a German childhood* (M. Chalmers, Trans.). New York: Other Press.

Fielding, M., & Moss, P. (2011). *Radical education and the common school: A democratic alternative*. London, England: Routledge.

Fisher, G. (2015, September 20). Working moms have more successful daughters and more caring sons, Harvard Business School study says. *Quartz*. Retrieved from qz.com/434056/working-moms-have-more-successful-daughters-and-more-caring-sons-Harvard-Business-School-study-says

Foner, E. (2015). *Gateway to freedom: The hidden history of the Underground Railroad*. New York: Norton.

Frank, T. (2004). *What's the matter with Kansas?* New York: Henry Holt.

Frank, T. (2016). *Listen, liberal*. New York: Metropolitan.

Freire, P. (1970). *Pedagogy of the oppressed* (M. B. Ramos, Trans.). New York: Herder & Herder.

Friedman, B. (2009). *The will of the people*. New York: Farrar, Straus and Giroux.

Friedman, H. L. (2013). When did competitive sports take over American childhood? *The Atlantic*. Retrieved from www.theatlantic.com/education/archive/2013/09/when-did-competitive-sports-take-over-american-childhood/279868/

Galston, W. (1991). *Liberal purposes: Goods, virtues and diversity in the liberal state*. Cambridge, MA: Cambridge University Press.

Galuszka, P. A. (2016, March 18). Shadows of the past, convergence: Diversity and inclusion. *Chronicle of Higher Education, 10*–15.

Gardner, J. W. (1984). *Excellence*. New York: Norton.

Gardner, L. C. (2008). *The long road to Baghdad: A history of U.S. foreign policy from the 1970s to the present*. New York: New Press.

Gardner, M. (1963). *The annotated Alice*. New York: World.

Gardner, M. (1983). *The whys of a philosophical scrivener*. New York: Quill.

Geiger, R. L. (2015). *The history of American higher education*. Princeton, NJ: Princeton University Press.

Gilligan, C. J. (1982). *In a different voice*. Cambridge, MA: Harvard University Press.

Glaude, E. S., Jr. (2016). *Democracy in black: How race still enslaves the American soul*. New York: Crown.

Gordon, R. J. (2016). *The rise and fall of American growth*. Princeton, NJ: Princeton University Press.

Gregory, M. R. (2014). The procedurally directive approach to teaching controversial issues. *Educational Theory, 64*(6), 627–648.

Groenhout, R. E. (2004). *Connected lives: Human nature and an ethics of care*. Lanham, MD: Rowman & Littlefield.

Grubb, W. N. (Ed.). (1995). *Education through occupations in American high schools* (vols. 1 & 2). New York: Teachers College Press.

Gutmann, A. (1987). *Democratic education*. Princeton, NJ: Princeton University Press.

Hacker, A. (2016, February 2). The wrong way to teach math. *New York Times Sunday Review*, 2.

Hadamard, J. (1954). *The psychology of invention in the mathematical field*. New York: Dover.

Hartshorne, H., & May, M. (1928–1930). *Studies in the nature of character; Studies in deceit; Studies in the organization of character*. New York: Macmillan.

Hax, C. (2016, May 1). Tell me about it. *Asbury Park Press*, 11E.

Heath, S. B. (1983). *Ways with words*. New York: Cambridge University Press.

Held, V. (2006). *The ethics of care: Personal, political, and global*. Oxford, England: Oxford University Press.

Heller, N. (2016). The big uneasy: What's roiling the liberal-arts campus? *New Yorker*. Retrieved from www.newyorker.com/magazine/2016/05/30/the-new-activism-of-liberal-arts-colleges

Hirsch, E. D. (1967). *Cultural literacy: What every American needs to know*. Boston, MA: Houghton Mifflin.

Hirsch, E. D. (1996). *The schools we need: Why we don't have them*. New York: Doubleday.

Hixon, R. (2015, January). Henry and George Jacobsen. *Keys Life Magazine, 14*, 34.

Hoffer, E. (1951). *The true believer*. New York: Harper & Row.

Hoffman, M. (2000). *Empathy and moral development: Implications for caring and justice*. New York: Cambridge University Press.

Hume, D. (1983/1751). *An enquiry concerning the principles of morals*. Indianapolis, IN: Hackett.

Jacoby, S. (2004). *Free thinkers*. New York: Metropolitan.

Jaschik, S. (2005, February 18). What Larry Summers said. *Inside Higher Ed*. Retrieved from www.insidehighered.com/print/news/2005/02/18/summers2_18

Kant, I. (1966/1781). *Critique of pure reason* (F. M. Muller, Trans.). Garden City, NY: Doubleday Anchor.

King, J. E. (2016). We may well become accomplices: To rear a generation of spectators is not to educate at all. *Educational Researcher, 45*(2), 159–172.

King, M. L., Jr. (1969). Letter from Birmingham city jail. In H. A. Bedau (Ed.), *Civil disobedience* (pp. 27–48). New York: Pegasus.

Kingsolver, B. (1989). *Homeland and other stories*. New York: Harper Perennial.

Kingsolver, B. (2012). *Flight behavior*. New York: Harper Collins.

Kish-Gephart, J. J., & Campbell, J. T. (2015). You don't forget your roots: The influence of CEO social class background on strategic risk taking. *Academy of Management Journal, 58*(6), 1614–1636. Retrieved from dx.doi.org/10. 5465/amj. 2013. 1204

Kliebard, H. (1999). *Schooled to work: Vocationalism and the American curriculum 1876–1946*. New York: Teachers College Press.

Kohlberg, L. (1981). *The philosophy of moral development*, Vol. 1. San Francisco, CA: Harper & Row.

Kohn, A. (1999). *The schools our children deserve*. Boston, MA: Houghton Mifflin.

Krugman, P. (2015, November 9). Despair, American style. *New York Times*, A23.

Kruse, K. M. (2015). *One nation under God*. New York: Basic Books.

Kuhmerker, L. (1991). *The Kohlberg legacy for the helping professions*. Birmingham, AL: R. E. P.

Kurlansky, M. (1997). *Cod*. New York: Penguin.

Lehane, D. (2008). *The given day*. New York: Harper Collins.

Leonhardt, D. (2014, January 23). Upward mobility has not declined, study says. *New York Times*. Retrieved from www.nytimes.com/2014/01/23/business/upward-mobility-has-not-declined-study-says.html

Levi, P. (1988). *The drowned and the saved* (R. Rosenthal, Trans.). New York: Vintage.

Litsky, F. (2002, September 11). Johnny Unitas, NFL's genius of the huddle, dies at 69. *New York Times*. Retrieved from www.nytimes.com/2002/09/12/sports/johnny-unitas-nfl-s-genius-of-the-huddle-dies-at-69.html

Mann, T., & Ornstein, N. (2012). *It's even worse than it looks: How the American constitutional system collided with the new politics of extremism.* New York: Basic.

Manning, K. R. (1983). *Black Apollo of science: The life of Ernest Everett Just.* New York: Oxford University Press.

Martin, J. R. (1992). Critical thinking for a humane world. In Stephen P. Norris (Ed.), *The generalizability of critical thinking* (pp. 163–180). New York: Teachers College Press.

Matthews, C. (2014, October 31). Wealth inequality in America: It's worse than you think. *Fortune.* Retrieved from fortune.com/2014/10/31/inequality-wealth-income-us/

McCrum, R. (2011, March 27). EF Schumacher: Cameron's choice. *The Guardian.* Retrieved from www.theguardian.com/politics/2011/mar/27/schumacher-david-cameron-small-beautiful

McLuhan, M. (1967). *The medium is the massage.* Berkeley, CA: Gingko Press.

Mill, J. S. (1993/1859). *On liberty and utilitarianism.* New York: Bantam.

Mill, J. S. (2007). Moral influences in early youth: My father's character and opinions. In C. Hitchens (Ed.), *The portable atheist.* Philadelphia, PA: Da Capo Press.

Milner, H. R., IV, Delale-O'Connor, L. A., Murray, I. E., & Farinde, A.A. (2016). Reflections on *Brown* to understand *Milliken v. Bradley*: What if we are focusing on the wrong policy questions? *Teachers College Record, 118*(3).

MIT Admissions Blog. (2015, September 3). Picture yourself as a stereotypical male. Retrieved from mitadmissions.org/blogs/entry/Picture-yourself-as-a-stereotypical-male

Monbiot, G. (2015, September 24). Meet the ecomodernists: Ignorant of history and paradoxically old-fashioned. *The Guardian.* Retrieved from www.theguardian.com/environment/georgemonbiot/2015/sep/24/meet-the-ecomodernists-ignorant-of-history-and-paradoxically-old-fashioned

Monroe, G. (2001). *The highwaymen: Florida's African-American landscape painters.* Gainesville: University Press of Florida.

National Governors Association Center for Best Practices & Council of Chief State School Officers. (2010). *Common Core State Standards for English language arts & literacy in history/social studies, science, and technical subjects.* Washington, DC: National Governors Association Center for Best Practices, Council of Chief State School Officers.

National Science Board. (2016). *Science and engineering indicators 2016.* Arlington, VA: National Science Foundation.

Nearing, S., & Nearing H. K. (1970). *Living the good life.* New York: Schocken.

Nearing, S., & Nearing, H. (1979). *Continuing the good life.* New York: Schocken.

Nearing, S. (2000). *The making of a radical: A political autobiography.* White River Junction, VT: Chelsea Green.

Neill, A. S. (1960). *Summerhill*. New York: Hart.

New, J. (2014). Spelman College builds up student health initiative in years after leaving NCAA. *Inside Higher Ed*. Retrieved from www.insidehighered.com/news/2014/10/15/spelman-college-builds-student-health-initiative-years-after-leaving-ncaa

Niederle, M., & Vestlund, L. (2010, Spring). Explaining the gender gap in math test scores: The role of competition. *Journal of Economic Perspectives, 24*(2), 129–144.

Noddings, N. (1989). *Women and evil*. Berkeley: University of California Press.

Noddings, N. (1992). *The challenge to care in schools*. New York: Teachers College Press.

Noddings, N. (1993). *Educating for intelligent belief or unbelief*. New York: Teachers College Press.

Noddings, N. (2002a). *Starting at home: Caring and social policy*. Berkeley: University of California Press.

Noddings, N. (2002b). *Educating moral people*. New York: Teachers College Press.

Noddings, N. (2006). *Critical lessons: What our schools should teach*. Cambridge : Cambridge University Press.

Noddings, N. (2012). *Peace education: How we come to love and hate war*. Cambridge: Cambridge University Press.

Noddings, N. (2013/1984). *Caring: A relational approach to ethics and moral education*. Berkeley: University of California Press.

Noddings, N. (2013). *Education and democracy in the 21st century*. New York: Teachers College Press.

Noddings, N. (2015a). *A richer, brighter vision for American high schools*. Cambridge: Cambridge University Press.

Noddings, N. (2015b). *Philosophy of education* (3rd ed.). Boulder, CO: Westview Press.

Nucci, L., & Narvaez, D. (Eds.). (2008). *Handbook of moral and character education*. New York: Routledge.

Oakes, J. (2005). *Keeping track: How schools structure inequality* (2nd ed.). New Haven, CT: Yale University Press.

Oakes, J., & Rogers, J. (2006). *Learning power: Organizing for education and justice*. New York: Teachers College Press.

Oakley, M. A. B. (1972). *Elizabeth Cady Stanton*. Brooklyn, NY: Feminist Press.

Onuf, P. S., & Gordon-Reed, A. (2016). *"Most blessed of the patriarchs": Thomas Jefferson and the empire of the imagination*. New York: Liveright.

Orwell, G. (1958/1937). *The road to Wigan pier*. San Diego, CA: Harcourt.

Paley, V. G. (2004). *A child's work*. Chicago, IL: University of Chicago Press.

Payne, R. K. (2005/1996). *A framework for understanding poverty*. Highlands, TX: aha! Process.

Pew Research Center for the People & The Press. (2012, September 27). *Trends in news consumption: 1991–2012: In changing news landscape, even television is vulnerable*. Retrieved from www.people-press.org/2012/09/27/in-changing-news-landscape-even-television-is-vulnerable/

Piaget, J. (1954). *The construction of reality in the child*. New York: Basic.

Piaget, J. (1970). *Genetic epistemology*. New York: Norton.

Pinckney, D. (2016, February 11). The anger of Ta-Nehisi Coates. *New York Review of Books*, 28–30.

Pinker, S., & Spelke, E. (2005). *The science of gender and science*. An *Edge* special event. Retrieved from www.edge.org/3rd_culture/debate05/debate05_index.html

Plato. (1987). *Republic* (D. Lee, Trans.). Harmondsworth, England: Penguin.

Putnam, R. D. (2015). *Our kids: The American dream in crisis*. New York: Simon & Schuster.

Rankin, J. (2015, January 21). Davos—A complete guide to the World Economic Forum. *The Guardian*. Retrieved from www.theguardian.com/business/2015/jan/21/-sp-davos-guide-world-economic-forum

Rappaport, A. (2015, November 11). Philosophers (and welders) react to Marco Rubio's debate comments. *New York Times*. Retrieved from www.nytimes.com/politics/first-draft/2015/11/11/philosophers-and-welders-react-to-marco-rubios-debate-comments/

Ravitch, D. (2010). *The death and life of the great American school system*. New York: Perseus.

Rawls, J. (1971). *A theory of justice*. Cambridge, MA: Harvard University Press.

Rawls, J. (1993). *Political liberalism*. New York: Columbia University Press.

Reiss, T. (2012). *The black count: Glory, revolution, betrayal, and the real count of Monte Cristo*. New York: Crown.

Remarque, E. M. (1982/1929). *All quiet on the western front*. (A. W. Wheen, Trans.). New York: Fawcett.

Rhoden, W. (2012, October 22). Seeing through the illusions of the sports hero. *New York Times*. Retrieved from www.nytimes.com/2012/10/22/sports/seeing-through-the-illusions-of-the-sports-hero. html?_r=0

Richmond, E. (2015, November). The reality of the philosophers vs. welders debate. *The Atlantic*. Retrieved from www.theatlantic.com/education/archive/2015/11/philospher-vs-welders/415890/

Ricoeur, P. (1969). *The symbolism of evil* (E. Buchanan, Trans.). Boston, MA: Beacon Press.

Ripley, A. (2013, September). The case against high-school sports. *The Atlantic*. Retrieved from www.theatlantic.com/education/archive/2013/09/when-did-competitive-sports-take-over-american-childhood/279868/

Rivoli, P. (2009/2015). *The travels of a t-shirt in the global economy: An economist examines the markets, power, and politics of world trade*. Hoboken, NJ: Wiley.

Roberts, D. (2015, December 31). Here's how the NFL might combat concussions. *Fortune*. Retrieved from http://fortune.com/2015/12/31/nfl-concussion-technology/

Ruddick, S. (1989). *Maternal thinking: Toward a politics of peace*. Boston, MA: Beacon Press.

Russell, B. (1963). What is an agnostic? In L. Rosten (Ed.), *Religion in America*. New York: Simon & Schuster.

Rybczynski, W. (1986). *Home: A short history of an idea*. New York: Viking.

Sacks, P. (2007). *Tearing down the gates: Confronting the class divide in American education*. Berkeley: University of California Press.

Safina, C. (2011). *The view from Lazy Point*. New York: Holt.

Scarry, E. (2014). *Thermonuclear monarchy*. New York: Norton.

Schumacher, E. F. (1973/1989). *Small is beautiful: Economics as if people mattered*. New York: HarperPerennial.

Shipler, D. K. (2004). *The working poor: Invisible in America.* New York: Knopf.

Siddle Walker, V., & Snarey, J. R. (Eds.). (2004). *Race-ing moral formation: African American perspectives on care and justice.* New York: Teachers College Press.

Simmons, A. (2016, April). Literature's emotional lessons. *The Atlantic.* Retrieved from www.theatlantic.com/education/archive/2016/04/educating-teenagers-emotions-through-literature/476790/

Slote, M. (2007). *The ethics of care and empathy.* New York: Routledge.

Sola, K. (2015, November 11). Sorry, Rubio, but philosophers make 78% more than welders. *Forbes.* Retrieved from http://www.forbes.com/sites/katiesola/2015/11/11/rubio-welders-philosophers/

Spock, B. (2001). *On parenting.* New York: Pocket Books.

Stanton, E. C. (1993/1895). *The woman's Bible.* Boston: Northeastern University Press.

Stewart, A. (2013). *The drunken botanist: The plants that create the world's drinks.* Chapel Hill, NC: Algonquin.

Stone, O., & Kuznick, P. (2012). *The untold history of the United States.* New York: Simon & Schuster.

Teachout, Z. (2014). *Corruption in America.* Cambridge, MA: Harvard University Press.

Thoreau, H. D. (1969/1849). On the duty of civil disobedience. In H. A. Bedau (Ed.), *Civil disobedience* (pp. 27–48). New York: Pegasus.

Tillich, P. (1952). *The courage to be.* New Haven, CT: Yale University Press.

Toffler, A. (1970). *Future shock.* New York: Bantam.

Trethewey, N. (2012). *Thrall: Poems.* New York: Houghton Mifflin Harcourt.

Tronto, J. (1993). *Moral boundaries: A political argument for an ethic of care.* New York: Routledge.

True, M. (1995). *An energy field more intense than war.* Syracuse, NY: Syracuse University Press.

Turner, J. (1985). *Without God, without creed.* Baltimore, MD: Johns Hopkins University Press.

Vincent, P., & Grove, D. (2012). Character education: A primer on history, research, and effective practices. In P. M. Brown, M. W. Corrigan, & A. Higgins-D'Alessandro (Eds.). *Handbook of prosocial education.* Lanham, MD: Rowman & Littlefield.

Voosen, P. (2016, April 22). "If America wants to kill science, it's on its way": Hope Jahren on women, research, and life in the lab. *Chronicle of Higher Education,* B14.

Walzer, M. (2015). *The paradox of liberation: Secular revolutions and religious counterrevolutions.* New Haven, CT: Yale University Press.

Ward, G. C., & Burns, K. (1999). *Not for ourselves alone: The story of Elizabeth Cady Stanton and Susan B. Anthony.* New York: Knopf.

Watson, M. (2003). *Learning to trust.* San Francisco, CA: Jossey-Bass.

Watson, P. (2010). *The German genius.* New York: HarperCollins.

Weisberg, J. (2016, February 25). We are hopelessly hooked. *New York Review of Books, 63*(3), 6–9.

Westheimer, J. (Ed.). (2007). *Pledging allegiance: The politics of patriotism in America's schools.* New York: Teachers College Press.

Westheimer, J. (2015). *What kind of citizen?* New York: Teachers College Press.

Wheatley, P. (1773). *Poems on various subjects, religious and moral.* Project Guten-
berg EBook retrieved from www.gutenberg.org/cache/epub/409/pg409-images
.html.

White, J. T. (1909). *Character lessons in American biography.* New York: The Character Development League.

Wilson, E. O. (2006). *The creation: An appeal to save life on earth.* New York:
Norton.

Wilson, E. O. (2016). *Half-earth: Our planet's fight for life.* New York: Liveright.

Winslow, B. (2010, Spring). The impact of Title IX. *History Now 23.* Retrieved from
www.gilderlehrman.org/history-now/

Wood, G. S. (2011). *The idea of America.* New York: Penguin Press.

Woolf, V. (1966/1938). *Three guineas.* New York: Harcourt Brace.

Wulf, A. (2015). *The invention of nature: Alexander von Humboldt's new world.*
New York: Knopf.

Yourgrau, P. (2005). *A world without time.* New York: Basic.

Zeisler, A. (2016). *We were feminists once: From Riot Grrrl to CoverGirl®, the buying and selling of a political movement.* New York: PublicAffairs.

Zezima, K. (2014, May 29). How Teddy Roosevelt helped save football. *Washington
Post.* Retrieved from www.washingtonpost.com/news/the-fix/wp/2014/05/29/
teddy-roosevelt-helped-save-football-with-a-white-house-meeting-in-1905/

Zinn, H. (1968). *Disobedience and democracy.* New York: Random House.

Index

About the Authors

Nel Noddings is Lee Jacks Professor of Education, Emerita, at Stanford University. Her books include *Education and Democracy in the 21st Century, When School Reform Goes Wrong, The Challenge to Care in Schools, Educating Citizens for Global Awareness, Educating for Intelligent Belief or Unbelief,* and *Educating Moral People.*

Laurie Brooks is a member of the board of directors of Provident Financial Services and serves on the advisory boards for the Enterprise Risk Management program at North Carolina State University and the quantitative finance program at Rutgers University. She has more than 30 years' experience in petroleum engineering and financial risk management and has taught many different grade levels.